Q&A
Commercial
Law

Routledge Questions & Answers Series

Each Routledge Q&A contains questions on topics commonly found on exam papers, with comprehensive suggested answers. The titles are written by lecturers who are also examiners, so the student gains an important insight into exactly what examiners are looking for in an answer. This makes them excellent revision and practice guides.

Titles in the series:

Q&A Company Law
Q&A Commercial Law
Q&A Contract Law
Q&A Criminal Law
Q&A Employment Law
Q&A English Legal System
Q&A Equity and Trusts
Q&A European Union Law
Q&A Evidence
Q&A Family Law
Q&A Intellectual Property Law
Q&A Jurisprudence
Q&A Land Law
Q&A Medical Law
Q&A Public Law
Q&A Torts

For a full listing, visit www.routledge.com/cw/revision

Q&A Commercial Law

Jo Reddy and Rick Canavan

Routledge
Taylor & Francis Group

LONDON AND NEW YORK

Eighth edition published 2016
by Routledge
2 Park Square, Milton Park, Abingdon, Oxon OX14 4RN

and by Routledge
711 Third Avenue, New York, NY 10017

Routledge is an imprint of the Taylor & Francis Group, an informa business

First edition published by Cavendish Publishing 1994
Seventh edition published by Routledge 2012

British Library Cataloguing in Publication Data
A catalogue record for this book is available from the British Library

Library of Congress Cataloging-in-Publication Data
A catalog record for this title has been requested

ISBN: 978-1-138-85487-1 (pbk)
ISBN: 978-1-315-72069-2 (ebk)

Typeset in TheSans
by Wearset Ltd, Boldon, Tyne and Wear
Printed and bound by CPI Group (UK) Ltd, Croydon, CR0 4YY

Contents

Table of Cases

Table of Legislation

▪ EU Legislation

▪ Secondary Legislation

Guide to the Companion Website

www.routledge.com/cw/revision

Visit the Law Revision website to discover a comprehensive range of resources designed to enhance your learning experience.

The Good, The Fair, & The Ugly

Good essays are the gateway to top marks. This interactive tutorial provides sample essays together with voice-over commentary and tips for successful exam essays, written by our Q&A authors themselves.

Multiple Choice Questions

Knowledge is the foundation of every good essay. Focusing on key examination themes, these MCQs have been written to test your knowledge and understanding of each subject in the book.

Bonus Q&As

Having studied our exam advice, put your revision into practice and test your essay writing skills with our additional online questions and answers.

Introduction

This book is intended to be of help to students studying commercial law who feel that they have acquired a body of knowledge, but do not feel confident about using it effectively in exams. This book sets out to demonstrate how to apply the knowledge to the question and how to structure the answer. Students often find the technique of answering problem questions particularly hard to grasp, so this book contains a large number of answers to such questions. This technique is rarely taught in law schools and the student who comes from studying science or maths A levels may find it particularly tricky. Equally, a student who has studied English literature may find it difficult to adapt to the impersonal, logical, concise style that problem answers demand. A student who has done largely project work will often find a three-hour unseen paper written examination very daunting. It is hoped that this book will be particularly useful at exam time, but may also prove useful throughout the year. The book provides examples of the kind of questions that are usually asked in end-of-year examinations, along with suggested solutions. Each chapter deals with one of the main topics covered in commercial law courses and contains typical questions on that area. The aim is not to include questions covering every aspect of a course, but to pick out the areas that tend to be examined because they are particularly contentious or topical. Many courses contain a certain amount of material that is not examined, although it is important as providing background knowledge. It cannot be overemphasised enough that it will help students to have an awareness of the general context of the subject and what issues are currently topical or controversial. Examiners are always impressed if an answer alludes to a current issue to illustrate an argument, particularly if it is not one the lecturer has raised.

PROBLEM AND ESSAY QUESTIONS

Some areas tend to be examined only by essays, some mainly – although not invariably – by problems, and some by either. The questions chosen reflect this mix, and the introductions at the beginning of each chapter discuss the type of question usually asked. It is important not to choose a topic and then assume that it will appear on the exam paper in a particular form unless it is in an area where, for example, a problem question is never set. If it might appear as an essay or a problem, revision should be geared to either possibility: a very thorough knowledge of the area should be acquired, but also an awareness of critical opinion in relation to it. In most cases, unless there has been a change of personnel or revision of the syllabus, past exam papers should always be looked at carefully. Reading the rubric and understanding it is absolutely essential. Students should not assume that all questions will be confined to a single area of the subject – commonly in Commercial Law there may well be an issue about exemption clauses or damages alongside, for example, an issue about the application and scope of the implied terms in **ss 12–15** of the **Sale of Goods Act 1979**.

LENGTH OF ANSWERS

The answers in this book are about the length of an essay that a good student would expect to write in an exam. Some are somewhat longer and these will also provide useful guidance for students writing assessed essays, which typically are between 2,000 and 3,000 words. In relation to exam questions, there are a number of reasons for including lengthy answers: some students can write long answers – about 1,800 words – under exam conditions; some students who cannot nevertheless write two very good and lengthy essays and two reasonable but shorter ones. Such students tend to do very well, although it must be emphasised that it is always better to aim to spread the time evenly between all four essays. Therefore, some answers indicate what might be done if very thorough coverage of a topic were to be undertaken.

THE FOOTNOTES

Some of the questions also provide footnotes exploring some areas of the answer in more depth, which should be of value to the student who wants to do more than cover the main points; it would not be expected that any one student would be able to make all of the points they contain, but they demonstrate that it is possible to choose to explore, say, two interesting areas in more depth in an answer once the main points have been covered. It cannot be emphasised enough that the main points have to be covered before interesting, but less obvious, issues can be explored.

EXPRESSING A POINT OF VIEW

Students sometimes ask, especially in an area such as say international sales (for example, 'CIF contracts should properly be described as contracts for the sale of documents. Discuss.') whether they should argue for any particular point of view in an essay. It will be noticed that the essays in this book tend to do this. In general, the good student does argue for one side but he or she always uses sound arguments to support his or her view. Further, a good student does not ignore the opposing arguments; they are considered and, if possible, their weaknesses are exposed. Of course, it would not be appropriate to do this in a problem question or in some essay questions but, where an invitation to do so is held out, it is a good idea to accept/reject it rather than sit on the fence. Individual expression is not something to be avoided but should be based on reasoned and rationale arguments.

EXAM PAPERS

Commercial law exam papers vary in relation to the number of substantive topics included in the syllabus; for example, some syllabuses will deal with Agency but others not. This book will include questions on each of the main areas of the syllabus. For example, a typical paper might include problem questions on the implied terms (**ss 12–15** of the **Sale of Goods Act 1979** if the contract is business-to-business), passing of property and risk (**ss 16–20** of the **Sale of Goods Act 1979**), the *nemo dat* rule and its exceptions (**ss 21–25** of the **Sale of Goods Act 1979**, **s 2** of the **Factors Act 1889**, **Pt III** of the **Hire Purchase Act 1964**), if dealt with, retention of title (Romalpa clauses), and some aspects of remedies. As said, subsidiary issues such as the validity of an exclusion clause in a business-to-business contract might appear. If Agency is within the syllabus, a question on the authority of an agent, and the rights and obligations of an undisclosed principal are favourites. Some courses include Consumer Credit law, others will not or will treat it as part of a separate consumer law module, so do not be surprised to find in this book answers to questions on areas you will not have dealt with in the module offered by your Law School. Therefore, the questions have to be fairly wide-ranging in order to cover a reasonable amount of ground on each topic. Some answers in this book therefore have to cover some of the same material, especially where it is particularly central to the topic in question, for example, the scope and application of the implied term as to satisfactory quality in **s 14(2)** of the **Sale of Goods Act 1979**.

SUGGESTIONS FOR EXAM TECHNIQUE

Below are some suggestions that might improve exam technique; some failings are pointed out that are very commonly found on exam scripts. A pre-question plan is a very useful idea particularly in a problem question, as many marks are lost by bad technique as are lost by lack of knowledge. A very good example of this is a question of tracking a series of transactions to determine whether the buyer at the end of a line of sub-sales has obtained a good title, involving the *nemo dat* rule and its exceptions – it is all too easy to miss a transaction or leave a party out if a proper structure plan is not prepared indicating the main points and cases to discuss.

(1) When tackling a problem question, do not write out the facts in the answer. Quite a number of students write out chunks of the facts as they answer the question – perhaps to help themselves to pick out the important issues. It is better to avoid this and merely to refer to the significant facts.

(2) It is your personal choice whether you use an impersonal style in both problem and essay answers (of course, examiners may differ in their views on this point). In an answer, you could use the word 'I' or you could say 'it is therefore submitted that' or 'it is arguable that'. If you prefer 'I believe that' or 'I feel that', that's fine.

(3) In answers to problem questions, try to explain at the beginning of each section of your answer what point you are trying to establish. You might say, for example: 'In order to show that liability under **s 1** will arise, three tests must be satisfied.' You should then consider all three, come to a conclusion on each and then come to a final conclusion as to whether or not liability will arise. If you are really unsure whether or not it will arise (which will often be the case – there is not much point in asking a question to which there is one very clear and obvious answer!), then consider what you have written in relation to the three tests. Perhaps one of them is clearly satisfied, one is probably satisfied and the other (arising under, for example, **s 1(8)**) probably is not. You might then say: 'As the facts give little support to an argument that **s 1(8)** is satisfied, it is concluded that liability is unlikely to be established.'

(4) You do not get double the marks for saying the same thing twice – you waste time and may not complete the paper – say what you have to say and move on to the next question – if a little unsure about whether you wish to say more leave some space and come back to the question – try and avoid tacking on bits to a question at the end of the paper, as these can obviously be overlooked. Equally, avoid contradicting yourself – it is surprising the number of students who change their mind in the course of an answer and do not correct an earlier statement so initially say 'X obviously has a good claim' but then on the next page 'It is clear X cannot succeed'!

(5) Remember essays and exam papers are also an exercise in writing the English language – try and avoid over-long complex sentences. Use paragraphs and break up the work – have a structure – in simple terms a beginning, middle and end. Avoid overly pretentious language wherever possible. Use simple English. Avoid what can be called the 'stream of consciousness approach', just pouring out material in a more or less continuous fashion with few or no paragraph breaks and very long sentences – if an examiner can read and follow your answer easily it may well reflect in a better mark.

(6) Particularly in essays, a good strong conclusion is helpful – you need not come down on one side or the other but you want to leave the examiner in no doubt that you are aware of the issues involved – again in essays proposals for changes or reform will usually gain extra marks. Do not leave things in the air – if the question has asked you to critically evaluate, you want to show you have done so and not be simply descriptive or just let the essay tail off into nowhere.

(7) Answer the question set and not the one you would have liked to be set. For example, if the question asks you to discuss the issues of 'satisfactory quality' in **s14(2)** of the **Sale of Goods Act 1979** and you have learnt a lot about 'sales by description' in **s13** of the **Sale of Goods Act 1979** and this has not come up elsewhere on the paper, you waste time and will fail the question, probably, if you spend a lot of time talking about **s13** and little or no time discussing **s14(2)**, however happy you feel that you have shown the examiner that you are fully on top of **s13**!

(8) A statement of the obvious but often overlooked – use a good writing implement. If you have very small writing using a pale blue biro with a thin nib does not help!

Common Pitfalls

The most common mistake made when using Questions & Answers books for revision is to memorise the model answers provided and try to reproduce them in exams. This approach is a sure-fire pitfall, likely to result in a poor overall mark because your answer will not be specific enough to the particular question on your exam paper, and there is also a danger that reproducing an answer in this way would be treated as plagiarism. You must instead be sure to read the question carefully, to identify the issues and problems it is asking you to address and to answer it directly in your exam. If you use your Q&A book to focus on your question-answering skills and understanding of the law applied, you will be ready for whatever your exam paper has to offer!

1

General Questions

INTRODUCTION

This chapter contains four questions which are not confined to one particular part of the syllabus but are broader. Such questions are often included in examinations in order to test your knowledge of recent developments in the subject or simply to give you an opportunity, which most questions in law papers do not, to demonstrate a wider knowledge of the syllabus. The first question poses an important general question as to whether it is possible to define commercial law. Questions 1 and 2 are of a general type often found in examinations, inviting the student to take an overview of commercial law and its function in the business world. Question 3 requires a good knowledge of the recent Consumer Rights Act 2015.

QUESTION 1

'No matter what impression may be given by textbooks, there is no such thing as English Commercial Law. There are only a number of loosely connected areas of private law, which are lumped together and called "Commercial Law" without any thought given to whether or not they form a coherent area of law.'

▶ **Discuss.**

How to Answer this Question

This is a challenging question and one to which there can be no definitive answer. This is because commercial law means different things to different textbook authors. We do not know *why* some topics are included while others are not dealt with or are categorised as being only 'ancillary' to commercial law.

The problem we face is that England does not have a self-contained body of principles and rules specific to commercial transactions. English commercial law has been developed by common law, and its principles are all over the place in case reports. It is almost impossible to rely on law reports alone. We depend on academic textbooks, practitioner texts and journals but such materials do not form a commercial code. Authors do not create law; they merely explain it. Students need to set their own boundaries in answering this question and the challenge is to engage in the discussion rather than striving to a conclusion as to its definition.

Applying the Law

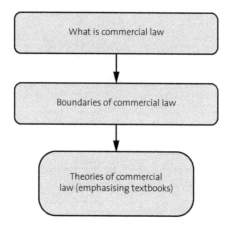

ANSWER

The reason why textbooks do not and cannot provide a definition of commercial law is because the UK does not have a code. It does not have a self-contained integrated body of principles and rules specific to commercial transactions (unlike the American Uniform Commercial Code). It is the absence of anything resembling either a commercial code or the commercial part of a civil code which makes defining the boundaries of commercial law difficult. Defining commercial law by looking at the approach taken by textbooks is over-simplistic. The obvious problem with defining commercial law in this way is that we do not know *why* some topics are included while others are not dealt with or are categorised as being only 'ancillary' to commercial law. Most commercial textbooks do not try to define commercial law; they do not set out the theories of commercial law.

Different commercial textbooks contain different topics. The various topics however reveal an enduring theme. In all aspects of commercial law, the focus is on transactions. Some commercial law (for example, sale of goods) regulates transactions directly. Other areas (for example, banking and insurance law) concern mechanisms necessarily ancillary to such transactions. Others (for example, product liability) stem from the consequences of transactions even where the party seeking the help of the law is not a direct party in the transaction.

But the selection of topics depends on authors' ideas of what business activity is. Perhaps authors are not sure where some topics should be placed. Most commercial law courses are a sort of 'miscellaneous section', that is, topics put together because they do not fit conveniently into courses of their own (unlike, for example, company law, revenue law).

In any event, the textbook approach gives rise to boundary problems. Authors draw boundaries in different ways. For example, Professor Goode limits boundaries of commercial law to law that governs commercial transactions (for example, contract law, sale of goods). He excludes the law governing commercial institutions (for example, company law and partnership law). The difficulty with this is that the boundary between transactions and institutions is not clear. It is arguable, for instance, that the **Companies Act 2006** is no more than the application of general agency principles (and so is transactional law and, yes, qualifies as commercial law). Equally arguable is that the Companies Act is crucial to the structure and function of companies (and so classifies as institutional law).

CONCLUSION

Taking a textbook approach to defining commercial law is over-simplistic. If we take the textbook approach, then commercial law is predominantly doctrinal (or 'black-letter') in its methodology and orientation. All we can say is that commercial law textbooks reinforce ideas about what commercial law is. But the selection of topics depends on authors' own ideas of commercial law and what business activity is. The obvious problem with defining commercial law in this way is that it is subjective.

QUESTION 2

'The strength of English commercial law has been its concern to provide solutions to practical problems facing commercial parties.'

▶ **Discuss.**

How to Answer this Question

This question is not an opportunity to discuss commercial law in a general way. A good answer requires you to identify what the needs of the commercial community are and then identify how the courts and legislature have responded to those needs. You should illustrate these points by drawing examples from a range of areas of commercial law.

Applying the Law

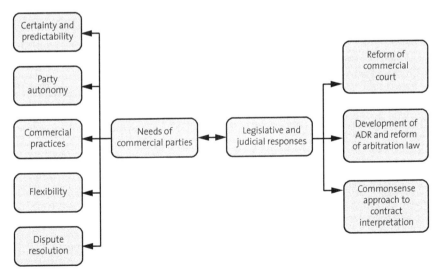

This diagram illustrates the main factors to consider for both commercial parties and possible legal responses.

ANSWER --

In order to answer the question, it is necessary to identify what problems commercial parties face and how English commercial law helps them by providing solutions. If commercial law is about commercial activity, then the fundamental purpose of commercial law is the facilitation of commercial activity.[1]

(1) CERTAINTY AND PREDICTABILITY

The commercial community values legal certainty above all.[2] Business people want to know that courts will be reliable and will consistently interpret transactions in a particular way. This allows for planning and anticipation of liability. Many transactions (many of high value) are undertaken on the basis that courts will continue to follow rules laid down in preceding cases. Business people do not want the law to be based on a random application of local custom and idiosyncrasies of individuals. Of course, this is not guaranteed because judges' thinking will change over time but, on the whole, courts have consistently promoted certainty of outcome over those of fairness and justice. This is what business people want.

As Lord Mansfield said, it is more important that a rule is certain than what the rule is.[3] An example is the postal rule (*Adams v Lindsell* (1818)). It does not matter if acceptance is deemed to take place at the time of posting or receipt. Parties to a contract merely need to know.

If the law is clear and certain, the outcome of a dispute may be predicted and parties may resolve it without having to litigate. If litigation is necessary, at least disputes can be dealt with quickly. This is especially important in a price fluctuation market.

The use of documentary credits is an example of courts' approach to ensure certainty.[4] Documentary credit is a bank's assurance of payment against presentation of specified documents. It is the most common method of payment in international sales. Although the **Uniform Customs and Practice for Documentary Credits**[5] only applies if it is expressly incorporated into a contract, because of its wide acceptance amongst international bankers, courts are likely to view the UCP as impliedly incorporated as established usage. There are two general principles involved with documentary credits. First, the doctrine of strict compliance dictates that a banker must comply exactly with its client's (the buyer)

---

1 As with every essay question, the provision of a brief outline of the issues to be discussed is the first step to ensure that your essay has a structure.

2 Where the question is about practical problems/implications, emphasise the practical aspects of a question. This shows that you are focused on the relevant issues.

3 *Vallejo v Wheeler* (1774): 'In all mercantile transactions the great object should be certainty; and therefore, it is of more consequence that a rule should be certain, than whether the rule is established one way or the other. Because speculators in trade then know what ground to go upon.'

4 The provision of a concrete example is a good way to illustrate the issues raised by the question and demonstrates understanding.

5 The current, seventh, edition, is often known as **UCP 600**.

instructions as to payment. Even if the value of some documents required by the buyer is questionable, 'it is not for the bank to reason why'.[6] Even a minor discrepancy will disentitle the banker to reimbursement from its client. A clear example is the case of *Equitable Trust v Dawson* (1927) where the buyer's instruction was payment against a certificate signed by experts, whereas the banker paid against documents signed by one expert. The House of Lords held that the banker had acted against his instructions and was thus not entitled to reimbursement.[7]

Second, the principle of autonomy of credit dictates that a bank is not concerned with any dispute that the buyer might have with the seller. As Lord Denning said[8] in *Power Curber v National Bank of Kuwait* (1981), a letter of credit ranks as cash and must be honoured. Courts have consistently defended the autonomy principle on grounds that an irrevocable letter of credit is the 'life-blood of international commerce'. It thus must be honoured and be free from interference by the courts, otherwise trust in international commerce would be damaged. The commercial value of the documentary credit system lies in the fact that payment under a letter of credit is virtually guaranteed (subject to the strict compliance principle). Certainty of payment is of paramount importance to the business community, thus irrevocable credits are treated like cash by courts.

(2) PARTY AUTONOMY

Business people should be free to make their contracts and they are entitled to receive what they bargained for. The aim of commercial law is to enforce the intention of the parties, not frustrate that intention by a rigid set of rules.[9]

Courts take a non-interventionist approach, justified on the basis that it promotes certainty. Courts should only intervene if the contract terms are so restrictive or oppressive that it offends public interest. Whenever there is a contest between contract law and equity in a commercial dispute, contract law wins hands down. This is one reason why so many foreigners select English law to govern their contracts and English courts to decide the case. Business people know where they stand with English law and English judges.[10]

Courts are, however, encouraged to take a more interventionist approach in some types of contracts. This is because of the development of a 'consumer society'. For example, although the **Consumer Rights Act 2015** ('**CRA**')[11] serves primarily to consolidate much of

....

6 Devlin J in *Midland Bank v Seymour* (1955).

7 Lord Sumner: 'There is no room for documents which are almost the same, or which will just do as well.'

8 Stating by whom a legal principle was stated in a case demonstrates a deeper knowledge and is likely to attract additional marks.

9 Lord Goff of Chieveley in an article analysing the objectives of judges when interpreting commercial contracts in *Commercial Contracts and the Commercial Court* (1984): 'We are there to help businessmen, not to hinder them; we are there to give effect to their transactions, not to frustrate them; we are there to oil the wheels of commerce, not to put a spanner in the works, or even grit in the oil.'

10 Around 65% of disputes heard before the Commercial Court involve only foreign parties, that is, parties have expressly chosen England as the jurisdiction for dispute resolution.

11 See Question 3.

the existing law in one statute, it does make significant changes to the law in some areas. Overall, the Act represents a substantial increase in the rights of consumers and in the powers of the court. Business-to-business contracts are kept separate, however, and the **Sale of Goods Act 1979** continues to govern the relationship. There is now a clearer difference between pure commercial transactions and business-to-consumer contracts.

(3) RECOGNITION OF COMMERCIAL PRACTICES

Courts have always recognised and given legal effect to customs and practices of the business community. The most common way is by implying a term into the contract, for example where the parties are in the same trade and there is a particular custom of that trade. By judicial recognition, commercial practice has become part of the common law.[12] An example is the agency doctrine of the undisclosed principal.[13] In this situation, the existence of an agency is not disclosed to the third party, who therefore thinks he is contracting only with the agent in his own right and is unaware that the agent is acting for another. Nevertheless, the general rule is that the principal can intervene and enforce contract with the third party. This is an exception to doctrine of privity under the common law.[14] It is important to bear in mind that the initial contract is between the agent and the third party. The undisclosed principal intervenes in an existing contract. The justification for the doctrine of the undisclosed principal has been the subject of much discussion by academic writers. It is generally accepted that although it runs against the fundamental principles of privity of contract (that is, there must be agreement between the parties), the doctrine is justified on grounds of commercial convenience. Generally, in commercial law, courts assume that buyers and sellers are willing to buy/sell to anyone. Contracts are not personal and business people are not concerned about the identity of the other contracting party.[15] There is no reason for the undisclosed principal rule other than that courts recognise that this is what business people do. It is purely a matter of recognising commercial practice.

(4) FLEXIBILITY

Commercial people keep finding new ways of doing business. The Internet is a good example.[16] The Internet environment is constantly changing and the law must respond. Business people need the law to adapt to accommodate these changes. The English courts have been flexible. Legislation has also been flexible; whenever reform is proposed, extensive consultation takes place with the business community before a Law Commission report is produced. For example, amendments to the **Sale of Goods Act 1979** include s 20A.[17] Business buyers had complained that they had paid for goods but

---

12 For example, the bill of lading is recognised as a document of title to goods at common law.

13 The provision of a practical example demonstrates understanding of the law and will attract a good mark.

14 This is not an exception under the **Contracts (Rights of Third Parties) Act 1999**, because the undisclosed principal is not identified or identifiable at the time of the contract, so the Act does not apply.

15 Lord Lindley in *Keighley, Maxsted v Durant* (1901): 'in the great mass of contracts it is a matter of indifference to either party whether there is an undisclosed principal or not'.

16 Placing the essay question into its practical, wider context is another way to demonstrate knowledge and understanding.

17 Inserted as an amendment by the **1995 Act**.

where the seller became insolvent before delivery, their claim against the receiver failed on grounds that the buyer has no property in unascertained goods. Commercial people wanted this change. **Section 20A** essentially gives a buyer who has paid for goods before delivery some measure of protection if the seller becomes insolvent. The buyer acquires property in an undivided share and he becomes an owner in common of the bulk pro rata.

However, flexibility is often at the expense of certainty. For example, **s 15A** says that if the breach of description or quality of the goods is so slight that it would be unreasonable for the buyer to reject the goods, such a breach may be treated as a breach of warranty only. Although this allows for some flexibility, its application is uncertain.

More recently, BIS (Department for Business, Innovation and Skills) consulted businesses (amongst other groups) on options to simplify the law in relation to the supply of goods, services and digital content supplied under a contract. This resulted in the **Consumer Rights Act 2015** ('**CRA**') which came into force on 1 October 2015. The **CRA** treats consumer contracts for digital content as a separate category of content with its own statutory rights and remedies for the first time.[18] The consumer now has a number of rights which are implied into the contract or not dealt with expressly.

(5) RESOLUTION

No matter how certain and predictable the law is, there will always be disputes. What commercial people need is a quick, inexpensive and efficient way to deal with problems. This need has been met in several ways. For example, commercial courts are special courts. These are separate courts of the Queen's Bench Division. They do nothing but hear commercial disputes. The procedure is flexible with relatively little formality. Courts themselves have been willing to develop new remedies, for example, the development of the *search and seize order*, allowing seizure of evidence which might otherwise be destroyed.[19]

(6) FAIRNESS AND GOOD FAITH

A contemporary argument is that the law should promote fairness and good faith (especially if commercial law is to include consumer transactions). But English law has developed without a general duty of good faith. Examples include *The Mihalis Angelos* (1971), where a party can exercise the right to terminate a contract for breach even though the breach causes him no loss. This is so even if the sole motive for termination is market price fluctuation.[20]

---

18 See Question 3.

19 Other ways developed to deal with disputes include arbitration and alternative dispute resolution (such as mediation).

20 Another example is *White & Carter v Macgregor* (1962) where a party can perform his obligations against the other party's wishes and remains entitled to claim the full value of the contract price.

Many countries have a general duty of good faith. In England, the idea of good faith is the subjective standard of honesty, rather than an objective one of fair dealing. Partly because of harmonisation of commercial law in the European Union, there is a growing reference to an objective standard of good faith. For example, in relation to consumer contracts under the **Consumer Rights Act 2015**, the test is no longer *you* are being unfair, merely *it* looks unfair (**s 62**).

SUMMARY[21]

The main challenge for commercial law is to strike the right balance between these competing principles to provide solutions to problems faced by commercial parties. Where the balance should lie depends on the circumstances of the case. For example, if the parties involved are multinational corporations in the shipping trade, certainty might take precedence, whereas if there is a significant imbalance between the parties (if one party is a consumer), some certainty may be sacrificed in favour of fairness or flexibility.

Tensions are unavoidable. Business people want the law to be predictable in its application. But this is not always possible. More predictability means more detailed rules. At the same time, business people want flexibility, to allow them to develop new ways of doing business. This is very well, but how does commercial law deal with these competing principles? Essentially, it is a balancing act. Commercial law rules need to be sufficiently predictable to generate confidence so business people can depend on it. At the same time, the law must be responsive and flexible enough to allow the development of new markets. On the whole, English commercial law does provide solutions to practical problems facing commercial parties.

QUESTION 3

The **Consumer Rights Act 2015** has been described by the UK government as 'the biggest overhaul of consumer law for a generation'. What are the key changes introduced by the Act in relation to the implied contract terms for satisfactory quality, description, fitness for purpose, remedies and unfair terms.

How to Answer this Question

This question is designed to test your knowledge of the new **CRA**. It is important, however, not just to write down all you know about the **CRA**. You are explicitly asked to concentrate on a particular perspective, that is, the implied terms as relates to quality, description and fitness for purposes. Note that the question does not restrict your answer to just goods, so it is advisable to deal with the implied terms for goods, services as well as digital content. You also need to include a discussion of the changes made to consumer remedies and unfair terms. It is a matter to some extent of your own judgment as to how much space you can afford to give to each of these issues.

---

21 Ending your answer with a conclusion, ie, a summary of the results of your discussion/analysis, ensures that you present a complete picture to the examiner.

Applying the Law

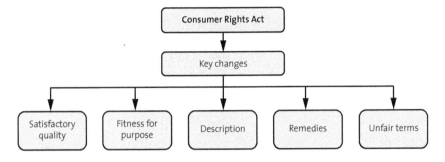

ANSWER

The **Consumer Rights Act 2015** ('**CRA**') replaces much of the existing UK legislation relating to the sale of goods and services to consumers and unfair contract terms. It introduces consistent definitions of key concepts (such as who classifies as a 'trader' or 'consumer'), introduces new statutory rights and a series of tiered remedies for consumers, as well as bringing it into line with developments in technology.

The **CRA** constitutes a major reform of consumer protection law. Whilst the Act echoes the previous law when it comes to implied contract terms for satisfactory quality, description, fitness for purpose and other standards, it adds a number of new provisions including introducing for the first time specific rights and remedies for digital content.

GOODS

The **CRA** continues to imply terms into consumer contracts that goods will be of satisfactory quality (**s 9**), fit for a particular purpose (**s 10**) and as described (**s 11**). The **CRA** introduces a requirement that, unless differences are bought to a customer's attention pre-contract, goods must match a model seen/examined by the consumer (**s 14**).

The **CRA** also introduces **s 12** which is an implied term regarding the information which must be provided pre-contract as required under the Consumer Contracts Regulations 2013 (which differs depending on whether goods are sold at a distance or face-to-face). Pre-contractual information includes, for example, point of sale materials, details regarding payment, delivery and after-sales service.

If the trader installs the goods, the **CRA** provides that the goods will not conform to the contract unless they are installed correctly (**s 15**).

The right to reject goods which do not conform to the contract has changed significantly. Previously, there was no defined period in which a consumer can reject goods, merely that a consumer must reject goods supplied in breach of contract within a 'reasonable time'. This has been interpreted differently and that has led to uncertainty. In contrast, **ss 20–24** of the **CRA** creates a tiered system of remedies in the event the consumer's statutory rights are breached. In essence, these comprise:

❖ A **short-term right to reject** the goods and claim a full refund for up to 30 days after purchase (shorter in the case of perishable goods) (**s 22**). The 30 days can be extended by the trader, but not shortened. If the consumer requests that the goods be repaired or replaced (see below), the 30-day period stops temporarily. Once the goods are repaired or replaced, the consumer then has the remainder of the 30-day period or seven days (whichever is longer) to check whether the repair or replacement has been successful and to decide whether to reject the goods.

❖ If the fault is discovered after 30 days of purchase or the consumer requests the trader to **repair or replace** within 30 days of purchase, the trader must do so at the trader's cost, and within a reasonable time and without causing significant inconvenience to the consumer (**s 23**). Note that the consumer cannot enforce this right if the repair or replacement would be impossible, or the associated costs would be disproportionate compared to the consumer's other remedies. The trader has only *one* opportunity to repair or offer one replacement.[22] If the trader refuses to repair or replace the goods or the trader's one attempt at repair fails or the first replacement is also defective, or if the consumer cannot enforce this right as it would be impossible or disproportionate, the remedies move on to the next tier.

❖ The consumer has the right to an appropriate **price reduction** (up to the full price paid by the consumer), or a **final right to reject** (**s 24**). The final right to reject is subject to a right of deduction for use, to take into account the use the consumer has made of the goods since they were delivered. If a consumer exercises the final right to reject in the first six months, the trader must make a full refund (unless the goods in question are a motor vehicle). It is only after this six month period that the trader may reduce the refund to take account of the use the consumer has had of the goods.

If the trader fails to supply pre-contractual information required by **s 12**, the above tiered remedies do not apply. The consumer may, however, recover costs incurred by the consumer as a result of the trader's breach, up to the price of the goods.

The burden lies on the consumer to prove that the goods do not conform to the contract if they are exercising their short-term right to reject. However, goods are presumed not to conform to the contract if a consumer exercises their right to a repair or replacement, price reduction or final right to reject within six months of delivery. If more than six months have passed, the consumer must prove that the defect was present at the time of delivery.

---

22 The fact that the consumer has the right to a price deduction or to reject the goods/services after only one unsuccessful repair or replacement is a significant development and one particular area that is causing some anxiety for businesses.

Unless agreed otherwise, goods must be delivered without undue delay or no more than 30 days after the date of the contract.

SERVICES

The **CRA** continues to imply terms into consumer contracts for the supply of services that the service will be performed with reasonable skill and care (**s 49**), the price will be reasonable if not fixed (**s 51**) and the service will be performed within a reasonable time if not fixed (**s 52**).

The **CRA** introduces a new provision that anything said or written by the trader to the consumer about the trader or the service is an implied term of the contract if it influences the consumer to buy the service or make any decision about the service after entering into the contract. Previously, where representations are made by a trader, they do not form part of the contract. This meant that a consumer was limited to a claim for misrepresentation. Under the **CRA**, statements made by the trader become contractual terms, that is, they will give rise to a breach of contract claim. This is significant because such claims are usually easier to prove than those based on misrepresentation.

If the service is not performed with reasonable care and skill or in line with pre-contractual information provided by the trader, the consumer is entitled to *repeat performance* of the service. Where repeat performance is requested, the work must be done at no cost to the consumer, within a reasonable time and without causing the consumer significant inconvenience. If a repeat performance is not possible (or cannot be done within a reasonable time and without causing significant inconvenience), a *price reduction* can be claimed.

This is a significant development in consumer rights. Previously, there were no specific statutory remedies. The new remedies under the **CRA** do not exclude common law remedies such as damages but, needless to say, a consumer cannot recover twice for the same loss.

DIGITAL CONTENT

For the first time, the **CRA** covers contracts for the supply of digital content (such as software, music, computer games, ebooks and 'apps') as a separate category from other goods and services, with their own statutory rights and remedies. Broadly, the implied terms mirror those for goods, that is, digital content must be of satisfactory quality (**s 34**), fit for a particular purpose (**s 35**) and as described (**s 36**).

If digital content does not satisfy these requirements, a consumer does not have the right to reject it[23] but instead has:

---

23 Note this important distinction – a consumer has no right to reject digital content. This is because digital content cannot be returned and there is no requirement that the consumer delete the content from their device.

❖ The right to **repair or replacement** of the content. The rules are the same as the rules for goods (above), except that the trader is not limited to one attempt to repair or replace the content, provided it can do so within a reasonable time and without causing significant inconvenience to the consumer.

❖ The right to a **price reduction** of an 'appropriate amount'. The rules are the same as the rules for goods (above).

❖ The right of a **refund**, but only in cases where the trader is in breach of the statutory warranty that it has the right to supply the content (**s 41**).

A consumer is also entitled to claim compensation for damage where digital content causes damage to an electronic device or other digital content owned by a consumer (for example, through a virus), if the consumer can show that the trader did not exercise reasonable care and skill in the provision of the digital content. The trader must either repair the damage or failing that pay compensation to cover the cost of replacing the device and/or any digital content that is damaged.

Previously, there was potentially a wide discrepancy in the treatment of digital content, depending on whether it is downloaded or provided in tangible form. The **CRA** makes clear that digital content can be supplied either in a physical format (such as a music CD) or in an intangible format (such as music downloaded to a computer). It is worth noting that where digital content is mixed with tangible goods (for example, a television or a microwave) these are considered as 'mixed contracts'. In such cases, if the digital content does not meet the necessary standards, the *whole* item will be treated as not conforming to the contract and the remedies available to the consumer are those provided as if the item were goods. This is important because this gives a consumer a right to reject that is not available solely for defective digital content.

UNFAIR TERMS

The **CRA** both consolidates and clarifies existing consumer legislation on unfair contract terms, removing conflicting overlaps between the **Unfair Contract Terms Act 1977** and the **Unfair Terms in Consumer Contracts Regulations 1999** (the latter is fully revoked). The provisions cover consumer contracts and now extend to consumer 'notices'. A consumer notice (which may either be written or oral) includes announcements and other communications intended to be read by a consumer (so will include, for instance, renewal notices and customer promotions).

As with previous legislation, the **CRA** prevents exclusion of certain types of liability, so that, for example, a trader cannot exclude liability in relation to terms as to quality, description etc for the supply of goods (**s 31**) or digital content (**s 47**); nor can a trader exclude or restrict liability for death or personal injury resulting from negligence (**s 65**). These 'black listed' terms will automatically be unenforceable against the consumer.

The **CRA** requires all terms (or notices) of a consumer contract to be fair. The assessment of fairness continues to be based on whether the term causes a significant imbalance in the parties' rights and obligations under the contract to the detriment of the consumer (**s 62**). Significantly, the assessment is no longer limited to non-negotiated terms.

The **CRA** also sets out a 'grey list' of the types of terms that might be regarded as unfair. As previously, this list is non-exhaustive and is only indicative of the types of terms which may be found to be unfair. **Schedule 2** sets out 20 potentially unfair terms – three of which are new.[24]

One of the aims of the **CRA** is to improve transparency for consumers and all written terms offered to a consumer must be 'transparent'. An important change introduced by the **CRA** is that terms which specify the main subject matter of the contract or set the price are not subject to the 'fairness' test (**s 64**) if the terms are both transparent *and* prominent.[25] A term is transparent where it is expressed in plain and intelligible language and be legible (if in writing). The prominence of the term will be determined by how it was brought to the consumer's attention. It must be in such a way that the 'average consumer' would be aware of it. An average consumer is one who is 'reasonably well-informed, observant and circumspect'. Previously, there was no requirement for 'prominence'. For example, if a trader sets a higher price than a competitor but the trader has made this price term both transparent and prominent, the price term may not be assessed for fairness.

It is worth noting that under the **CRA**, courts must consider the fairness of contract terms even if the parties to the proceedings do not raise fairness as an issue.

SUMMARY[26]
Although the **CRA** serves primarily to consolidate and simplify existing UK consumer legislation, it makes significant changes to the law in some areas. The **CRA** represents a substantial increase in consumer rights. Some provisions, such as consumers' rights in contracts for goods and services will be familiar as they are largely drawn from the **Sale of Goods Act 1979** and the **Supply of Goods and Services Act 1982** but other provisions, such as consumers' rights in contracts for digital content, are totally novel.

....

24 The presence of a term on the grey list will not automatically mean the term is unfair. It will need to be assessed for fairness by the court.

25 Although the price paid for goods is not subject to a test of fairness, the new wording clarifies that other aspects of the payment may be subject to scrutiny. For example, the timing and method of payment may now fall within the court's consideration of fairness. This clarifies the decision of *Financial Conduct Authority v Abbey National plc* (2009). In this case, the Supreme Court held that charges for unauthorised overdrafts were exempt from an assessment for fairness because they were price terms pursuant to the now-revoked **reg 6** of the **Unfair Terms in Consumer Contracts 1993 Regulations**. The charges will now be subject to a fairness assessment under the **CRA** if they are not prominently displayed to consumers when the relevant agreement is made.

26 It is always good to finish your answer with a conclusion which summarises your findings.

2

Description and Quality

INTRODUCTION

The questions in this chapter relate to the statutory implied terms as to description, quality and fitness for purpose, to exclusion clauses and also to product liability. In some courses, the law of trade descriptions is dealt with in questions which also raise contractual issues. This has not been done in this book because a number of sale of goods courses do not include trade descriptions in their syllabuses.

The **Consumer Rights Act 2015** ('**CRA**') came into force on 1 October 2015. It primarily consolidates much of the existing law in one statute, but it does make significant changes to the law in some areas. Note straightaway that the **CRA** only applies to business-to-consumer ('B2C') contracts. Overall, the Act represents a substantial increase in the rights of consumers and in the powers of the court. In relation to consumer contracts, the **CRA** replaces the **Unfair Contract Terms Act 1977** ('**UCTA**'), most of the **Sale of Goods Act 1979** ('**SGA**') and the **Supply of Goods and Services Act 1982** ('**SGSA**'). Significant changes have been made to consumer remedies in respect of faulty goods and the exclusion of price terms from scrutiny for unfairness.

Business-to-business ('B2B') contracts (as well as consumer-to-consumer contracts) remain governed by the **UCTA**, **SGA** and **SGSA**.

In all contracts, the **Unfair Terms in Consumer Contracts Regulations 1999** are revoked.

Commercial law courses tend to concentrate on B2B contracts and this is reflected in this book. You need to be clear as to which type of contract you are being examined on. If the contract is a B2C, the **CRA** applies. Under **s 2** of the **CRA**, a 'consumer' as an *individual* acting for purposes that are wholly or mainly outside that individual's trade, business, craft or profession. Small businesses (including sole traders) will have to look to the **SGA** for protections against the purchase of defective goods or services. **CRA Pt 1** deals with consumer contracts for goods, digital content and services. **Part 2** deals with unfair terms. **Part 3** contains miscellaneous provisions, including enforcement powers. This book concentrates on B2B contracts, though **Question 7** illustrates the situation of a B2C contract.

QUESTION 4

Longworth plc recently bought two used cars, each six months old, for its executives to drive. Lee, managing director of Longworth plc, first saw the two cars at Shoddy's Garage a month ago, when he noticed that one, a Kuga, had an engine oil leak and the other, a Galaxy, had a water leak in the boot. He did not, however, look in the boot of the Kuga. Shoddy assured him: 'They are good little buses; you can rely upon them.' After test-driving both cars, Lee, on behalf of Longworth plc, signed two contracts of purchase, one for each car. Lee left the Kuga with Shoddy to have the oil leak repaired and drove away in the Galaxy. Two weeks later, he returned the Galaxy for its boot leak to be repaired and collected the Kuga. The next day, he discovered, first, that the Kuga had a water leak in its boot; second, that the engine oil leak had not been repaired and was irreparable (meaning that a new engine was necessary); and, third, that soon after delivery to its first buyer, the Galaxy had been in an accident and subsequently treated by its owner's insurance company as a 'write-off'. Upon learning these facts, Lee informed Shoddy's Garage that he was rejecting the cars and demanded the return of the purchase price to Longworth plc.

▶ **Advise Longworth plc.**

How to Answer this Question

This question follows a certain style of setting questions, which involves a lot of points being included. The question is testing your ability to spot each of the issues raised as well as your ability to deal with them. Thus, a good answer must acknowledge each of the points raised and must not concentrate on some of the issues to the exclusion of the others.

The issues raised in this question are:

❖ liability for breach of the conditions as to satisfactory quality and fitness for purpose;

❖ liability (for an express term and/or misrepresentation) arising out of the statement about the cars being 'good little buses', etc;

❖ the remedies available to the buyer and, in particular, whether there has been acceptance of the goods so as to preclude rejection.

A sensible order of treatment is:

❖ implied conditions in **s 14**;

❖ express term/misrepresentation;

❖ remedies.

Applying the Law

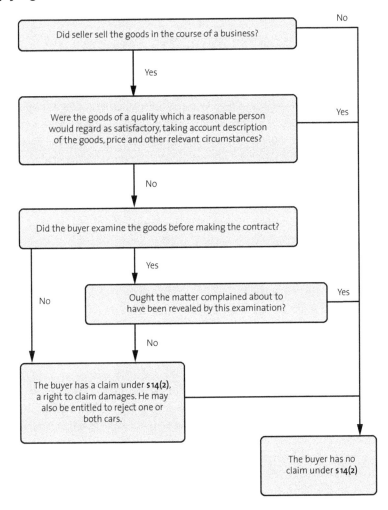

This diagram illustrates how to consider the application of the **SGA s 14(2)** *in this scenario. You will also have to touch on liability for misrepresentation and/or breach of an express term and* **s 14(3)** *(fitness for purpose). In addition, rights of rejection and remedies for breach of the contract will have to be considered.*

ANSWER

This question raises issues of liability for express and implied terms of the contract, for misrepresentation and the extent of any remedies available to Longworth plc. There may be liability in respect of the implied conditions as to satisfactory quality and fitness for purpose, liability for breach of an express term that the cars were 'good little buses' and liability for misrepresentation arising out of the same assertion by Shoddy. These possible liabilities will be considered, as will the remedies that may be available to Longworth plc.

It is to be observed that a separate contract was signed in relation to each car and, therefore, presumably the parties intended two distinct contracts. This answer will proceed upon that assumption.[1]

SATISFACTORY QUALITY

Because Shoddy sells in the course of business, terms regarding satisfactory quality and fitness for purpose are implied as conditions into the contracts of sale negotiated with Longworth plc. However, one condition, in **s14(2)** of the **Sale of Goods Act 1979**, is not implied as regards any defect specifically drawn to the buyer's attention before the contract was made or, given that Lee made a pre-purchase examination of the cars, as regards any defect which 'that' examination ought to have revealed. The engine oil leak in the Kuga and water leak in the boot of the Galaxy both appear to be defects falling into one or both of these categories, most clearly the latter category, since we are told that Lee noticed them. Assuming the water leak in the Galaxy can be repaired, it seems clear that in respect of that leak, no reliance can be placed by Longworth plc upon **s14(2)**.

The engine oil leak of the Kuga has turned out, however, to be irreparable without a complete engine replacement. This suggests that the true nature and/or extent of the defect was not something which was either drawn to Lee's attention or which ought to have been revealed by his pre-contract examination of the car. Neil LJ in *R and B Customs Brokers v United Dominions Trust* (1988) indicated, *obiter*,[2] that a defect of which the buyer is aware but which he reasonably (and mistakenly) believes will be rectified at no cost to himself is not excluded from the effect of **s14(2)**. It seems therefore that Longworth plc can rely upon the condition in **s14(2)** as regards the engine oil leak in the Kuga. The condition as to satisfactory quality might also apply to the water leak in the boot of the Kuga and to the fact that the Galaxy had been an insurance 'write-off'. The first of these *might* be a defect which Lee's pre-purchase inspection *ought* to have revealed. It seems clear that that inspection did not in fact reveal it because Lee did not in the course of that inspection look into the boot of the Kuga. In *Thornett and Fehr v Beers* (1919), it was held that a buyer who had, before the purchase, inspected the outside of some barrels but not the inside was precluded from relying on the condition as to satisfactory quality as regards defects which would have been revealed if he had inspected the inside. It is submitted, however, that a minor change to the wording of **s14(2)** effected in 1973 (to the then **Sale of Goods Act 1893**), namely, the change from 'such examination' to 'that examination' has reversed the effect of the 1919 case. Thus, Longworth plc is precluded from relying on those defects that ought to have been revealed by the examination which Lee actually made, but is not prejudiced by him having made a less extensive examination than he might have made. Put another way, the leak in the Kuga's boot was not a defect which ought to have been revealed by the examination which Lee actually made.

....

1 In your introduction, you should clearly identify the legal issues raised by the question. This is a good way to convince the examiner that you have understood what is relevant and will make him be positively inclined towards your answer.

2 Stating by whom or how (*obiter* or *ratio*) a particular legal principle was stated in a case demonstrates a deeper knowledge and will attract additional marks.

So, do the engine oil leak and boot leak in the Kuga make the car of unsatisfactory quality, and does the fact that the Galaxy was an insurance 'write-off' make the Galaxy of unsatisfactory quality? **Section 14(2A)** requires us to ask in each case whether the car reached a standard that the reasonable person would regard as satisfactory, taking account of any description given to the goods, the price and any other relevant circumstances. Undoubtedly, one of the relevant circumstances is the fact that, in each case, the car was not new but was six months old.[3] **Section 14(2B)** lists a number of aspects of the quality of the goods, including their 'fitness for all the purposes for which goods of the kind in question are commonly supplied'. Thus, the purposes for which a car is bought include not merely the purpose of driving it from place to place, but of doing so with the appropriate degree of comfort, ease of handling and pride in its outward and interior appearance (*Rogers v Parish* (1987)). This general approach applies also to second-hand cars and the question is whether, in this case, the defects were sufficiently serious to render even these second-hand cars of less than satisfactory quality. A second-hand car which, unknown to the buyer at the time of the contract, had been an insurance 'write-off' has been held for that reason not to have reached the necessary standard (*Shine v General Guarantee Corp* (1988)). The two leaks in the Kuga are less easy to decide upon. On the one hand, one is to expect minor defects in a second-hand car (*Bartlett v Sydney Marcus* (1965)). On the other hand, it could be said that the oil leak which requires a new engine for it to be remedied is actually a major defect. As regards the newly discovered water leak in the Kuga, much will depend upon its extent and the ease with which it can be repaired. Therefore, it is submitted that in the case of both cars, Longworth plc has a valid claim under **s14(2)**, but whether that extends to the boot leak in the case of the Kuga will depend upon the seriousness of the latter.

FITNESS FOR PURPOSE

Longworth plc's claim in respect of the defects discussed above might equally be made under **s14(3)**. Shoddy knows of the particular purpose for which Longworth plc wanted the cars, namely, the purpose of being driven by the company's executives. The defects already being relied upon under **s14(2)** render the cars not reasonably fit for that purpose. Longworth plc may have no claim under **s14(3)** in respect of defects of which it was aware (for example, the Galaxy's leaky boot) if Longworth plc placed no reliance upon Shoddy's skill and judgment in respect of them. It will still have a claim in relation to the other defect (*Cammell Laird v Manganese Bronze and Brass* (1934)).

'GOOD LITTLE BUSES'

Shoddy's assertion that the cars were 'good little buses' arguably implied that the cars were in good condition (*Andrews v Hopkinson* (1957)). This may have amounted to:

(1)   an express term, either a condition or a warranty, of the contract; and
(2)   a misrepresentation.

Assuming it was an express term of the contract, it is submitted that that express term was broken in the case of the Kuga by virtue of its engine oil leak necessitating a new engine.

....

3   In order to attract a good mark you need to ensure that you don't merely describe the law; you need to explain and apply it to the requirements of the question.

Whether the same can be said of water leaks in the boot is more problematic. Much will depend upon the seriousness of those leaks and the ease with which they can be repaired.

A claim for misrepresentation can succeed only if Lee relied upon Shoddy's statement. Did his pre-purchase examination of the cars indicate a lack of such reliance? Presumably not, because the statement appears to have been made *after* those examinations. Did Lee's subsequent test drives indicate that he was not relying on Shoddy's statement? It seems not, since Shoddy's statement referred to the cars' reliability (that is, presumably, over a period of time) and one or two test drives could not disclose the truth or otherwise of that. It is not necessary for Longworth plc to have relied exclusively upon Shoddy's statement. An untrue statement of fact by Shoddy which was one of the reasons Longworth plc was induced into buying will give Longworth plc a right to rescind the contract. If, however, Longworth plc wishes to claim damages for a misrepresentation, it may do so, either as an alternative to rescission (when the issue of whether to award damages is at the discretion of the judge – **s 2(2)** of the **Misrepresentation Act 1967**) or as an independent claim for damages under **s 2(1)**. In the latter case, Shoddy will have a defence if he can show, on a balance of probabilities, that at the time of the contract he had reasonable grounds to believe, and did believe, the statement to be true (**s 2(1)** of the **Misrepresentation Act 1967**).[4]

REMEDIES

Remedies for misrepresentation have just been discussed. For any breach of contract, there is a right to claim damages. Longworth plc has also purported to reject the cars and required the return of the price for each. Assuming that there was breach of the implied term in either **s 14(2)** or **s 14(3)**, Longworth plc undoubtedly had a right of rejection, since both of those terms are implied *conditions*. The same is not necessarily true of the express term encompassed by the words 'They are good little buses; you can rely upon them.' Assuming that this amounted to an express term of the contract, it would have to be decided whether the parties intended it to be a condition, that is, a term any breach of which would give Longworth plc the right to reject the goods and regard the contract as repudiated. The tendency of the courts is not to regard as a condition any express term (other than one as to the time of delivery), unless the parties have very clearly indicated it (*Cehave v Bremer, The Hansa Nord* (1976)). Thus, the test of whether Longworth plc had any right of rejection/repudiation for breach of the express term depends upon whether the breach was sufficient to deprive Longworth plc of substantially the whole of the benefit of the contract (*Hong Kong Fir v Kawasaki Kisen* (1962)). It is submitted that neither the boot leak in the case of one car nor the boot leak and the engine oil leak in the case of the other was sufficiently serious.

Assuming that Longworth plc was, because of the breach of the conditions in **s 14**, within its rights in rejecting the cars and demanding the return of the price, it will nevertheless have lost that right if, by the time it rejected the cars, it had already 'accepted' them within the meaning of **s 35**. Longworth plc rejected the Galaxy just over two weeks after

---

4   This burden is a very heavy one to discharge (*Howard Marine v Ogden* (1978)) and it is unlikely that Shoddy will manage to prove such a defence.

taking delivery. After a similar period of time, the buyer in *Bernstein v Pamson Motors* (1987) was held to have accepted the car. Even under the law as it then stood, that decision was controversial.[5] Since then, however, **s 35** has been amended so that, in determining what is a reasonable length of time, it is relevant to ask whether the buyer has had a reasonable opportunity to examine the goods for the purpose of ascertaining whether they comply with the contract. It is thus arguable that Longworth plc had not, in just over two weeks, had the Galaxy long enough to have examined it for that purpose. If it had not, then it was entitled to act as it did in rejecting it. Similarly, Longworth plc arguably had not had the car long enough that it could be said to have affirmed the contract – and thus was entitled to rescind the contract (and reject the car) for misrepresentation.[6]

Whatever may be a reasonable period of time for the buyer to examine the goods to see if they conform to the contract, there may be added to that period of time a further reasonable period. This may, for example, be a period during which the buyer investigates any apparent non-compliance (*Clegg v Andersson* (2003)) or a period during which the seller repairs the goods under an arrangement with the buyer (**s 35(5)**). So, Longworth plc clearly had not lost its right to reject the Kuga. Indeed, Longworth had taken delivery of the Kuga only one day before rejecting it.

Consequently, Longworth plc is entitled to the return of the Kuga's purchase price. It might also claim damages, although these are unlikely to be substantial in the case of the Kuga. In the case of the Galaxy, if Longworth plc is held to have lost its right to reject the car, the damages would be more substantial. Assuming that the breach in relation to the Galaxy was due to the fact that it had been an insurance 'write-off', the amount of damages would be the difference between the market value the car would have had it not got that particular history and the lower value it currently has.

QUESTION 5

Towning is a well-known dealer in antique vases. On 1 March, he went into China Emporium and asked the shop assistant if they had anything special. He was shown a vase described by the shop assistant as a 'Shing' vase and, after examining it behind a glass case, Towning agreed to buy it for £3,500 and took the vase with him. Towning was very pleased with the purchase because he had a customer who would pay handsomely for such a vase.

On 12 March, Towning left the vase with his customer to see if he would be interested in buying it for £4,000. The vase was returned two days later because it emerged that it was not genuine and that it was worth less than £250. A week later, during a dinner party, Towning discovered that water leaked from the vase which he was using to display a bunch of flowers.

---

5 Showing that you are aware of controversies surrounding a particular legal principle will set your answer apart from an average answer.
6 In *Feldarol Foundry v Hermes Leasing* (2004), the Court of Appeal held that a period of five to six weeks in relation to a defective car was not beyond a reasonable time in which to examine it, and thus the contract had not yet been affirmed.

Towning contacted China Emporium immediately, demanding his money back, and was told that it was not the shop's policy to make refunds in any circumstances.

▶ **Advise Towning.**

How to Answer this Question

The central issue in advising Towning is whether he is better off arguing that the pre-contractual statement that the vase was a 'Shing' vase had become part of the contract or suing for misrepresentation. Note that Towning is not dealing as a consumer, hence the **Consumer Rights Act 2015** does not apply to his contract with China Emporium. His contract is governed by the **Sale of Goods Act 1979**.

The main points that need to be considered are as follows:

❖ China Emporium's policy about not refunding money (was this part of the contract anyway?);
❖ description: s 13 of the **Sale of Goods Act 1979**;
❖ satisfactory quality: s 14(2);
❖ fitness for purpose: s 14(3);
❖ misrepresentation, common law and the **Misrepresentation Act 1967**;
❖ when a buyer loses the right to reject goods (acceptance/affirmation);
❖ remedies.

Applying the Law

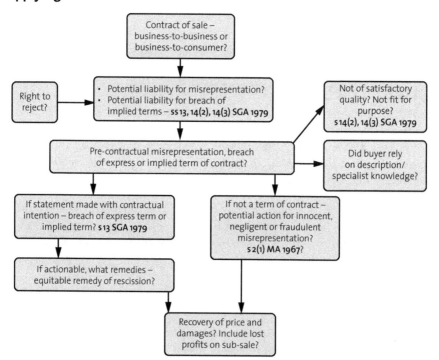

This diagram shows how to consider the contract of sale in relation to this scenario.

ANSWER

Towning has bought a vase which he now wishes to return and has been told that he is not entitled to a refund of the purchase price. It is clear that any attempt to restrict or limit liability is subject to the strict requirements of incorporation. China Emporium's policy of refusing refunds in any circumstances cannot be effective to prevent Towning from pursuing the matter against them if a term to that effect has not been incorporated into their contract. We are not told what the express terms and conditions were under the contract, or whether reasonable notice of the policy had been given before or at the time of the contract. Indeed, if there was such a notice displayed, perhaps in the shop, then such a term will be incorporated within their contract even if Towning did not read it. Assuming that there was no such notice, China Emporium is not entitled to rely on a policy which has not been disclosed to Towning, and the question of whether or not the policy is reasonable is not in issue. In any event, even if there were such a notice, it would probably be ineffective by virtue of the **Unfair Contract Terms Act 1977**.

It is clear that Towning was not dealing as a consumer.[7] Whether Towning has the right to return the vase will depend on finding a breach of a term of the contract or an actionable misrepresentation. There are four possible grounds here:

❖ description;
❖ satisfactory quality;
❖ fitness for purpose;
❖ misrepresentation.

DESCRIPTION

The relevant description in this case is that it was a 'Shing' vase. **Section 13** of the **Sale of Goods Act 1979** states that where goods are sold by reference to a description, it is an implied term that the goods should correspond with the description. In considering whether the sale is one by description, the court will have regard to *Harlingdon and Leinster v Christopher Hull Fine Art Ltd* (1990), that is, whether the seller in making the description has held himself out as having special knowledge and whether the buyer has relied on that description. In that case, a painting was sold described by art dealers, who were not experts in German art, as one by the German painter Gabriele Münter. The buyer, who did not make further inquiries but was an expert in German art, bought the painting for £6,000. It later transpired that the painting was a fake, worth less than £100, and the buyer rejected the painting on the ground that it did not comply with its description. The Court of Appeal held that the sale was not one by description since the description was not influential in the sale.[8]

---

7 **Section 2** of the **Consumer Rights Act 2015** defines a consumer as an individual acting for purposes that are wholly or mainly outside that individual's trade, business, craft or profession. Since we are told that Towning is a dealer in antique vases, when he bought the Shing vase, he did so in the course of his business. It was not therefore a consumer transaction.

8 Outlining the facts of a particular case is a good way to illustrate the relevant legal rules and thus strengthens your argument.

Applying the *Harlingdon* case to the question, although we are told that Towning is a well-known dealer in antique vases, we are not told whether China Emporium, with its name, was a known expert in this type of vase. Only if it was within the reasonable contemplation of the parties that Towning would rely upon the description 'Shing' could there be a sale by description. If China Emporium was, unlike the art dealers in *Harlingdon*, knowledgeable in 'Shing' vases, or held itself out to be, Towning would be entitled to reject the vase and claim damages.

We are told that Towning examined the vase before agreeing to buy it. A sale of goods is not prevented from being a sale by description solely because the buyer himself selects the goods (s13(3) and *Beale v Taylor* (1967)).

SATISFACTORY QUALITY

China Emporium clearly sells in the course of business so the implied term in s14(2) applies. The goods will not be of satisfactory quality if they do not meet the standard a reasonable person would regard as satisfactory, taking account of the price, any description and all other relevant circumstances (s14(2A)). One relevant aspect of their quality is their fitness for all the purposes for which goods of the kind in question are commonly supplied. The issue which needs to be looked at here is whether the vase was fit for the purposes for which it might commonly be supplied. Towning paid £3,500 for the vase. It is reasonable to assume that most people paying this high price for a vase will be buying it as an investment or for its resale value. Thus, the vase should be of satisfactory quality as an investment, but what of the fact that the vase is only worth £250? The Court of Appeal considered this point in the *Harlingdon* case, and Nourse LJ's view was that the purpose or purposes for which goods of this kind are commonly bought are the 'aesthetic appreciation of the owner or anyone else he permits to enjoy the experience'.[9] Thus, even if there was a defect in the quality of the vase, it was not one which made it 'unsaleable'. The question of whether goods are reasonably fit for resale cannot depend on whether they can or cannot be resold without making a loss. The test is an objective one, not dependent on the purpose for which Towning himself required the vase. It seems, therefore, that since most people would have bought the vase for its aesthetic appreciation, the fact that it was not a 'Shing' vase did not make the vase unfit for aesthetic appreciation which, despite its value being so much lower than the price, did not mean that the goods were of unsatisfactory quality.

We are told that Towning subsequently discovers that the vase leaks when he uses it to display a bunch of flowers. Can Towning claim that this rendered the vase of unsatisfactory quality? Before the 1994 amendments to s14, there was authority that the term as to merchantable quality did not require that the goods were reasonably fit for all the purposes for which goods of that description were commonly supplied, and that it was

....

9   The critical consideration of a statement given either in a case or by a noted expert is a good way to attract additional marks.

sufficient if they were fit for one of those purposes (*Aswan v Lupdine* (1987)).[10] Now, however, **s14(2B)** provides that one aspect of the quality of the goods is their fitness for all the purposes for which goods of that kind are commonly supplied. Certainly, vases are commonly supplied for use as display containers holding fresh flowers and water. It is difficult to know whether that is one of the purposes for which 'Shing' vases are commonly supplied. If it is, then the fact that the vase leaks suggests that it is not of satisfactory quality. If such vases are, however, commonly supplied for only one purpose, aesthetic appreciation (without containing fresh flowers), then the fact that it leaks will not make it of unsatisfactory quality.

FITNESS FOR PURPOSE

Section 14(3) provides that where goods are required for a particular purpose which has been made known to the seller, there is an implied term that the goods should be reasonably fit for that purpose. This will not apply if Towning did not rely or it was unreasonable for Towning to rely on China Emporium's skill and judgment in supplying the goods. In relation to the problem, two questions therefore need to be asked. First, did Towning make known to China Emporium the exact purpose for which the vase would be required? Second, if so, was it reasonable for him to rely on China Emporium's skill and judgment? The answer to the first question seems likely to be 'yes', as Towning is a well-known dealer and it is therefore reasonable to assume that if China Emporium is aware of this, it would also know that Towning would have bought the vase for resale as an antique item. The answer to the second question, however, is likely to be 'no', because, as was discussed in relation to 'description' (above), as between the parties, Towning was the expert in 'Shing' vases and it would be unreasonable for him to rely on China Emporium's skill and judgment. It seems, therefore, that China Emporium is not liable under **s14(3)**.

MISREPRESENTATION

The false statement that the vase was a 'Shing' vase may amount to an actionable misrepresentation, entitling Towning to rescind the contract and claim damages. The requirements of an actionable misrepresentation are that there was a false statement of an existing fact by one party which induced the other to enter the contract. It must be a statement of fact and not opinion, although an opinion which is not honestly held at the time or is based on facts which the maker of the statement ought to have known may be actionable.

It is clear from this question that the shop assistant did describe the vase as a 'Shing' vase. Towning's reliance on this description does not have to be reasonable. The court in *Museprime Properties v Adhill* (1990) held that the reasonableness of the reliance was relevant to determining whether there was actual reliance, but that the test of reliance is subjective (the more unreasonable the reliance, the less likely the court is to believe that it did actually affect the buyer's decision to enter into the contract). It is also clear that the

10 Showing an awareness of the historical development demonstrates your knowledge.

statement does not have to be the sole reason for entering into the contract: it is sufficient that it was one reason (*Edgington v Fitzmaurice* (1885)). It may be, therefore, that
Towning has a stronger claim in misrepresentation than under the implied conditions
under the **Sale of Goods Act**.

Once it has been established that an actionable misrepresentation has been made, the
remedies will depend on whether the misrepresentation was made innocently, negligently or fraudulently.[11] It is unlikely that the shop assistant will have made the statement that it was a 'Shing' vase fraudulently. Either he made it innocently (that is, in
genuine ignorance of the fact that it was untrue) or negligently (that is, he had no
reasonable grounds for believing that the statement was true) under **s 2(1)** of the **Misrepresentation Act 1967**.[12] If the misrepresentation was made innocently, Towning will
be entitled to rescission of the contract. If the misrepresentation was made negligently,
Towning will be entitled not only to rescission, but may recover for all losses caused by
the misrepresentation, unrestricted by the rules of remoteness (*Royscot Trust Ltd v Rog-
erson* (1991)). Moreover, following *Parabola Investments v Browallia* (2009), he will be
entitled to lost profits.

One final point which needs to be made is that whether Towning decides to pursue the
matter for breach of contract or for misrepresentation may depend on the fact that it was
some three weeks after he bought the vase that he tried to reject the goods against China
Emporium. Any action for breach of contract is subject to the rules of acceptance under
s 35 of the **Sale of Goods Act** which, *inter alia*, deems the buyer to have accepted the goods
if, after a lapse of reasonable time, he retains the goods without intimating to the seller
that he rejects them. In *Bernstein v Pamson Motors* (1987), a period of three weeks was
regarded as beyond a reasonable time in which to examine a motor car. Since then, **s 35**
has been amended and a reasonable period now will normally include a reasonable
opportunity for the buyer to examine the goods for the purpose of ascertaining whether
they conform to the contract. This may well mean that the reasonable period of time
before the buyer is taken to have accepted the goods will be longer than previously (*Clegg
v Andersson* (2003)). Towning had in fact had the vase for over three weeks before giving
notice of rejection. However, he discovered after two weeks that it was not a 'Shing' vase.
Assuming that that is a breach of condition, it is arguable that keeping it a further week
afterwards before rejecting it amounts to acceptance. If, however, he was using that week
in order to have experts examine it to confirm whether or not it was a 'Shing' vase
(although we are told nothing to suggest that he was), that would have the effect of
lengthening the reasonable period of time (*Truk v Tokmakidis* (2000)). If he has accepted
the goods, his only remedy for breach of contract would be a claim for damages, the

....

11 A detailed knowledge of misrepresentation is not usually required on commercial law courses, but bear in
mind that the examiner is entitled to test you on the general principles of contract law.
12 It is possible, of course, to bring the action under the common law, that is, under the rule in *Hedley Byrne v
Heller* (1964). Since the **Misrepresentation Act 1967**, however, **s 2(1)** is the preferable cause of action
because then the burden of proof is on the defendant to show that there were reasonable grounds for
believing that the statement was true.

amount of which would depend greatly on whether, on the one hand, he could establish a breach of contract arising out of the description 'Shing' vase or, on the other, was able only to rely on the fact that the vase leaked.

An action in misrepresentation is not subject to the acceptance rules and a buyer is only deemed to have lost his right to rescind if he has affirmed the contract which, after three weeks, it may be held that he has done. If it were established that the misrepresentation were fraudulent, then time would begin to run only from when Towning discovered the truth. It seems that Towning only knew of the lack of authenticity of the vase around 14 March (when his customer returned it to him) and it was only a week after that that he contacted China Emporium. Thus, if it was a fraudulent misrepresentation, Towning may be able to rescind the contract. He would in any case be entitled to damages for misrepresentation, to cover all his losses, not limited by the rules of remoteness.

QUESTION 6

Mary, in the course of her business, agreed to buy from Joseph '2,000 Christmas trees, Nordman Fir, five feet to six feet high, fair average quality for the season, packed 50 to a pallet, delivery to Mary's premises on 10–12 December'. The contract contained an exclusion clause which satisfied the requirement of reasonableness in the **Unfair Contract Terms Act 1977** and which excluded liability for any breach of the statutory implied conditions as to satisfactory quality and fitness for purpose. On 12 December, Joseph tenders delivery to Mary.

Consider the legal position on 12 December in each of the following alternative situations:

(a) 90% of the trees are between five feet and six feet high but 5% of them are slightly less than five feet and 5% are slightly over six feet high;
(b) a number of the trees are unevenly tapered in shape and are thus not 'fair average quality for the season';
(c) the trees are packed 75 to a pallet;
(d) the delivery tendered is of 2,020 trees.

How to Answer this Question

This question, with its exclusion clause, plainly effective to exclude the implied conditions as to satisfactory quality and fitness for purpose, is clearly concentrated on the implied condition as to description and to the (often) related issues that arise in relation to delivery of the wrong contract quantity or of contract goods mixed with non-contract goods. A simple approach here is to deal with each numbered part of the question in turn, taking care to refer back where necessary to an answer already given rather than to repeat issues that are the same in relation to the different parts of the question.

Applying the Law

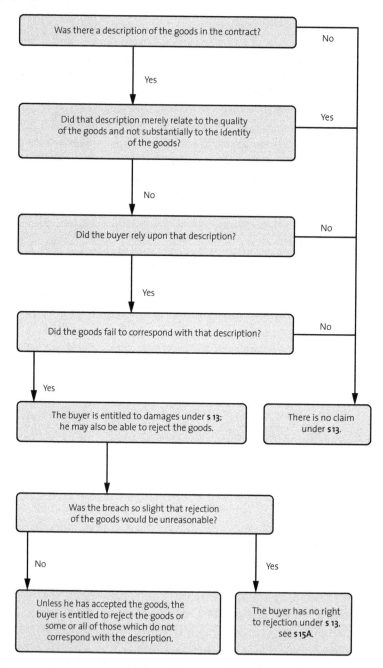

How the law relating to the right to reject can be understood in this answer can be seen above. In addition to the issue above, you will have to consider the impact of the express term re fair average quality, the effect of the exclusion clause and delivery of the wrong amount. The remedies available to the buyer will need to be looked at.

ANSWER

(A) 90% OF THE TREES COMPLY

The fact that 10% of the trees are outside the definition of 'five feet to six feet high' could cause the seller to be in breach of the condition, implied by **s 13** of the **Sale of Goods Act 1979**, that the goods must correspond with their description. So far as we are informed, the shortness or extra length does not render the trees of any less quality or likely to be less fit for any purpose for which Mary had indicated to Joseph that she wanted them. It seems clear that 'five feet to six feet high' was an express term of the contract as to description and thus any failure to comply would be a breach of the condition in **s 13**. We are not told how short of five feet or how much in excess of six feet the non-conforming trees measured, except that we are told that the deviation was 'slight'.[13] Joseph might seek to invoke the maxim *de minimis non curat lex* and thus argue that any deviation was so small that it ought to be ignored. However, the measurements of five feet to six feet, given in the contract description, are precise measurements and it has been held by the House of Lords that a contract requirement on the seller to supply staves 'half an inch thick' was exactly that and that supplying staves up to nine-sixteenths of an inch thick was a breach of the implied condition implied by **s 13** (*Arcos v Ronaasen* (1933)). If the seller had wished for a margin, he should have stipulated for it in his contract. In the present case, that reasoning can be taken further by the observation that there was a margin stipulated for in the contract, that is, anything from five to six feet high. Thus, it seems that Joseph is in breach of the condition in **s 13**.

Normally, a breach of condition entitles the buyer to reject the goods. In the case of a breach of the conditions in **ss 13–15** of the **Sale of Goods Act**, however, this is subject to **s 15A**. Mary will not be entitled to reject the goods if the breach was so slight that it would be unreasonable for her to reject them. Although we are told that some of the trees were 'slightly' over or under the contract height, we are not given enough facts to know if **s 15A** does apply – and it is for Joseph, the seller, to show that it does. If it does not apply, then Mary has a whole range of options open to her. First, she could waive her right to reject the goods (which would leave her in exactly the same position as if **s 15A** does apply) and simply claim damages for her loss, if any, arising from the fact that some of the trees were too short and some too long. If she suffered no damage or loss because of that, then she would be entitled only to nominal damages. Second, she could reject the whole consignment and, assuming that Joseph is unable to supply a complete consignment of complying trees by the end of the contractual delivery deadline (12 December), she could claim damages which would be assessed on the difference between what she was contracted to pay Joseph and the market price (if higher) on 12 December of 2,000 trees matching the contract description (**s 51**). Third, Mary could accept those trees which did conform to the contract description and reject some or all of the 10% which did not (**s 35A**). In this scenario, she must pay for those she accepts pro rata at the contract rate. She will also be

---

13 Noting the lack of information provided by the question and pointing out the likely implications of any such lack show an understanding of the area of law in question.

able to claim damages in relation to the 10% she rejects, the damages being the difference between the contract price for the number of rejected trees and, if higher, the market price on 12 December for that number of trees conforming to the contract description.

(B) SOME ARE NOT OF 'FAIR AVERAGE QUALITY FOR THE SEASON'

Given the facts that (i) Mary was not dealing as a consumer, and (ii) the exclusion clause satisfies the requirement of reasonableness, the implied conditions as to satisfactory quality and fitness for purpose cannot be relied upon by Mary. Unless there is some special statutory provision relating to Christmas trees or to trees, there are no other implied conditions as to quality (**s14(1)**). That leaves two possible causes of action available to Mary. The first is that Joseph is in breach of the condition as to description, in that the trees do not conform to the contract requirement that they be of 'fair average quality for the season'. However, it seems unlikely that the court would regard those words as part of the contract 'description' (*Ashington Piggeries v Christopher Hill* (1972)). This is because the contract description does not normally include quality requirements but is confined to those elements in the contractual requirements which help to 'identify' the goods.[14] The result of this, combined with the exclusion clause, is that reliance on the implied conditions as to description and quality is ruled out. This means that Mary is thrown back on her other possible cause of action, namely, a claim for breach of an *express* term of the contract, that is, a term that the trees be of fair average quality for the season. This term is unlikely, however, to be regarded by the court as a condition of the contract since the parties have not, it appears, indicated that it was their intention that any breach of the term would entitle Mary to regard the contract as repudiated. That being so, the term is only a warranty (or intermediate term) of the contract and Mary could not regard the contract as repudiated by a breach of that term unless the breach deprived Mary of 'substantially the whole benefit' of the contract (*Hong Kong Fir v Kawasaki Kisen* (1962); *Cehave v Bremer* (1976)).

We are told of neither the severity of the poor shape of the trees nor of the number affected. If more than half are affected and they are severely misshapen and if, as a result, Mary cannot sell them without damaging her own commercial reputation, then the court would very likely be prepared to regard the breach as a repudiatory one. If the breach is sufficiently severe to amount to a repudiatory breach, then Mary is entitled to accept those which conform to the contract and to reject some or all of those which do not. Whether Mary refuses to accept all or just some of the goods, the risk for her is that the court may subsequently hold that the breach did not deprive her of substantially the

---

14 Lord Diplock in that case said: The 'description' by which unascertained goods are sold is, in my view, confined to those words in the contract which were intended by the parties to identify the kind of goods which were to be supplied. It is open to the parties to use a description as broad or narrow as they choose. But ultimately the test is whether the buyer could fairly and reasonably refuse to accept the physical goods proffered to him on the ground that their failure to correspond with that part of what was said about them in the contract makes them goods of a different kind from those he had agreed to buy. The key to **s13** is identification.

whole benefit of the contract. In that case, then, Mary would herself be in breach of contract for refusing to take delivery and would be liable to Joseph for non-acceptance of the goods. The measure of damages would be the difference between the contract price for the number of trees rejected and the market price, if lower, on 12 December. Mary should therefore be advised to consider accepting the trees and reselling them for whatever she can get.[15] She would in those circumstances be able to claim damages for breach of the express term that the trees be of fair average quality for the season. Her measure of damages would, *prima facie*, be the difference in the value to her of the trees actually delivered and the higher value they would have had if they had been of fair average quality for the season (**s 53(3)**).

(C) TREES ARE PACKED 75 TO A PALLET

Even if the fact that the trees are packed 75 instead of 50 to a pallet renders them of unsatisfactory quality or unfit for their purpose, Mary will be unable to rely upon the implied conditions in **s 14** of the **Sale of Goods Act**, for the reasons just given in relation to the contract requirement that the trees be of fair average quality for the season.[16] Again, therefore, Mary has two possible causes of action. The first is for breach of an express term of the contract and the second is for breach of the implied condition as to description. As regards the former, again, it seems unlikely that the court would construe the express term as a condition of the contract and therefore any right of Mary to regard the contract as repudiated (and, hence, to reject the goods) must depend upon whether the breach (the trees being packed 75 instead of 50 to a pallet) deprives Mary of substantially the whole benefit of the contract. Unless there are some unusual facts which are not disclosed by the question as set, it seems unlikely that Mary has suffered such a breach. Thus, Mary's only right is to claim damages for breach of the express term, on the same basis as just explained in relation to the requirement that the trees be of fair average quality for the season. That is so, unless she can claim that Joseph is in breach of the condition as to description in **s 13**. Such a claim depends upon the requirement 'packed 50 to a pallet' being accepted by the court as being part of the contract 'description'. In *Re Moore and Landauer* (1921), a somewhat similar requirement was accepted by the Court of Appeal as being part of the contract description. This has the result that any deviation (even if quite a small one) from the requirement is a breach of condition and entitles the buyer to reject the goods. In *Re Moore and Landauer*, the buyer was held entitled to reject a consignment of tinned fruit because although the correct contract quantity had been delivered, some of them were packed in cases of 24 tins instead of (as the contract required) in cases of 30 tins.[17] That decision has, however, since been doubted in the House of Lords (*Reardon Smith Line v Hansen Tangen* (1976)). It is clear now that the courts are unlikely to find that an express term of the contract comprises part of the contract description unless it helps to 'identify' the goods. This means that the court is highly

---

15 Concluding your analysis with tailored advice to the advisee will ensure completeness of your answer.

16 Referring back to a previously drawn conclusion or an explanation made earlier not only demonstrates that you understand what is relevant, it also saves valuable time as you don't have to repeat yourself.

17 Providing an outline of a case which resembles the facts of the problem strengthens your argument/ conclusion.

unlikely to regard the requirement that the trees be packed 50 to a pallet as anything other than a warranty (or intermediate term) of the contract. Furthermore, **s 15A** has been added to the **Sale of Goods Act 1979** by the **Sale and Supply of Goods Act 1994** with the result that, even if there has been a breach of condition, Mary has no right to reject the goods if the breach was so slight that it would be unreasonable for her to reject them. Mary therefore should be advised not to reject the trees but to accept them and to claim damages for any loss as a result of the trees being packed 75 to a pallet.

(D) 2,020 TREES TENDERED

This part of the question seems no more than a straightforward example of the seller tendering more than the contract quantity. However, it must also inevitably be that the trees are not all 'packed 50 to a pallet', since 2,020 is not divisible by 50! For a discussion of that aspect of the matter, see the answer to (c) above. Leaving that issue aside, there remains the matter of the extra quantity. The normal rules on over-supply are as follows. First, Mary can reject all the goods for breach of the condition to supply 2,000 trees (**s 30(2)**). Second, she can accept the contract quantity and reject the surplus 20 (**s 30(2)**). Third, she could accept the whole lot and pay for the extra *pro rata* at the contract rate (**s 30(3)**). However, the operation of **s 30** is subject to any custom and practice between the parties and to any usage of the trade (**s 30(5)**). Even if there is no such relevant custom, practice or usage, the court may well regard the over-supply of 20 trees (that is, a mere 1% of the contract quantity) as *de minimis*. In that case, Mary has suffered no breach and will be required to pay nothing for the extra 20 trees.

Common Pitfalls

This question includes a lot of points. A good answer must acknowledge each of the points raised and must not concentrate on some of the issues to the exclusion of the others.

QUESTION 7 --

Yvette wants to buy a washing machine. She walks into a branch of Home Appliance Ltd for advice. She tells Andy, the shop assistant, that she needs a machine that has a quick wash cycle. Andy recommended the Helper because, on average, it requires just 30 minutes for a wash cycle at 50 degrees Celsius. The machine is delivered later that day.

It turns out that for a wash cycle at 50 degrees Celsius the machine in fact requires 60 minutes. Two weeks later, the machine is beginning to make funny noises and starts belching smoke. The load it is washing at the time is completely destroyed. When Yvette phones Andy to ask for her money back, Andy tells her that the contract Yvette signed included a clause stating: 'All conditions relating to the quality or condition of any machine are hereby excluded. The seller accepts no liability in respect of any statements made prior to the contract unless such statements have been put in writing.'

▶ **Advise Yvette.**

How to Answer this Question

Unlike the other questions in this chapter, Question **7** deals with a business-to-consumer contract. There is nothing in the question to suggest that Yvette is anything but an individual buying the washing machine for private purpose. Her purchase from Home Appliance Ltd is thus a consumer transaction to which the **Consumer Rights Act 2015** applies.

The issues raised in this question are:

- ❖ liability for breach of the conditions as to description, satisfactory quality and fitness for purpose;
- ❖ liability (for an express term and/or misrepresentation) arising out of the statement about the washing machine needing only 30 minutes for a wash cycle;
- ❖ the remedies available to the consumer;
- ❖ the exclusion clause. The method of dealing with it is, after quickly acknowledging that it was incorporated into the contract, to deal with the interpretation of the clause and then the effect under the **Consumer Rights Act 2015**.

Applying the Law

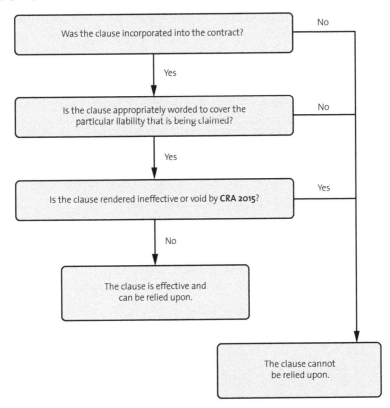

The diagram illustrates how the exemption clause can be considered in this question once the status of the contract has been determined.

*In addition to the issue of the exemption clause you will have to consider the status of the statements by the employee and whether the item was of satisfactory quality (**s 9(2)**). Also whether the machine can be rejected and the consumer remedies for breach of contract.*

ANSWER

This question raises issues of liability for express and implied terms of the contract and the extent of any remedies available to Yvette, bearing in mind the seller has purported to exclude liability.

DESCRIPTION

When Yvette told Andy she needed a washing machine capable of a quick wash cycle, he recommended the Helper because, he said, it needed just 30 minutes for a wash cycle. This may have amounted to an express term. This means that the washing machine supplied must be as described. Assuming it was an express term of the contract, it is clear that that express term was breached in Yvette's case because the wash cycle, in fact, took 60 minutes. This would also constitute a breach of a trader's obligation to supply goods as described under **s 11** of the **Consumer Rights Act 2015** ('**CRA**').[18] We are told that Andy recommended the Helper but we are not told if Yvette had actually seen a Helper on display in the shop. If she had, **s 14** requires that the machine delivered to her matches the model on display.

For any breach of contract, there is a right to claim damages. Although it seems clear there was a breach of the express term as to description, it would have to be decided whether the breach deprived Yvette of substantially the whole benefit she was entitled to expect under the contract to determine whether she could reject the goods and regard the contract as repudiated. It would be much easier for Yvette to bring her claim under the **CRA**. Yvette bought the machine just over two weeks ago. **Section 22** of the **CRA** gives the consumer a short-term right to reject goods and claim a full refund for up to 30 days after purchase. This is further discussed under 'Remedies' below.

SATISFACTORY QUALITY

Because Home Appliance Ltd trades in the course of business, terms regarding satisfactory quality and fitness for purpose are implied as conditions into the sale contract with Yvette. Under **s 9(2)** of the **CRA**, there is an implied term that goods sold should be of satisfactory quality.

The machine belched smoke, ruining the load it was washing at the time. A reasonable person would not regard the machine as satisfactory, taking account of any description

---

18 Furthermore, **s 11** requires that certain information relating to the main characteristics of the goods must be provided to the consumer pre-contract. We are not told whether Andy gave this information to Yvette, although much of the information required is usually obvious when a consumer such as Yvette enters a store to purchase goods (eg a poster displaying the key features of the washing machine).

given to the goods, the price and any other relevant circumstances (**s 9(2)**). We are not told what price Yvette paid for the machine or whether it was bought as new or second-hand goods. The general approach is that the higher the price paid, particularly for new goods, the higher the standard the buyer can expect. However, in Yvette's case, the defects are sufficiently serious to render even second-hand goods of less than satisfactory quality (*Crowther v Shannon Motors* (1975)). Furthermore, no reasonable person would regard the washing machine as satisfactory if after such a short period of time (two weeks) it makes funny noises and starts belching smoke. The washing machine can hardly be described as safe or durable.

It is unlikely that Andy specifically drew the defects to Yvette's attention before the contract was made. We are not told whether Yvette made a pre-purchase examination of the washing machine, as regards any defect which 'that' examination ought to have revealed. Even if she did examine the machine, it is unlikely this would have revealed the defect.

Therefore, it is submitted that Yvette has a valid claim under **s 9(2)**.

FITNESS FOR PURPOSE

Yvette's claim in respect of the defects discussed above might equally be made under **s 10(3)**. Since the description of the goods ('washing machine') points to one purpose only, the washing machine must be fit for that particular purpose (*Priest v Last* (1903)) and it is clear that the defects already being relied upon under **s 9(2)** render the washing machine not reasonably fit for that purpose and thus a breach of the implied condition in **s 10(3)**. In addition, Yvette told Andy that she needs a machine that has a quick wash cycle. The machine recommended to her was not capable of this. Since it is reasonable for Yvette to place reliance upon Andy's skill and judgment in respect of his recommendation, Yvette will have a claim under **s 10(3)**.

EXCLUSION CLAUSE

Like any exclusion clause, the clause in this case will not have any effect unless it satisfies each of the following requirements:

❖ it was incorporated into the contract;
❖ as a matter of interpretation, the wording of the clause is effective to exclude liability which otherwise the seller would incur;
❖ the clause is not rendered invalid by the **CRA**.

In the present case, the first of these requirements is satisfied as we are told that Yvette had signed the contract (*L'Estrange v Graucob* (1934)).

INTERPRETATION OF THE CLAUSE

As regards the second requirement, the first sentence of the clause would clearly exclude liability for breach of the implied condition as to satisfactory quality in **s 9** of the **CRA**. Does it also exclude liability for the condition of fitness of purpose? The *contra proferentem* rule of construction which the courts use in construing exclusion clauses requires that, where a clause is ambiguous, the meaning which gives the clause the lesser effect is adopted. Referring to the wording of the clause, the condition as to fitness is excluded if it relates to the 'quality or condition' of a machine. Clearly, on the facts of the problem given, it is the quality that is in issue and, undoubtedly, the quality of a washing machine can affect its fitness for a particular purpose. However, the fitness for purpose condition implied by **s 10(3)** is not confined to matters of quality or condition. A machine can be of excellent quality and in excellent condition and still not be fit for a particular purpose for which the buyer has indicated she wants it. Here, Yvette told Andy that she wants a machine capable of quick wash cycles. Applying the *contra proferentem* rule, therefore, it seems likely that a court would hold that the fitness for purpose condition was not excluded.

It appears then that the first sentence of the clause, as a matter of interpretation, does exclude liability for breach of the condition as to satisfactory quality, but may well not do so as regards the condition of fitness for purpose.

Let us turn to the matter of Home Appliance Ltd's possible liability in respect of the pre-contract statement about the washing machine being capable of a 30-minute wash cycle. The second sentence of the clause would appear to exclude that liability, since there is no indication that Andy's statement was put into writing. There is, however, an argument which might prevent such a conclusion. It is possible that Andy's words might give rise to liability for breach of an express term of the contract (*Andrews v Hopkinson* (1957)). The clause refers to statements made 'prior to the contract'. It does not refer to statements which are part of the contract itself, which an express term – even one not reduced to writing – would undoubtedly be. So it might be argued that the clause was not intended to exclude express terms. The point is clearly an arguable one, since it could alternatively be said that the intention of the clause is to exclude all liability in respect of pre-contract statements, including terms of the contract itself, unless those terms are in writing.

CRA

Assuming that the clause is effective at common law to exclude at least some possible liabilities, is it robbed of that effect by the **CRA**? **Section 31** is quite clear: a term purporting to exclude or restrict the trader's liability for unsatisfactory goods or unfit goods is not binding on the consumer. Since Yvette dealt as a consumer in buying the washing machine, Home Appliance Ltd cannot exclude their liabilities in relation to **s 9** and **s 10** implied terms.

Let us turn to the effect of the **CRA** on the clause insofar as it purports to exclude liability for breach of unwritten express terms of the contract. Andy's assurance the washing machine has a quick wash cycle amounts to a consumer notice which, under **s 61**, includes unwritten communications. Thus the second sentence of the clause is subject to the requirement of fairness. The effect of **s 62** will render the exclusion clause of no effect since, contrary to a requirement of good faith, the clause causes a significant imbalance in the parties' rights and obligations to the detriment of the consumer. The exclusion clause in question is likely to be declared 'unfair'.

REMEDIES

Under **s 22**, Yvette has the *right to reject* the washing machine for breach of **s 9(2)** or **s 10(3)** and claim a full refund for up to 30 days after purchase. Yvette telephoned Andy two weeks after the washing machine was delivered. No particular form of words is necessary in order to treat the contract as terminated. Yvette merely needs to make it clear to Andy that she rejects the washing machine. Home Appliance Ltd is under a duty to refund Yvette in full without undue delay.[19] Since nothing indicated otherwise in the purchase contract, Yvette does not have to return the rejected washing machine. All Yvette now has to do is to make the washing machine available for collection by Home Appliance Ltd.

Alternative to rejecting the washing machine, Yvette could claim a remedy of repair or of replacement of the machine (**s 23**) which, if not successful or the associated costs would be disproportionate compared to Yvette's other remedies, she will then have the right to an appropriate *price reduction* (up to the full price paid by Yvette) or a *final right to reject* (**s 24**). The final right to reject is subject to a right of deduction for use, to take into account the use Yvette has made of the machine since it was delivered. It appears that these additional rights are not what Yvette wishes to claim for. We are told that she wants her money back, that is, she wants to reject the washing machine. Because the fault is obvious there is no need for further testing and Home Appliance Ltd must agree to provide a refund.

Yvette undoubtedly has a right of rejection under the **CRA**, since both **s 9(2)** or **s 10(3)** are implied terms. The same is not necessarily true of the express term (that the wash cycle is complete in 30 minutes), since it would have to be decided whether the parties intended it to be a condition, that is, a term any breach of which would give Yvette the right to reject the goods and regard the contract as repudiated. The test of whether Yvette had any right of rejection/repudiation for breach of the express term depends upon whether the breach was sufficient to deprive Yvette of substantially the whole of the benefit of the contract (*Hong Kong Fir v Kawasaki Kisen* (1962)). It is possible that the fact that the machine needs more than 30 minutes to complete the wash cycle was not sufficiently serious. This does affect Yvette's right to treat the contract as an end for breach of **s 9(2)** or **s 10(3)** under the **CRA**.

CONCLUSION[20]

The exemption clause in the contract will be of no effect to Yvette's claim. Yvette has already phoned Andy asking for her money back. She has rejected in a way clear enough to be understood by Home Appliance Ltd and Yvette is entitled to a refund without undue

---

19 **Section 20(15)** goes on to provide that the refund is due to the consumer at the latest within 14 days from when the trader agrees the consumer is entitled to it. Since the washing machine is clearly defective and in breach of the implied terms under the **CRA**, Home Appliance Ltd needs to refund Yvette within 14 days following the phone call to Andy.

20 It is always good to finish your answer with a conclusion which summarises your findings.

delay and within 14 days. Yvette's obligation is then to make the washing machine available for collection by Home Appliance Ltd (since we are not told whether under the contract there was a provision otherwise).

Yvette may also claim damages, in particular, for the load the machine was washing but which was completely destroyed. Such damages would not be too remote under the rule in *Hadley v Baxendale* (1854).

3 Passing of Property and Risk

INTRODUCTION

This chapter covers the passing of property and risk. The **Consumer Rights Act 2015** has not affected these rules.

QUESTION 8

Vinco Wines Ltd is a wine merchant. Its stock in its warehouse a month ago was:

❖ 100 bottles of 1990 Château Rayas;
❖ 200 bottles of 1921 Vintage Armagnac which, unknown to Vinco Wines Ltd, were the last bottles of that vintage remaining unconsumed anywhere in the world;
❖ 350 bottles of 2000 Château-Grillet;
❖ assorted other wines.

In the last month, Vinco Wines has made and received no deliveries of wine, but has made the following agreements to sell wine:

❖ '100 bottles of 1990 Château Rayas' to Hotel Anatoly;
❖ '200 bottles of 1921 Vintage Armagnac' to Viktor plc;
❖ '300 bottles of 2000 Château-Grillet, currently in Vinco Wines' warehouse' to Sergei Bank;
❖ '50 bottles of 2000 Château-Grillet' to Restaurant Gleb.

As regards payment: Anatoly paid Vinco Wines when it made the contract; Viktor agreed to pay upon collecting the goods from Vinco Wines' warehouse; Sergei and Gleb each agreed to pay upon delivery by Vinco Wines to their respective premises.

Yesterday, Vinco Wines despatched to Gleb 50 bottles of 2000 Château-Grillet. Unfortunately, the lorry (Vinco Wines' own) crashed en route and all the wine on board was lost. Last night, a fire destroyed Vinco Wines' warehouse and its contents.

▶ **Advise Hotel Anatoly, Viktor plc, Sergei Bank and Restaurant Gleb.**

How to Answer this Question

This question is plainly concerned with the issue of whether risk had passed from the seller to the buyer. However, the answer must not be confined to that, because it is important to know whether the contracts are still binding and, if not, what the position is. The relevant provisions under the **Sale of Goods Act 1979** need to be discussed.

Note that the buyers in the question are not dealing as consumers. Under the **Consumer Rights Act 2015**, consumers are defined as being individuals and it appears that the buyers in the question are businesses.[1]

Applying the Law

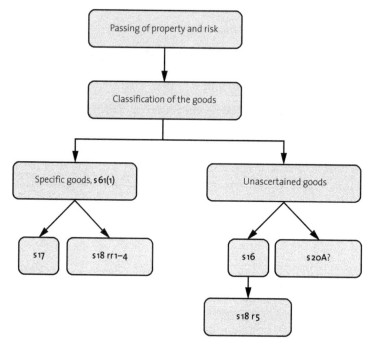

This diagram illustrates how passing of property is discussed in the answer.

ANSWER

Each of the buyers will be advised as to whether the risk in the goods had passed to them and, if not, whether the contract is still binding.

We are not told whether the contracts contained any provision stating when risk was to pass to the buyer or when property was to pass. It will be assumed that there was no such provision. In any case, even if there were a provision that property was to pass to the buyer at a particular stage, that provision could not, in the case of a contract for the sale

---

1 If any of the buyers were a consumer, it is not the **Sale of Goods Act** that applies but the **Consumer Right Act 2015** ('**CRA**'). Under **s 29** of the **CRA**, risk passes to the consumer only when goods come into the physical possession of the consumer or designated person.

of unascertained goods, come into effect until those goods were ascertained (**s 16** of the **Sale of Goods Act 1979**).

In the absence of contrary agreement, and subject to a couple of provisos, risk passes with property (**s 20**). Subject to **s 16** just mentioned, property passes when the parties intend it to (**s 17**) and, unless a different intention appears, property passes according to the rules in **s 18**. The application of these rules depends upon whether the contract in question was for specific goods or unascertained goods.

SPECIFIC OR UNASCERTAINED GOODS?

The time for determining whether goods are specific or unascertained goods is that at which the contract is made. If the contract is for goods which are 'identified and agreed upon' at the time the contract is made, then it is one for the sale of specific goods (**s 61(1)**). The agreement which Hotel Anatoly has is not one for specific goods, since, even if the parties had expected that Anatoly's contract would be fulfilled from Vinco Wines' stock, there was apparently no contractual agreement to that effect, but simply an obligation on Vinco Wines to deliver '100 bottles of 1990 Château Rayas'. Thus, if Vinco Wines chose to keep for itself the 100 bottles in its stock at the time of the contract or if it chose to supply them to another customer, it could still comply with its contractual commitments to Hotel Anatoly by getting hold of 100 other bottles of 1990 Château Rayas and supplying those to Hotel Anatoly. That makes it a contract for the sale of unascertained goods, since the contract did not identify the 100 bottles in Vinco Wines' stock as the contractual bottles (*Re London Wine Shippers* (1986)).

Similarly, the contract with Viktor plc did not identify the 200 bottles of 1921 Vintage Armagnac in Vinco Wines' stock as being the contractual bottles. Had it been possible to do so, Vinco Wines could have bought a further 200 bottles and used those to fulfil its contract with Viktor plc. It is submitted that it is irrelevant that it would in fact have been impossible to buy more such bottles. It may be argued that a contract to buy 'a painting of the *Mona Lisa* by Leonardo da Vinci' is no different from a contract to buy 'the painting of the *Mona Lisa* by Leonardo da Vinci', since there is only one such painting. However, in the present case, Vinco Wines was unaware that the bottles in its warehouse were the only ones in existence and, in those circumstances, it cannot be said that the 1921 Vintage Armagnac bottles were 'identified and agreed upon at the time the contract was made' as being the contractual goods, since, so far as the parties were concerned, the contract allowed other goods to be supplied which corresponded with the contract description. Thus, Viktor plc's contract also was for the sale of unascertained goods.

The contract with Sergei Bank did identify Vinco Wines' stock as the source from which Sergei Bank's bottles must come. However, it did not identify which of the 350 bottles in its stock were to be supplied to Sergei Bank. Thus, Sergei Bank's contract was also a contract for the sale of unascertained goods (*Re Wait* (1927)).

Gleb Restaurant's contract, apparently, did not even require his bottles to be supplied from Vinco Wines' current stock. So, for the same reasons as applied to Hotel Anatoly's contract, Gleb Restaurant's was a contract for the sale of unascertained goods.

SECTION 20A

Section 20A provides for the buyer to obtain an undivided share of goods in unascertained goods from an identified bulk. There is, however, no question of **s 20A** applying to any of the goods in this problem.[2] There is only one lot of goods which are to come from a bulk which is identified by the parties, either in the contract or subsequently. Those are the 300 bottles that Sergei Bank has agreed to buy. **Section 20A** does not apply to these goods, because it comes into operation only when the buyer pays for the goods and Sergei Bank is not due to pay until delivery occurs. It follows that the passing of ownership and risk will be determined by reference to what the parties may have agreed and, failing that, by reference to **ss 16–19**.

PASSING OF PROPERTY

It may be that, in the case of Hotel Anatoly, the parties intended property to pass at an early stage, since Hotel Anatoly paid for the goods at the time of making the contract. However, nothing was done to ascertain which bottles were to be supplied to Hotel Anatoly. Therefore, no property ever passed to Hotel Anatoly, since no property can pass in goods until and unless they are ascertained (**s 16**).

Where, after the making of the contract, goods become ascertained, property will not pass (unless a contrary intention appears) until goods are unconditionally appropriated to the contract by one party with the assent of the other (**s 18 r5**). In the case of Viktor plc, so far as we are told, nothing was done to appropriate the goods to the contract. Therefore, there being nothing to indicate a contrary intention on the part of the parties, property never passed to Viktor plc. If, contrary to the opinion advanced above,[3] the sale to Viktor plc was in fact a sale of specific goods, then, assuming that the contract was an 'unconditional' one,[4] and that the wine was in a deliverable state, property will have passed to Viktor plc at the time the contract was made. At least, that is so according to **s 18 r1**, which states that it is immaterial that payment or delivery or both are postponed. However, the application of that rule coupled with the rule in **s 20** would mean that risk had passed to Viktor plc even though the goods were still in Vinco Wines' warehouse. That would be an unsatisfactory result to achieve unless the parties had very clearly indicated it to be their intention, as it would be quite likely that Vinco Wines was covered by insurance for the loss of or damage to its goods on its premises, and quite unlikely that a buyer would expect to have to take out insurance cover for goods of which he had yet to take delivery and for which he had yet to make payment. Maybe it was for that sort of consideration that Diplock LJ said in *Ward v Bignall*

---

2   The explanation of why a particular legal principle is not applicable in relation to a question is as important as the explanation of why a particular legal rule is applicable in relation to a question: on the one hand, this is because it narrows your analysis down to what is relevant; on the other hand, this is because it demonstrates understanding.

3   Considering different possibilities/solutions is a good way to attract marks as it shows that you have understood the potential implications of a particular legal rule.

4   That is, the contract does not contain a condition preventing **s 18 r1** from applying. In *Varley v Whipp* (1900), since the seller did not own the goods which were the subject of the contract, it was held that this was a conditional contract, ie a contract with the condition that the seller needed to acquire the goods first before property could pass to the buyer.

(1967) that in the case of specific goods, very little is needed to give rise to the inference that the parties intended property only to pass upon payment or delivery. If the court found the parties' intention by that means, then **s18 r1** would not apply, since the **s18** rules apply only where the intention of the parties is not apparent. Therefore, it is submitted that even if the sale to Viktor plc were of specific goods, property was intended to pass only upon delivery and payment and that therefore no property in the wine passed to Viktor plc.

It could be that, in the case of Sergei Bank, its 300 bottles became ascertained by exhaustion (see *Karlshamns Olje Fabriker v Eastport Navigation Corp, The Elafi* (1982)). This is because the contract requires its bottles to be supplied from the 350 in stock and as soon as the 50 are despatched to Restaurant Gleb, Sergei Bank's have become ascertained as being the remaining 300. However, although no property can pass before the goods become ascertained, it does not follow that the parties intended that property should pass as soon as the goods became ascertained. Unless the intention of the parties appears otherwise, property does not pass unless there is unconditional appropriation of the goods to the contract. It might be argued that Vinco Wines made the unconditional appropriation by despatching the 50 bottles to Restaurant Gleb, since Vinco Wines was thereby effectively committing itself to delivering the remaining 300 to Sergei Bank. In that case, however, it would seem that Vinco Wines was unconditionally appropriating the 50 bottles to Restaurant Gleb. But was it really? Certainly, it would have been had it consigned the 50 bottles to an independent carrier to deliver to Restaurant Gleb (see **s18 r5(2)**). Is this still the case when it sends its own lorry? If this was an unconditional appropriation of the 50 bottles to Restaurant Gleb, then it is submitted that there was an unconditional appropriation of the remaining 300 to Sergei Bank. In that case, it seems likely that we can infer that Sergei Bank impliedly assented in advance to that appropriation (as is possible; see *Aldridge v Johnson* (1857)), since it must have assumed that Vinco Wines was free to dispose of all but 300 of its stock of 2000 Château-Grillet. It is arguable, however, that consigning the goods to Restaurant Gleb on Vinco Wines' own lorry did not amount to an unconditional appropriation and that such an appropriation would occur only upon delivery by Vinco Wines' lorry to Restaurant Gleb. If the lorry had been recalled, for example by Vinco Wines calling the driver via a mobile telephone in the lorry's cab, then Vinco Wines would still have 350 bottles from which to select Sergei Bank's. Thus, the despatch of 50 bottles in Vinco Wines' own lorry did not, it is argued, demonstrate an intention to attach those 50 irrevocably to Restaurant Gleb's contract, or the remaining 300 irrevocably to Sergei Bank's. It is submitted that, therefore, property did not pass to either Sergei Bank or to Restaurant Gleb. Even if the despatch to Restaurant Gleb did amount to an unconditional appropriation, it would still be the case that no property would have passed to Restaurant Gleb (as opposed to Sergei Bank), since there is nothing from which to infer Restaurant Gleb's assent given in advance to such an appropriation (as was the case in *Pignataro v Gilroy* (1919)) and thus his assent would only be given upon delivery to him, which never occurred because of the lorry crash.

PASSING OF RISK

It has been argued that no property passed to any of the buyers in the problem. It follows that no risk passed to them either (**s 20**) unless delivery was delayed for any of their faults (**s 20(2)**). It is possible that delivery to Viktor plc was delayed through its fault, depending upon whether it had taken more than the agreed (or else a reasonable) time in coming to collect its wine. If it was due to Viktor plc's delay, then the 200 bottles of Vintage Armagnac were at Viktor plc's risk, since their loss in the fire is certainly something that might not have happened if Viktor plc had collected them earlier (**s 20(2)**; *Demby Hamilton v Barden* (1949)).

Risk not having passed (except possibly to Viktor as argued above), Vinco Wines is not excused from having to deliver to Hotel Anatoly and to Restaurant Gleb wine which corresponds to the descriptions in their respective contracts. Nothing has rendered their contracts impossible to perform, because they were contracts for the sale of purely generic goods. If Vinco Wines does not carry out those contracts, it will be liable to the buyers for non-delivery.

On the other hand, both Viktor plc's and Sergei Bank's contracts have become impossible for Vinco Wines to carry out: Viktor plc's because there is no more of that wine left in the world and Sergei Bank's because the contract provided for the goods to come from a particular source and that source is now an impossibility (*Howell v Coupland* (1876)). The contracts being for unascertained goods, **s 7** will not apply, but the contracts are frustrated at common law, assuming the frustration was not self-induced, that is, that the fire was not Vinco Wines' fault. That being so, Vinco Wines is not liable for non-delivery and nor are Sergei Bank and Viktor plc liable to pay the price. Even if (that is, in Viktor plc's case) the contract had been for the sale of specific goods, the result would have been the same (that is, provided that risk had not passed) by virtue of **s 7**.

If risk had passed to Viktor plc, that is, if delivery was delayed because it was contractually late in collecting, then Viktor plc's contract will not have terminated for frustration or void for **s 7**, but instead it will be liable for the price.

QUESTION 9

(a) 'The rules in the **Sale of Goods Act 1979** relating to the passing of risk do not always place the risk upon the party who should sensibly bear it.'

▶ **Discuss this statement.**

(b) Green enters into a contract for the sale to Browne of 600 bags of fava beans out of the 800 bags of Green's fava beans currently stored in Whyte's warehouse. On receiving a cheque for the purchase price, Green gives Browne the receipt and written delivery authority. A month later, when Browne goes to collect the fava beans, it is discovered that, since the contract was made, 400 of Green's bags have been stolen. Browne is offered delivery of the remaining 400 bags and seeks your advice.

▶ **Advise Browne.**

How to Answer this Question

Many law examiners do not indicate how many marks are allocated to each half of the question. The only safe guide to adopt in such a case is that either the (a) and (b) parts carry equal marks, or else there will not be a very great disparity between the marks allocated to each part. It is certainly unreasonable to assume that, because the question in (a) is shorter, the answer should be.

The answer to (a) is to some extent a matter of taste. There is certainly no right answer. One could mount a good case for the rules being sensible. The approach taken in this model answer is to attack the rules on the basis that if you can come up with some plausible criticisms of the area of law under scrutiny, it is usually easier to attack the state of the law than it is to defend it. Note that Part (a) specifically refers to the **SGA 1979**. This means that the rules to be discussed relate to business-to-business contracts because if business-to-consumer contracts are concerned, the **Consumer Rights Act 2015** applies (and s 29 of the **CRA** provides that risk remains with the trader until goods come into the physical possession of the consumer).

Part (b) is a typical problem on the passing of risk. The most common cause of students throwing away marks on problems on this topic is a failure to do any more than consider who bears the risk, that is, a failure to spell out the consequences, such as a possible frustration of the contract and whether the buyer still has to pay the price. The plan adopted in (b) is to consider on whom the loss of the theft falls, and then to consider the possible consequences of it falling on Green or Browne.

Applying the Law

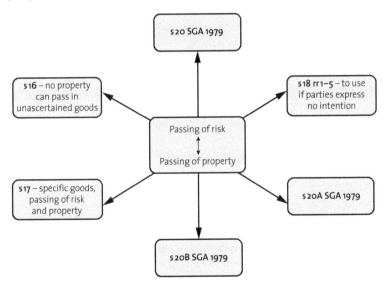

This mind map illustrates the key aspects of the **SGA** *to consider in relation to passing of risk and property in this answer.*

ANSWER

(A)

Apart from the addition of **ss 20A** and **20B** in 1995, the rules referred to in the question have remained virtually unchanged since the first **Sale of Goods Act** was passed in 1893. That Act was itself a codifying Act which sought to put into statutory form rules that had been arrived at by judges deciding individual cases.[5] Thus, they do not result from a considered comprehensive approach to the whole range of issues that ought to bear upon a piece of legislation. They do, however, reflect the basic 'freedom of contract' philosophy which imbued the decisions in commercial cases by nineteenth-century judges. This accounts for the opening words of **s 20** ('unless otherwise agreed') which allow the parties to determine the rules within their own contract. To that extent, the comment in the question is unjustified, since it is surely sensible to have risk borne by the party who it has been agreed in the contract should bear it.

Where the matter is more debatable is in those cases where the contract is silent as to who bears the risk. In this situation, apart from two exceptions specifically provided for in **sub-ss (2)** and **(3)**, the basic approach adopted is to tie the passing of risk to the passing of property. This approach is flawed because the passing of property is significant for other purposes as well as for determining the passing of risk – those other purposes include the seller's right to maintain an action for the price (see **s 49**) and the right of the relevant trustee in bankruptcy to take the goods in the event of one or other of them becoming bankrupt.[6] The rules on the passing of property are themselves subject to the freedom of contract principle which allows the parties to agree when they intend property to pass. In that case, the rules on the passing of risk and the passing of property are not lacking in sense, since the parties can presumably remember to cater for the one when making a specific provision for the other. It would certainly be quite absurd of the parties to include a retention of title clause whereby the seller retains title (that is, property) long after delivery to the seller without also including a clause stating that the risk passes with delivery.[7]

It is where the parties do not remember or think to include express provisions on these matters that the rules in **s 20** (on the passing of risk) and the related rules in **ss 16–19** (on the passing of property) appear particularly flawed. The plain fact is that it would be logical (apart from the clear justice of the exceptions in **s 20(2)** and **(3)**) to link the passing of risk with physical delivery of the goods, unless the parties have expressly agreed otherwise.[8] There are two very sound reasons for this. First, it is obvious that in the vast majority of cases, it is the person in possession who has the greatest ability to take care of the goods to see that they

---

5   Showing an awareness of the development of the area of law in question demonstrates both knowledge and understanding.

6   Be prepared to challenge the assumptions made by the question, don't merely agree with the statement made because it is easy. You are assessed on the ability to think critically, that is, your ability to consider opposing arguments.

7   Critical consideration is a good way to attract additional marks.

8   Indeed, this is the situation where the buyer is a consumer. Under the **CRA 2015**, risk passes to the consumer only on physical delivery of goods to him.

are not stolen, burnt, damaged, etc. If he has to bear the risk of any loss, then he has the consequent incentive to exercise that care. The second reason is that it is likely to be much easier to secure insurance cover for goods on your own premises or otherwise within your own possession.[9] Of course, it is possible to secure insurance cover when they are elsewhere. One does wonder, however, how many businesses fail to insure goods of which they are not in possession but for which they are bearing the risk. The notion of insuring goods where, although the risk of loss or damage is borne by the insured, the property in the goods is with someone else may raise problems of whether the insured had in law an insurable interest. If that is a problem, then the law on insurable interest needs changing. Not only do the rules in **ss 16–20** not tie the passing of risk and of property to the transfer of possession of the goods, they expressly recognise that the passing of property and/or risk can occur independently of whether delivery has occurred – see the wording of **s 18 r 1** and **s 20**. There is undoubtedly something inconsistent about saying, as **s 20** does in its principal rule in **sub-s (1)**, that it is immaterial whether delivery has been made or not and then saying in an exception to that rule that where delivery is delayed due to the fault of one of the parties, any loss which might not have occurred but for the delay is to be borne by the party at fault.

There is, however, a further difficulty which would more commonly arise if the rule tying the passing of risk to the passing of property in the absence of contrary agreement were abolished.[10] This is the absurdity where, while the risk is with one party and the property is with the other, the goods are destroyed or damaged by the negligence of a third party; the party who suffers the loss is unable to maintain an action for damages against the culprit (*Leigh and Sillivan v Aliakmon Shipping Co* (1984)).

Finally, it must be acknowledged that the somewhat complicated rules relating to the sale of a specified quantity of unascertained goods out of an identified bulk were a sensible amendment to the law. They were introduced in 1995 and are stated in **ss 20A** and **20B**. They were designed to deal with the situation where the buyer has paid for the goods and where they are still unseparated from the identified bulk at the time when the bulk is damaged or lost in whole or in part. Now, unless the parties have agreed something to the contrary, the buyer will no longer be a mere unsecured creditor in the event of the seller's insolvency. So far as risk is concerned, each buyer may have to bear the risk of loss or damage to his share of the bulk, even though the goods remain unascertained.

(B)

The question requires us to establish, if possible, at whose risk the goods were when 400 bags were stolen. Much depends upon whether they were stolen before or after Browne paid for the goods (that is, gave over his cheque to Green).[11]

....

9 Where the question relates to practical problems, emphasise the practical aspects of a question in your answer. This shows that you are focused on the relevant issues.

10 Showing an appreciation of the wider implications of a particular principle is a good way to attract marks. However, remember to focus on the relevant issues; don't simply write down all you know.

11 Pointing out omissions in the information provided by the question and considering the impact these omissions might have on the outcome of your analysis will attract a higher mark as it demonstrates your understanding.

THEFT OCCURRED BEFORE BROWNE PAID

We turn first to the situation where the theft occurred before Browne paid Green. In this situation, Browne had not at that time acquired any property or any undivided share in the goods. That is because **s16** of the **Sale of Goods Act 1979** is quite clear. Property in unascertained cannot pass to the buyer until and unless goods have been ascertained. Since the 600 bags Browne agreed to buy remain unascertained, property cannot have passed to him. This is so even if the bulk (Whyte's warehouse) is identified: *Re Goldcorp* (1995). Thus, the risk will have at that time been with Green. In that case, frustration becomes a possibility. **Section 7** of the **Sale of Goods Act 1979** will not apply because it refers only to contracts for the sale of specific goods. It is possible, however, for the contract to be frustrated at common law if it is a contract for the sale of unascertained goods out of a specific bulk (*Howell v Coupland* (1876)). This would certainly be the case where the whole of the bulk was lost or stolen. In that case, Green would not be liable for non-delivery and Browne would not be liable to pay the price.[12]

However, the court may infer an intention on the part of the parties that, where only part of the bulk has been lost, the contract should not be regarded as frustrated, but that there was an implied term that: (a) the seller was excused from his obligation to deliver the whole contract quantity of 600 bags; and (b) the buyer was to have the option of buying what was left at a *pro rata* proportion of the contract price (*Sainsbury v Street* (1972)). The solution adopted in this latter case would leave Browne with a choice as to whether to take the remaining 400 bags at two-thirds of the contract price or to decline to take any at all. **Section 30(1)** entitles Browne to reject all the goods anyway, because he had agreed to buy 600 bags, not the 400 tendered. But this is subject to **s30(2A)** which says that a buyer is not so entitled if the shortfall/excess is only slight. If Green tenders to Browne 400 bags, the shortfall (200 bags) is not so slight, so Browne has the option of rejecting the 400 bags tendered. However, Brown should be advised that he needs to mitigate his loss, so if the price of fava beans was going up, he'd be better off taking delivery of whatever Green can offer him and delivery of the balance of the 200 bags will be deemed an impossibility.

The solution adopted in *Sainsbury v Street* might not be quite so simple for a court to adopt in Green's and Browne's case if Green had in fact also made a contract to sell the other 200 bags to someone else. In that case, the option allowed to the two buyers, Browne and B2, would presumably be an option to take a proportion (in Browne's case, 75%) of the remaining 400 bags and pay for them *pro rata* at the contract rate. Or could it be that, in the event of the other purchaser not wanting to take his proportion of the 400 bags, Browne would be given the option of taking all 400? These are some of the possible difficulties in the court adopting a *Sainsbury v Street* approach and could lead the court instead simply to decide that the contract is frustrated. In the latter case, Browne would have no right to take any of the remaining 400 bags, but might be able to negotiate a new contract with Green about them.

....

12 In which case the remedies under *Fibrosa* or the **Law Reform (Frustrated Contracts) Act 1943** would apply. Since we are told Browne paid the price after the frustrating event, he is entitled to recover his payment on grounds of total failure of consideration.

THEFT OCCURRED AFTER BROWNE PAID

If the bags were stolen after Browne paid Green, then **ss 20A** and **20B** are relevant. These sections apply where there is a sale of a specified quantity (here, 600 bags) out of a bulk which is identified in the contract (here, Green's fava beans stored in Whyte's warehouse). Their effect is that, upon payment of the price, the buyer (Browne) acquires property in an undivided share of the bulk and he becomes an owner in common of the bulk *pro rata*. It appears therefore that if Browne fully paid the price for 600 bags, he would have become owner in common of 75% of the bulk.[13] What is not clear however is, when **s 20A** applies, whether risk passes to a buyer when he acquires an undivided share or only later when he acquires property by ascertainment and appropriation. The **Sale of Goods Act** does not actually deal with this point. There are arguments both ways.[14] Some say that that risk passes to the buyer at the time the buyer acquires an undivided share, based on *Sterns v Vickers* (1923) discussed below. The preferable view, however, is that risk does not pass to a buyer at that time. This is because **s 20B(3)** says that **s 20A** does not affect the rights of any buyer under his contract. This must mean that Browne remains entitled to his contractual rights of delivery of 600 bags which conform in all respects. If this latter interpretation is correct, risk of the loss is on Green. Had all 800 bags been stolen, the contract would have been frustrated at common law and both Green and Browne are excused from further performance. But only 400 bags were stolen, leaving 400 available bags in Whyte's warehouse. The problem does not state that there is any other buyer to whom Green has agreed to sell any of the bulk. So, assuming Browne was the only buyer of the bags stored in Whyte's warehouse, it is possible that **s 18 r 5(3)** applies so that property in the remaining 400 bags passes to Browne by a process of exhaustion.[15] Green will not be able to supply the shortfall of 200 bags from elsewhere because, in order for **s 18 r 5(3)** to apply, there must have an agreement to buy goods from a specified bulk (that is, Whyte's warehouse). Since Green will not be able to do so, this will entitle Browne to claim damages for non-delivery of the 200 bags, calculated as the difference between the contract price and the market price at the time delivery was to be made.

The result will be very different if Green can rely on **s 20(2)** or if it can be said that the arrangement over giving the delivery authority to Browne indicated that the parties intended risk to pass on the handing over to Browne of the delivery authority. In either of those two eventualities, Browne and Green would bear the loss in the proportions of their respective interests in the bulk: 75% and 25%. As regards **s 20(2)**, we are told that Browne went to collect the fava beans 'a month later', that is, presumably a month after being given the written delivery authority. It is quite possible that a month was an unreasonable delay and that therefore one could describe delivery as having been delayed through Browne's 'fault'. If so, Browne has to bear the consequences of the theft if that loss might

....

13 The size of Browne's share of the bulk depends on the quantity of bags paid for and the quantity of the bags then in Whyte's warehouse. It is assumed here that Browne had fully paid the price for all 600 bags.

14 The consideration of possible alternative solutions makes your answer stand out from the rest and demonstrates both deeper knowledge and understanding.

15 **Section 18 r 5(3)** gives statutory authority to the ascertainment by exhaustion case of *The Elafi* (1982).

not have occurred if he had collected the goods within a reasonable period of time (say, within a week). We are not told when the theft occurred. If it is established that it occurred before the lapse of what would have been a reasonable length of time for Browne to turn up to collect the goods, then Green cannot rely on **s20(2)**. If it occurred after a lapse of that length of time, or if it might have done, then it is a loss which 'might' not have occurred if Browne had collected on time and **s20(2)** applies.[16] Alternatively, the arrangement over the giving of the delivery authority, and Browne thus taking on the task of collecting the goods, could well be something which a court would take as indicating the intention of the parties that risk should pass to Browne upon the handing over to him of the delivery authority (*Sterns v Vickers* (1923)). In the situation where either **s20(2)** applies or else the theft occurred after the parties intended risk to pass (for example, on the handing over of the delivery note), the result is as in *Sterns v Vickers*, namely, that all 800 bags were *pro rata* (that is, 75%) at Browne's risk. This is because he had agreed to buy 75% of the 800 bags. In that case, he has to bear 75% of the loss of 400 bags, that is, the loss of 300 bags. In that case, he is entitled to take delivery of a further 300 bags, but must pay the full contract price. In this scenario, there is no possibility that the contract has become frustrated by virtue of the theft, since the only way to make sense of the rule that Browne has to bear the risk is to make him pay for the goods, despite the fact that some of them have been stolen.

We now consider the situation if Green had agreed to sell the remaining 200 bags to another buyer (B2) who had also paid for them before the theft from Whyte's warehouse. In that situation, both Browne and B2 would have an undivided share in the bulk in the proportions 75% and 25% respectively. Whether they bear the loss in those proportions is unclear. As discussed above, when **s20A** applies, there are arguments which suggest risk passes to a buyer when he acquires an undivided share and there are arguments that risk only passes to a buyer when he acquires property by ascertainment and appropriation. If risk passes to the buyer at the time the buyer acquires an undivided share, based on *Sterns v Vickers* (1923), this would mean that Browne and B2 would suffer the loss as follows: Browne would lose 300 bags and B2 would lose 100. Thus they would each be entitled to take from the remaining bulk 300 and 100 bags respectively. In that scenario, Browne would be entitled to 300, not 400, of the remaining bags. He would not, however, be entitled to any repayment of the price he has paid. Taking the contrary view (that is, risk does not pass to a buyer at the time he acquires property in an undivided share), risk remains with Green and the loss lies with Green. The contract with Browne is then frustrated at common law since it is a contract for the sale of unascertained goods out of a specific bulk. Alternatively, the court implies a term that Green is excused from his obligation to deliver the whole contract quantity of 600 bags but Browne is to have the option of buying what was left at a *pro rata* proportion of the contract price (*Sainsbury v Street* (1972)).

....

16 Considering different options is a good way to attract marks as it shows that you have understood the potential implications of a particular legal rule.

4

Nemo Dat Quod Non Habet

INTRODUCTION

This chapter covers the *nemo dat* principle and the exceptions to it, in particular:

❖ estoppel;
❖ mercantile agents (**s 2(1)** of the **Factors Act 1889**);
❖ voidable contracts;
❖ seller in possession (**s 8** of the **Factors Act** and **s 24** of the **Sale of Goods Act 1979**);
❖ buyer in possession (**s 9** of the **Factors Act** and **s 25** of the **Sale of Goods Act**);
❖ **Part III** of the **Hire Purchase Act 1964**;
❖ the law enabling an owner to sue in conversion;
❖ the implied condition as to title in **s 12** of the **Sale of Goods Act** (**s 17** of the **Consumer Rights Act 2015** where the buyer is a consumer).

QUESTION 10

Wallace left his car for repair at Smithfield Garage, carelessly leaving the car's registration document in the glove compartment which was unlocked. While the car was at Smithfield Garage, Smithfield telephoned Wallace and informed him that another customer had seen the car and wished to buy it for £3,000. Wallace said that he had not intended to sell the car, but that if Smithfield were to receive an offer in excess of £4,000, he would be interested. Without again contacting Wallace, Smithfield sold the car for £3,500 to Marion, handing over the registration document and the ignition key.

▶ **Consider the legal position.**

How to Answer this Question

This question requires an understanding of the *nemo dat quod non habet* rule and the exceptions to it, in particular, the estoppel exception and the case law on **s 2(1)** of the **Factors Act 1889**. Sometimes, examiners allow you in the examination to refer to the statutory provisions. Without a knowledge of the case law, those provisions will take you only so far. Indeed, the question requires consideration of some possible distinctions between the facts of the problem set and those of a couple of the cases.

The sensible layout of an answer is very straightforward indeed. It is to consider first who now owns the car (no definite answer, however, can be given to that). That involves considering the two relevant exceptions to the *nemo dat* principle. Many candidates answering this type of question are content to leave it there. The question does, however, ask you to consider the legal position and that must also involve setting out the rights of the parties vis-à-vis each other in the light of the conclusion (or different possible conclusions) you come to as to who now owns the car. It is often important in questions such as this to consider possible claims in conversion and claims under **s17** of the **Consumer Rights Act 2015** *where the buyer is a consumer.*

Applying the Law

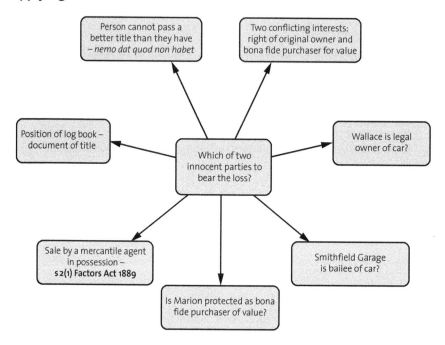

This mind map illustrates the key factors to consider in determining who will bear the loss in this scenario.

ANSWER

It is necessary first to establish who now owns the car, and then to advise the parties as to the legal position flowing from that.

TITLE

Wallace, we assume, owned the car to start with and since he has never agreed to sell it, he is still the owner unless one of the exceptions to the *nemo dat* principle applies. The *nemo dat quod non habet* principle states that someone who lacks title to goods (for example, Smithfield Garage) cannot transfer that title. Only if one of the exceptions to that principle applies will Smithfield Garage have conferred good title upon Marion. Two such possible exceptions present themselves for discussion: estoppel and the mercantile agent exception.

The first of these can be quickly dismissed, since it is now clearly established that the mere act of the owner of letting someone have possession of his goods is insufficient to enable an estoppel to be raised against him. The position is still the same even if the owner (here, Wallace) has parted not only with possession of the goods (here, a car), but also the ignition key and the registration book; the registration book is not a document of title (*Central Newbury Car Auctions v Unity Finance* (1957)). Nothing in the question suggests that Wallace by his conduct represented that Smithfield Garage was the owner, so *Eastern Distributors v Goldring* (1957) can be distinguished. Even if it was argued that Wallace negligently left his registration document in an unlocked glove compartment, that in itself would not invoke the estoppel doctrine to deprive Wallace of his ownership of the car (*Mercantile Credit v Hamblin* (1964)).

Does the mercantile agent exception apply? There are a number of requirements, each of which must be complied with before this exception, in **s 2(1)** of the **Factors Act 1889**, will apply. First, Smithfield Garage must have been a mercantile agent, that is, someone having, in the customary course of his business as an agent, authority to sell. On the given facts, it seems likely that Smithfield Garage as a car dealer had such customary authority, including the customary authority to sell the goods in his own name (*Rolls Razor v Cox* (1967)). Second, Smithfield Garage must have been in possession of the goods (or documents of title) with the consent of the owner (Wallace) at the time of the sale to Marion, which he clearly did, since he had possession of the car. Smithfield Garage must have also been at that time in possession of the car in his (Smithfield Garage's) capacity as mercantile agent. There is some ambiguity about this in the question, since originally Wallace left his car with Smithfield Garage for repair and therefore not with a view to Smithfield Garage selling it, or seeking offers for it. However, after Smithfield Garage's telephone call, Wallace could be said to have left the car with Smithfield Garage in two different capacities, one as a repairer and one as a factor (that is, authorised to seek and/or consider offers). This is because Wallace in that telephone call clearly contemplated the possibility of Smithfield Garage receiving further offers. **Section 2(1)** does not require that Smithfield Garage 'obtained' possession with the consent of the owner, merely that he was (that is, at the time of the disposition to Marion) in possession with that consent. The same presumably applies to the judicial gloss on the section which requires him to have been in possession in his capacity as a mercantile agent. Furthermore, there does not seem to be any logical reason why Smithfield Garage should not have been in possession in two capacities at the same time.

There is, however, a problem over the registration document. It is not a document of title but, for the mercantile agent exception to operate, the seller (here, Smithfield Garage) must be in possession of the goods, not just in his capacity as a mercantile agent, but also in such a way as to clothe the seller with apparent authority to sell; in the case of a motor vehicle, that really requires the seller to be in possession not just of the vehicle, but also of its registration document (*Pearson v Rose and Young* (1951)). This also ties in with the further requirement for the exception to apply, namely, that the seller in selling acts in the normal course of business of a mercantile agent. It was said in *Stadium Finance v Robbins* (1962) that selling a car without its registration document would not be a sale in the ordinary course of business. On the given facts, Smithfield Garage was in possession of the registration document which, together with the ignition key, he handed over to Marion. However, it was held in *Pearson v Rose and Young* that not only must the seller be in possession of the registration book as well as the car, but also he must be in possession of the registration book (as well as of the car) *with the consent of the owner*. In *Pearson v Rose and Young*, the seller was in possession of the registration book, but did not have the consent of the owner to that possession, since the seller had obtained possession of it by a trick he played upon the owner. This was taken one stage further in *Stadium Finance v Robbins*, where it was held that the owner accidentally leaving the document locked in the glove compartment did not amount to the seller having possession of it with the consent of the owner. The only possible distinctions between that case and the present problem are: first, that in Wallace's case, the document was in an *unlocked* glove compartment; second, that very possibly the key to the glove compartment in Wallace's car was the same as the ignition key which Wallace presumably left with the car; third, that possibly (although we do not know) something was said in the telephone conversation between Smithfield Garage and Wallace which alluded to the registration document and indicated Wallace's 'consent' to Smithfield Garage's possession of it.

Subject to what has just been said about the registration book, it seems that all the requirements of the exception have been satisfied, including the requirement that Marion took the car in good faith without notice of Smithfield Garage's lack of authority to make the sale.[1] There is nothing in the stated facts of the problem to indicate that Marion should have been 'put on notice'; at least, that is so provided the sale price of £3,500 was not so low as itself to be a cause of suspicion. If there is a substantial doubt about Marion's good faith, that could cause her a problem, since the burden of proof to show that she took in good faith is upon Marion (*Heap v Motorists Advisory Agency* (1923)).

CONSEQUENCES

Assuming that all the requirements of **s 2(1)** of the **Factors Act** are satisfied, then Marion now has good title to the car. That means of course that Wallace, in any action for conversion, would fail against Marion. Wallace would, however, have a good claim for conversion against Smithfield Garage. This is a tort of strict liability and, since Smithfield Garage has effectively disposed of the car to Marion, could not result in an order for the goods to be returned to Wallace, but only in an award of damages. The *prima facie* measure of damages to which Wallace is entitled would be the value of the car at the time of the sale to Marion. This would be a matter of evidence, but presumably Wallace will try to insist that it was worth at least £4,000, since that was a figure he would have been interested in. The value, however, is not necessarily the car's value to Marion, but its market value. It is of course possible that, before selling the car, Smithfield Garage had carried out the repairs. In that case, the cost of the repairs will need to be taken into account in one way or another, either by a set-off of their cost or by deduction of an improvement allowance by virtue of the provisions of the **Torts (Interference with Goods) Act 1977**. That allowance

---

1 Drawing an interim conclusion is a good way of signposting the relevant issues and also helps you to structure your answer logically.

might well be less than the cost of the repairs, since it is the proportion of the value of the car (that is, at the time of the sale to Marion) which is attributable to the improvement effected by the repairs.

If Marion did not satisfy the requirements of **s 2(1)** of the **Factors Act**, she will not have acquired good title.[2] In that case, Wallace would be entitled to succeed against Marion in an action in conversion. It is assumed that the car was not unique. Therefore, the result of such an action would not be to compel Marion to return the car, but would be an award of damages (with Marion perhaps being given the option of returning the car). The damages would be calculated as in the case of the claim against Smithfield Garage just discussed. Thus, the improvement allowance (due to the repairs by Smithfield – assuming Smithfield Garage had effected those repairs) would be deducted. If Marion chose to return the car to Wallace, Wallace would be liable to pay the improvement allowance to Marion.

If Marion were to be held liable to Wallace in the way just outlined, Marion would have a claim against Smithfield Garage for breach of the condition as to title. Assuming Marion *was not buying the car for purposes of her trade, business, craft or profession*, her action for this breach falls under **s 17** of the **Consumer Rights Act 2015**. Marion would be entitled to the return of her purchase price without undue delay and in any event within 14 days of her rejection. The entitlement to the return of the purchase price is based upon the notion that, since Marion never got title, she has suffered a total failure of consideration. This is true even if she has had some months' use of the car before having to surrender it to Wallace, for example, if it was some considerable time before the truth was discovered and the car's whereabouts traced to Marion.

QUESTION 11

Benedict had a car on hire purchase terms from Logbook Finance. He still owed three monthly instalments on the car when four months ago he sold it to Albert, a car dealer, who bought it for his wife to use as a runabout to do the shopping and collect the children from school. Before buying the car, Albert had a check done by HPI, of which he was a member. HPI responded that the vehicle in question was not registered with HPI as being the subject of a credit agreement. Two months later, Albert sold the car to another car dealer, Ashwin, who has since sold it to Edward.

▶ Advise the parties as to who owns the car now and what claims and liabilities each might have.

How to Answer this Question

This is a problem dealing with the *nemo dat* principle and the exceptions to it. In this case, the problem is located in hire purchase and involves a consideration of the following: estoppel, **Part III** of the **Hire Purchase Act 1964**; **s 9** of the **Factors Act 1889** (and **s 25** of the **Sale of Goods Act 1979**) and the doctrine of feeding the title. The punchline at the end of

2 Pointing out different solutions is a good way to attract marks as it shows that you have understood the potential implications of a particular legal rule.

the question is unusually helpful because it alerts you to the need to deal not only with who now owns the car, but also with any claims which the parties may have between themselves. Always in this type of question, these latter matters involve a consideration of who can maintain an action for conversion against whom and similarly who can make a claim against his seller for breach of the implied condition as to title.

Applying the Law

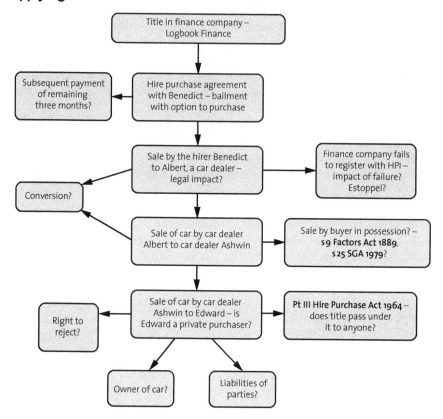

The flowchart illustrates the progress of the car from hirer to purchaser in this scenario and how this can be considered in relation to the nemo dat rule and possible exceptions.

ANSWER

It is assumed that Logbook Finance had good title to the car, since there is nothing in the question to suggest otherwise. First, we must try to ascertain who now has ownership. We will do so by dealing with the transactions in the problem in chronological order. Benedict did not have good title to the car because he had not yet completed his instalment payments or exercised his right to purchase. So, the *nemo dat quod non habet* principle means that he did not confer good title upon Albert unless it can be shown that the sale to Albert came within one of the exceptions to the *nemo dat* principle. Certainly, someone who has possession of goods under a hire purchase agreement is not a *buyer* in possession of the goods and, therefore, when he sells the goods, the buyer in possession exception (in **s 9** of the **Factors Act 1889** and **s 25** of the **Sale of Goods Act 1979**) cannot operate to defeat the title of the owner (*Helby v Matthews* (1895)).

Also, when Benedict sold the car to Albert, there is no question of **Pt III** of the **Hire Purchase Act 1964** applying, since Albert was a car dealer. That is so despite the fact that he bought the car for his own (or rather for his wife's) private use (*Stevenson v Beverley Bentinck* (1976)). Another means by which it might be argued that Albert obtained good title is by virtue of the doctrine of estoppel. That argument was used in a case involving very similar facts to this in *Moorgate Mercantile v Twitchings* (1976).[3] It failed because an estoppel has to rest upon a representation by the person to be estopped (here, Logbook Finance), and failing to register an agreement with HPI is not the same thing as making a representation. Rather, it is the opposite; it is an absence of doing something. Nor could it be said that the finance company was in breach of any duty of care in failing to register the agreement, since it was not under any duty to join HPI in the first place. We are not told anything about the current terms of membership of HPI. If, as at the time of the *Twitchings* case, the terms of membership do not impose a duty on members to register their credit contracts, then the result has to be the same, that is, Logbook Finance cannot be liable to Albert for failing to register and Albert cannot raise an estoppel against Logbook Finance.

In fact, the problem does not tell us that Logbook Finance failed to register with HPI the credit agreement it had with Benedict.[4] It is possible that the reason that Albert was given the response he was given by HPI was that this was due to negligence by HPI. We are not told the terms of the agreement between Albert and HPI. Depending upon what those terms are, HPI may well be liable to Albert in negligence or for breach of the implied term to a dealer such as Albert to carry out its service with reasonable care and skill (**s 13** of the **Supply of Goods and Services Act 1982**). Any exclusion clause in its contract purporting to exclude such liability will be subject to the requirement of reasonableness in the **Unfair Contract Terms Act 1977**.[5] Of course, even if the fault did lie with HPI, and even if HPI is liable in the way just canvassed, that will not alter the question of who owns the car. It will serve only to give Albert a claim in damages.

It seems unlikely then that any of the exceptions to the *nemo dat* principle will have served to give Albert good title. When Albert sold the car on to Ashwin, it seems very likely that Benedict had still not completed the payments to Logbook Finance under his hire purchase agreement, since when he bought the car, Benedict still had three monthly instalments to pay and Albert sold the car after having it for only two months. If Albert

··

3   When a problem scenario resembles what happened in a decided case, don't automatically assume that you have found the answer to the problem; this assumption might lose you valuable marks as the finer points of the question set might make an important difference to the analysis.

4   Pointing out omissions in the information provided by the question and considering the impact these omissions might have on the outcome of your analysis will attract a higher mark as it demonstrates your understanding.

5   If Albert was a consumer, the exclusion of liability would need to satisfy the unfairness test under the **Consumer Rights Act 2015**. See Question 3.

did not have good title, then he could not confer title upon Ashwin, unless some exception to the *nemo dat* principle applied. Again, **Pt III** of the **Hire Purchase Act 1964** will not apply because Ashwin also was not a private purchaser. However, does the 'buyer in possession' exception apply, that is, the exception stated in **s 9** of the **Factors Act 1889** and in **s 25** of the **Sale of Goods Act 1979**? Undoubtedly, Albert was a buyer (someone who had bought or agreed to buy) who obtained possession of the goods with the consent of the seller (Benedict). Albert delivered the car to Ashwin and, presumably, Ashwin took it in good faith unaware of the defect in title. Despite the fact that there was a compliance with the wording of the two sections, nevertheless, they do not apply. The House of Lords has held that the two sections can defeat the title only of an owner who has entrusted the possession of his goods to a buyer (*National Employers' Mutual General Insurance Association v Jones* (1988)). Thus, a disposition by Albert to Ashwin cannot by virtue of those two sections defeat the title of anyone except the owner who entrusted them to Albert. The two sections cannot defeat the title of Logbook Finance.

Ashwin sold the car to Edward. We are not told of Edward's status. If he was a private purchaser, he may be able to take advantage of **Pt III** of the **Hire Purchase Act 1964**. This is because although Edward did not buy the car from the hire purchase customer (Benedict), the Act gives its protection to the first private purchaser provided that that private purchaser bought the car *bona fide* and unaware of the hire purchase agreement (**s 27** of the **Hire Purchase Act 1964**, *Kulkarni v Manor Credit (Davenham) Ltd* (2010)). It is immaterial how expensive the vehicle was and it is immaterial whether Benedict's hire purchase agreement was a regulated agreement within the **Consumer Credit Act 2006**. There are no financial limits to the operation of **Pt III** of the **Hire Purchase Act 1964**. If, on the other hand, Edward was not protected by the **1964 Act** but he is a private purchaser (thus, a 'consumer'), he will have a claim for a full refund against Ashwin for breach of the right to supply goods under **s 17** of the **Consumer Rights Act 2015**.

There is a further way in which either Ashwin or Edward (if he is not a private purchaser) may have acquired good title to the car.[6] We are told that, four months before Ashwin sold the car to Edward, Benedict owed three monthly instalments on his hire purchase agreement. We are not told if Benedict subsequently paid those off and exercised his right to purchase. If he did, then he will have done what is necessary for title to pass from Logbook Finance to Benedict. If and when that happened, then title will have been fed automatically down the chain of buyers to Edward (*Butterworth v Kingsway Motors* (1954)). For this to happen, there is no need for the buyers to have been in good faith and, equally, it is immaterial if any or all of them were car dealers. If it did not, then we are left wondering whether Edward was a private purchaser or not.

CONSEQUENCES

If Edward was not a private purchaser, he will not have obtained good title unless Benedict has paid off his hire purchase instalments. If Edward did not get good title, Logbook Finance

---

6 The consideration of possible alternative solutions makes your answer stand out from the rest and demonstrates both deeper knowledge and understanding.

is entitled to succeed against Edward in an action in conversion. The measure of damages, however, would not be the value of the goods at the date of conversion (which is the usual measure of damages for conversion), but would be the lower of two amounts which are:

(a) the value of the car at the date of conversion (that is, when Edward bought it or refused to hand it over to Logbook Finance);

(b) the outstanding balance of the hire purchase price owed by Benedict to Logbook Finance.

This is the rule in *Wickham Holdings v Brooke House Motors* (1967), confirmed in *Chubb Cash Ltd v John Crilley & Son* (1983).

If Edward was not a consumer and is liable to Logbook Finance in the way just described, then he will have a claim for his losses against Ashwin under **s 12** of the **Sale of Goods Act** and Ashwin will, in turn, have such a claim against Albert and Albert will have such a claim against Benedict, although one guesses that the latter claim may not be worth much if Benedict has no means of paying.

If Edward was a private purchaser who obtained good title by virtue of the **1964 Act**, then Logbook Finance would have no valid claim against Edward, but would be entitled to succeed in conversion against either Ashwin or Albert. Indeed, even in the scenario just considered, that is, that Edward was not protected by the **1964 Act**, Logbook Finance would not be required to bring proceedings against Edward; the finance company could choose instead to sue Albert and/or Ashwin. They have each committed conversion by selling Logbook Finance's car. Conversion is a tort of strict liability and it is no defence to either of those dealers that, in selling Logbook Finance's car, they were unaware of Logbook Finance's interest in it. The measure of damages would again be calculated according to the rule in *Wickham Holdings v Brook House Motors*.

There is one further matter which is relevant if Edward does not have good title. It is that he is then entitled to reject the car and demand the whole of his purchase price back from Ashwin, who is entitled to do the same to Albert, who is entitled to do the same to Benedict (although, again, Benedict may not have the means to make the refund). The ability to reject the car depends upon the ruling in *Rowland v Divall* (1923) which, in the case of a breach of the condition as to title in **s 12** of the **SGA 1979**,[7] regards the buyer as having suffered a total failure of consideration.

QUESTION 12

Natasha owns a jewellery shop in Islington. Rafael came into the shop, selected a ruby bracelet and paid for it. Rafael explained to her that he had an appointment to play football that afternoon and asked if it would be all right to leave the bracelet with Natasha until after his football game. A little later that same afternoon, Weller, who looked the very image of Cristiano Ronaldo, the famous football player, and had a strong Portugese

---

7 **Section 17** of the **CRA** if Edward was a consumer.

accent, came into the shop and selected the very same bracelet (which by an oversight Natasha had failed to remove to be kept for Rafael). Natasha let Weller pay the £1,000 price by cheque, which Weller did – signing himself Cristiano Ronaldo. Subsequently, the cheque was dishonoured and Natasha informed the police, who traced the bracelet to Bean's shop in Croydon. It has turned out that Weller has a stall at Bermondsey market in south London and that he sold the bracelet (for £700) early one morning to Bean, a jewellery dealer, who considered at the time that he had a real bargain.

▶ **Advise Natasha.**

How to Answer this Question
The question deals with certain 'exceptions' to the *nemo dat* rule, namely:

❖ the position where a seller sells goods which the seller has already sold to an earlier buyer;

❖ when a buyer misrepresents (or a seller is mistaken as to) the buyer's identity;

❖ the rule (in **s 25** of the **Sale of Goods Act 1979**) dealing with a buyer in possession who sells the goods.

Also expected is the knowledge that the exception relating to market overt has been abolished. It is logical to deal with the transactions in chronological order. In that way, the passing of title can be traced through those transactions. As always in this sort of examination question, certain key facts are not given, with the result that the examinee cannot always be sure if an exception does or does not apply. This requires, as the answer progresses, copious use of the expressions 'if' or 'assuming that'.

Answer Structure

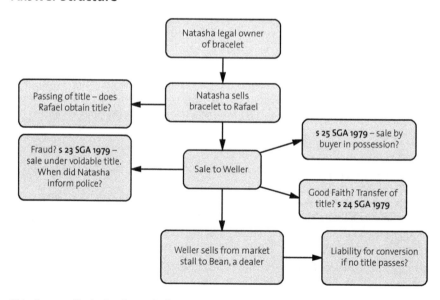

This diagram illustrates the main factors to consider in the sale of the bracelet.

ANSWER

As there is nothing in the question to suggest otherwise, it will be assumed that Natasha was at the outset the owner of the bracelet. Therefore, each of the transactions (the sales to Rafael and to Weller and the sale by Weller to Bean) must be examined to see whether it operated to pass title.

NATASHA'S SALE TO RAFAEL

Nothing suggests that the sale of the bracelet to Rafael was incomplete. Assuming nothing was agreed about when property in the bracelet was to pass, it is clear from **s18 r1** of the **Sale of Goods Act 1979** that property in the bracelet passed to Rafael at the time the contract with Natasha was made. Whether payment is made and when delivery is to occur is immaterial to the passing of property. We are told that in fact Rafael has paid but he asked Natasha to hold on to the bracelet until after his football game. Therefore, when Natasha subsequently sells the same bracelet to Weller, Natasha was no longer the owner. The question that arises is whether the subsequent events operate to transfer title from Natasha who did not have title so as to defeat the title of Rafael.

NATASHA'S SALE TO WELLER

The sale by Natasha to Weller appears to have been affected by fraud on the part of Weller, who passed himself off as being Cristiano Ronaldo. Whether or not he said anything to that effect, he certainly made a representation of it by signing himself as Cristiano Ronaldo. The effect of this was either to render the contract between himself and Natasha void for unilateral mistake or to render it voidable for fraud. In one case on somewhat similar facts (*Ingram v Little* (1961)), it was held that the contract was void for unilateral mistake. That case, however, is now generally regarded as having been decided on its own special facts. The law presumes that, as the parties were dealing face to face, Natasha intended to deal with the person there in the shop, albeit that she was mistaken as to that person's identity (*Lewis v Averay* (1972)). This is not a situation, like that in *Shogun v Hudson* (2001), where the parties were not face to face but contracted via an intermediary. Thus, there was an agreement between Natasha and Weller which, however, was a voidable contract, that is the agreement was valid unless and until Natasha avoided the contract for fraud. This was the result achieved in a case on remarkably similar facts, involving a sale of a ring by a jeweller (*Phillips v Brooks* (1919)). Thus, assuming for the moment that Natasha had title, good title passed to Weller, unless and until such time as Natasha rescinded the contract. In circumstances like those in the present case, it is impractical to suppose that the seller (Natasha) can contact the buyer (Weller) in order to rescind (set aside) the contract, since Natasha does not actually know who Weller was. If, however, the seller, when she realises the fraud, does her best to rescind the contract, for example, by informing the police, that will be regarded as rescinding the contract (*Car and Universal Finance v Caldwell* (1965)). This is what Natasha did. Giving such notice to a third party with an intention to rescind operates to rescind it and thus to cause the title to revert to the seller (Natasha). However, it will not have that effect if, as in *Phillips v Brooks*, the rogue buyer (Weller) has already sold the goods to a purchaser who was ignorant of the fraud and who bought in good faith. We are not told whether Weller sold the bracelet to Bean before or after Natasha informed the police of the fraud upon herself.[8] If it was afterwards, then Natasha informing the police will have operated to rescind her contract with Weller and to cause title to the bracelet to revert to Natasha. If Weller sold the bracelet to Bean before Natasha informed the police, then, since Weller had title at that time, Bean will have received title and, assuming that he was ignorant of the fraud and a purchaser in good faith, his title will be unassailable by Natasha. The fact that the price which Bean paid was low would not necessarily prevent him having been a purchaser in good faith. Indeed, one would expect prices in a street market to be significantly less than in, say, a more central London jewellers shop.

The position relating to the sale by Natasha to Weller is complicated by the fact that the bracelet in fact belongs to Rafael. If the transaction between Natasha and Weller was not avoided for fraud before Weller sold the bracelet on to Bean, the question arises as to whether that transaction operated to transfer title from Natasha who did not have title so as to defeat the title of Rafael. Natasha was a seller (she had sold to Rafael) and she continued being in possession of the goods with the consent of the buyer (Rafael). In those circumstances, if she sold and delivered the goods to another person who received them in good faith and without notice of the previous sale to Rafael, that transaction has the same effect as if Natasha had been expressly authorised by Rafael to make it (**s 24** of the **Sale of Goods Act** and **s 8** of the **Factors Act 1889**). Thus, it would operate to transfer Rafael's title to the innocent buyer. The question then arises as to whether Weller was 'in good faith'. In one sense, he very clearly was not acting in good faith because he was himself fraudulent. **Section 24** is clearly intended not to allow someone who takes in bad faith to benefit from the section. The difficulty is that if the absence of good faith prevents the sale from Natasha to Weller transferring title to Weller, it is not Weller who suffers but the person (Bean) to whom Weller sold. The requirement of good faith may possibly simply relate to the matter of the previous sale (in this case, to Rafael). It may mean that the buyer is not acting in good faith – and **s 24** does not operate – if the buyer (even though he may not have 'notice' of the previous sale) has reason to suspect that there is a previous sale. If that is what it means, then Weller was (in that limited sense) presumably acting in good faith (that is, without the slightest suspicion of any earlier sale of the bracelet by Natasha). In that case, if the sale by Weller to Bean took place before Natasha informed the police, Weller (and, through Weller, Bean) will have secured good title by virtue of **s 24**. In that case, Rafael will have lost title. Rafael will have a claim against Natasha for conversion damages but this does not detract from the fact that Bean may have good title.

WELLER'S SALE TO BEAN

It is necessary now to consider the position if the sale by Weller to Bean occurred after Natasha informed the police. In those circumstances, Weller was selling something to which he did not have title and, according to the *nemo dat quod non habet* principle, he

---

8 Pointing out omissions in the information provided by the question and considering the impact these omissions might have on the outcome of your analysis will attract a higher mark as it demonstrates your understanding.

will not have conferred title upon Bean. However, there is one exception to that principle which might have relevance. This is the possibility of Bean relying upon **s 25** of the **Sale of Goods Act**. First, however, it must be pointed out that the exception which used to exist in relation to any sale in market overt no longer exists, since **s 22** of the **Sale of Goods Act** was repealed in 1995. Thus, the fact that it was in Bermondsey market that Weller sold the bracelet is of no significance.

It is possible that Bean can claim good title by virtue of **s 25**, which is virtually identical in its wording to **s 9** of the **Factors Act 1889**. Assuming, as has been argued above, that the sale by Natasha to Weller was a voidable (and not a void) contract, then Weller was someone who had 'bought or agreed to buy'. He was in possession of the bracelet with the consent of the seller (Natasha) and he delivered the bracelet under a sale to Bean. That all being so, the conditions of **s 25** were all satisfied, apart from the requirement that Bean received the bracelet in good faith. It would seem that Bean's belief that he had a good bargain would not cast doubt on his *bona fides* unless the price of £700 was so low that it ought to have put him on notice. Once the conditions of the section are satisfied, the sale and delivery of the bracelet by Weller to Bean has the same effect as if Weller were a mercantile agent in possession of the goods with the consent of Natasha. This wording of **s 25** taken literally means that even if all the conditions of **s 25** were satisfied, Bean will have obtained good title only if the conditions for the passing of title by a mercantile agent (that is, under **s 2(1)** of the **Factors Act 1889**) were also satisfied. This means that **s 25** will operate to pass good title only if the buyer in possession (here, Weller) sells the goods in the normal course of business of a mercantile agent – that is, even if he was not in fact a mercantile agent. This seems to have been the approach adopted by the Court of Appeal in *Newtons of Wembley v Williams* (1965), where the buyer in possession sold the goods (a car) in a street market where mercantile agents commonly sold cars.[9] It was held in that case that **s 25** did operate to pass good title in circumstances (such as those in the present problem) where the buyer in possession had acquired the goods under a contract which was voidable for his own fraud, and which had in fact been avoided before the sale by the buyer.

However, **s 25** is probably of no use to Bean unless he can use it to defeat the title of Rafael as well as that of Natasha, since we have seen that Rafael appears to have obtained good title prior to Natasha agreeing to sell the bracelet to Weller. We are here dealing with the situation where it is after Natasha contacted the police that Weller sold the bracelet to Bean. In that situation, **s 25** is of no use to Bean, because **s 25** can be relied on to defeat the title only of the original owner (Natasha) who entrusted the goods to the buyer (Weller) who has then sold them on to the innocent purchaser (Bean) (*National Employers' Mutual General Insurance Association v Jones* (1988)).

CONCLUSION

Thus, Natasha is advised that Rafael obtained title by virtue of having bought the bracelet from her. If Natasha informed the police and thus avoided her contract for fraud with

---

9 Considering a case which resembles the facts of the problem strengthens your argument/conclusion.

Weller before he sold the bracelet to Bean, then Rafael still has that title. The sale to Bean will not operate to transfer title to Bean because: (a) the market overt exception to the *nemo dat* rule had been abolished; and (b) **s 25** cannot operate to transfer to the buyer (Bean) any title other than that of the person (Natasha) who entrusted goods to the seller (Weller). It will not operate to defeat Rafael's title. In those circumstances, Rafael could then demand return of the bracelet from Bean and, failing its return, would be entitled to succeed in an action against Bean in conversion. If Natasha did not inform the police before Weller sold the bracelet to Bean, then (subject to the correct interpretation of the expression 'in good faith' in **s 24**) Bean will have obtained good title by virtue of having bought from someone (Weller) who obtained good title by virtue of **s 24** of the **Sale of Goods Act**. In those circumstances, Natasha will be liable in conversion to Rafael for having sold his bracelet.

5

Performance and Remedies

INTRODUCTION

This chapter deals with remedies for breach of a contract of sale of goods, including coverage of the measure of damages.

The following topics should be prepared in advance of tackling the questions:

❖ the provisions in **ss 11(4)**, **35** and **35A** of the **Sale of Goods Act 1979** on acceptance and rejection;
❖ the measure of damages and rules thereon in **ss 50** and **51** of the **Sale of Goods Act 1979**;
❖ the effect of an anticipatory breach;
❖ severable contracts and **s 30** of the **Sale of Goods Act 1979**.

QUESTION 13

On 1 January, Ted had 2,000 widgets in stock. On that date, Dougal contracted with Ted to buy 1,000 widgets from Ted's current stock for £1,000, delivery to take place at Dougal's premises on 1 February. On 25 January, when the market price of widgets had dropped to 50 pence per widget, Dougal sent a fax to Ted informing him that Dougal no longer wanted the widgets. On 26 January, the market price of widgets began to rise and thereafter it fluctuated, so that on the succeeding days it was as follows: 26 January, 60 pence per widget; 27 January, 65 pence; 28 January, 70 pence; 29 January, 60 pence; 30 January, 80 pence; 31 January, 85 pence; 1 February, 90 pence. On 27 January, Dougal telephoned Ted stating that after all, he did need the widgets. Ted stated, however, that he could not supply them because he had already sold and delivered his whole stock of widgets to Doyle.

Advise Dougal in each of the following alternative situations:

(a) that Ted sold and delivered his stock of widgets to Doyle on 24 January;
(b) that Ted sold and delivered his stock of widgets to Doyle on 26 January.

How to Answer this Question

With a question such as this, where there is a single problem but a sub-set of questions, it cannot be assumed that the length of answer for each question is necessarily to be the same. Indeed, here, some of the same principles require discussion in each of the two different scenarios. The whole question is concerned with repudiation of the contract and the consequent measure of damages. Given that the two scenarios are clearly alternatives, it makes sense to take them separately.

Applying the Law

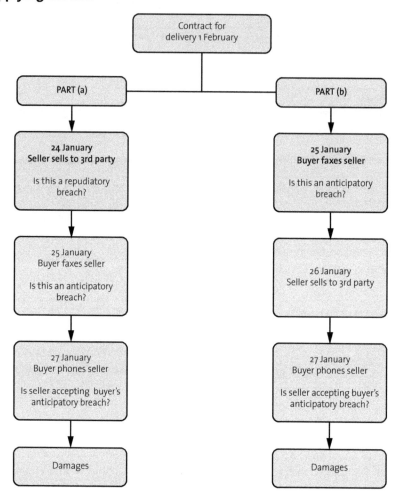

ANSWER

This question is concerned with anticipatory repudiation, who is liable to whom and for how much.

(A) TED DELIVERED HIS STOCK OF WIDGETS TO DOYLE ON 24 JANUARY

In this first scenario, this must have been a repudiatory (and anticipatory) breach by Ted of his contract with Dougal, since it was an act which was totally inconsistent with Ted's continuing ability to perform his contract with Dougal. It seems, however, that Dougal did not accept that repudiation as ending the contract, since it appears that Dougal was unaware of it. This seems clear from the fact that the next day Dougal sent a fax stating that he no longer wanted the widgets. Thus, that fax appears itself to have been a repudiatory breach by Dougal. For the moment, it will be treated as such in this answer. The question then arises as to whether Ted accepted Dougal's breach as terminating the contract. It is arguable that he did, since he informed Dougal two days later on the telephone that he could not (that is, was not going to) supply the widgets.

In those circumstances, Ted is entitled to claim damages for the anticipatory breach by Dougal. The damages claimable are for non-acceptance of the goods, and the *prima facie* measure of damages is the difference between the contract price (£1 per widget) and the (lower) market price on the date when, under the contract, delivery was due to take place (90 pence) (**s 50(3)**). That is still the relevant measure of damages, even where the buyer's non-acceptance takes the form of an anticipatory breach which has been accepted by the seller as putting an end to the contract (*Tai Hing Cotton Mill v Kamsing Knitting Factory* (1978)). Thus, the *prima facie* measure of damages available to Ted is 1,000 × 10 pence, which is £100.

This *prima facie* measure of damages is based upon an assumption that the seller waits until the contractual date for delivery under the contract and then goes out into the market and sells on that day. Even if that is not what the seller has in fact done, the measure of damages is nevertheless based on the assumption that it is. Thus, if the seller chooses to sell in the market either earlier or later than the contractual date for delivery, that fact will normally make no difference to the measure of damages (*Pagnan v Corbisa* (1970)). However, in the present case, the seller, Ted, had already sold the goods, that is, before the repudiation by Dougal, and in doing so had disabled himself from being able to perform the contract with Dougal. In those circumstances, the *prima facie* measure of damages can be reduced. We are not told the price at which Ted sold the widgets to Doyle. Given that on 25 January, the market price was 50 pence per widget, it would seem likely that Ted sold at about that price. In those circumstances, the question arises as to by how much, if at all, the measure of damages should be reduced. By selling to Doyle on 24 January, Ted actually increased his own losses, since he sold at a much lower figure than he would have done if he had held on until the contractual delivery date under his contract with Dougal. So, at first sight, this would seem to be far from a case for *decreasing* the *prima facie* measure of damages. The fact, however, is that Ted, by virtue of having sold the widgets to Doyle, had already (that is, before Dougal's repudiation) disabled himself from fulfilling his contract to Dougal. Thus, Dougal's later repudiation did not cause Ted any loss at all. According to this analysis, Ted is entitled only to nominal damages (see *The Mihalis Angelos* (1971) and *Gill and Duffus v Berger & Co* (1984)).

There is a possible different analysis of the above facts which would, however, produce a not dissimilar result. This analysis rests upon the principle that if a party to a contract relies upon a bad reason for treating the contract at an end when in fact there was available to him a valid reason, his treatment of the contract as at an end will not be regarded as wrongful (see *The Mihalis Angelos* (1971) and *Glencore Grain Rotterdam BV v Lebanese Organisation for International Commerce* (1997)). Applying this principle, Dougal's fax indicating that he did not want the widgets was not a wrongful repudiation of the contract, but was a rightful one because of Ted's repudiation in selling the stock elsewhere. That Ted's act in selling his stock elsewhere did amount to a repudiation of his contract with Dougal cannot really be doubted, given that the contract with Dougal required Ted to deliver not just any widgets but 1,000 widgets from Dougal's current stock. Thus, Dougal is entitled to maintain an action against Ted for non-delivery of the widgets. Dougal's subsequent change of mind and request on 27 January to reinstate delivery do not alter that position, since his request was declined by Ted. The measure of damages to which Dougal is entitled is *prima facie* the difference between the contract price and the market price, if higher, on the day when delivery was due to occur (**s 51(3)** and *Tai Hing Cotton Mill v Kamsing Knitting Factory*). According to this rule, however, Dougal has suffered no loss since the market price on 1 February (the day when delivery ought to have taken place) was 90 pence per widget, which is less than the contract price of £1. Thus, Dougal is entitled to only nominal damages.

(B) TED DELIVERED HIS STOCK OF WIDGETS TO DOYLE ON 26 JANUARY

In this scenario, there is no doubt that Dougal committed a wrongful repudiation by his fax on 25 January, since at that time Ted had not resold the goods. Taking it that Ted by his response on the telephone to Dougal on 27 January accepted Dougal's repudiation as putting an end to the contract, the question arises as to the measure of damages. Again, the *prima facie* measure is the difference between the contract price and the market price on the day due for delivery (**s 50(3)** and *Tai Hing Cotton Mill v Kamsing Knitting Factory*). So this will produce a figure of 1,000 × 10 pence, that is, £100. However, in this case, Ted has himself sold the widgets elsewhere prior to the contractual date (1 February) for delivery. It must be determined what effect, if any, that has on the *prima facie* measure of damages. Normally, the fact that the seller chooses to sell at an earlier or later time than the contractual date will make no difference (*Pagnan v Corbisa*). That principle is subject to the principle that the innocent party (here, Ted) who accepts the other party's wrongful repudiation as putting an end to the contract becomes under a duty to take reasonable steps to mitigate his loss. With the benefit of hindsight, we can say that Ted's sale on 26 January was mistaken, because it left him with a larger loss than if he had waited until 1 February to resell. In *Hoffberger v Ascot International Bloodstock Bureau* (1976), in very different circumstances from those in the present problem, the seller was held entitled to recover, as part of the damages awarded, the extra loss which his reasonable attempt to minimise his loss had in fact caused. If Ted's sale on 26 January can be described as a reasonable attempt to mitigate his loss – albeit one which as events turned out increased that loss – then the court may, in its discretion, award a measure of damages fixed by reference to some date other than the contractual date for delivery (*Johnson v Agnew* (1979)). That date would clearly then be the date (26 January) when Ted sold the widgets to Doyle. This would result in a higher measure of damages which would be the difference between the contract price (£1) and the market price on 26 January (60 pence), namely, 1,000 × 40 pence, which is £400. It is difficult to know whether the sale on 26 January *was* a reasonable attempt to mitigate damages. Clearly, if the price (60 pence) of widgets on 26 January appeared to be the 'top' of a brief strengthening of market confidence, then it would be plausible to describe the sale as a reasonable attempt to mitigate. But how does a market 'appear'? How, at any one time, can a seller predict whether the market will continue to rise or is about to turn?

There is one important fact which we do not know, namely, the price at which Ted sold to Doyle. We know that the market price on the date in question (26 January) was 60 pence. If in fact the sale to Doyle was at a higher price than that (for example, 70 pence), then that would lend some support to the suggestion that the sale was Ted taking a good and sensible opportunity to minimise his loss. Of course, in such a case, if the court did exercise its discretion not to apply the *prima facie* rule, it obviously would fix the measure of damages not by reference to the market price (60 pence) on 26 January, but by reference to the higher price actually obtained by Ted on his sale to Doyle. Leaving aside the possibility that Ted sold at above the market price on 26 January, our conclusion is that Ted is entitled to damages and that either he will receive £100 damages (that is, according to the *prima facie* measure set out in **s50(3)** of the **Sale of Goods Act 1979**) or £400 (that is, if in its discretion the court considers Ted's sale to Doyle on 26 January a reasonable attempt to mitigate his loss).

QUESTION 14

Kane agreed to sell to Marley 900 oak desks. The contract required delivery to be made in three equal instalments on 20 January, 25 January and 30 January. It also contained the clause 'This entire contract is governed by English law'. On 20 January, Kane delivered 280 desks (260 oak desks and 20 walnut desks). Today is 25 January and Kane has delivered 250 oak desks. Marley has now found a cheaper supplier and wishes to return all the desks delivered so far and to cancel delivery of the third consignment.

▶ **Advise Marley.**

What difference, if any, would it have made to your advice if today is 3 February and Kane has only just delivered the second consignment?

How to Answer this Question

There are two particular issues in the question which, on the facts given, it is impossible to determine for sure. These are: 'has Marley accepted the first consignment within the meaning of **s35** of the **Sale of Goods Act 1979**?' and 'is the contract severable or entire?'. Because of this, it is important not just to point these things out, but also to identify the position in the different possible eventualities. Thus, it is essential to use that wonderful word 'if', which is so often useful to examinees in law examinations.

As the question gives a story of two defective deliveries, the structure adopted for the answer here is to deal with them each in turn and then, at the end, to deal with the rider to the question.

Applying the Law

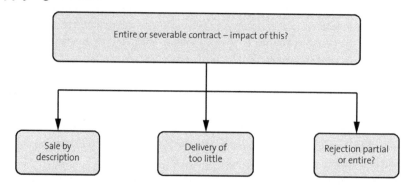

ANSWER

It is proposed to deal initially with the effect of the defective first delivery five days ago and then with the effect of today's defective delivery.

THE FIRST DELIVERY[1]

When Kane delivered the first consignment, he was in breach of contract in one or both of two respects. First, 20 of the desks were not oak and therefore did not comply with what must have been part of the contract description. That put Kane in breach of the express term as to description as well in breach of the condition implied by **s 13** of the **Sale of Goods Act 1979**.[2] Second, one can say that Kane delivered too small a quantity of the contract goods (that is, oak desks). Either way, there has been a breach of condition, giving the buyer the right to reject the goods (see **s 30(1)** of the **1979 Act**) and this, we are told, is what Marley wishes to do. There are, however, two problems with that. First, it is not clear whether the contract is a severable one. If it is, the defective first delivery may not give Marley the right to reject the later two consignments. Second, it is possible that Marley may have lost his right to reject the goods because he may be held to have 'accepted' the first defective delivery.

To take the second of these issues first, a buyer who accepts the goods or part of them is precluded from rejecting the goods (**s 11(4)** of the **Sale of Goods Act 1979**). **Section 35** of the **1979 Act** states three things which will amount to acceptance. The problem simply gives us no information on the first two, namely, whether Marley has either intimated to Kane his acceptance of the goods or else done any act inconsistent with rejecting them. As to the third thing (**s 35(4)**) listed in **s 35**, it is debatable whether a lapse of a reasonable length of time has occurred. Marley has had the desks for five days. It is true that a reasonable period of time will not have elapsed if Marley has not had the goods long enough to have

---

1. Clear signposting of the issues discussed (for example, by using headings) enhances the readability of your answer and helps to achieve clarity of expression.
2. It is reasonable to assume here that the contract between Kane and Marley is a not a consumer transaction, otherwise breach of the implied condition would fall under **s 11** of the **Consumer Rights Act 2015**.

been able to examine them to see if they conform with the contract. However, it must have been fairly obvious almost immediately upon delivery that: (a) 20 of the desks were missing; and (b) 20 of those which were delivered were walnut and not oak. It is arguable in those circumstances that five days is more than a reasonable period of time in which to reject. Certainly, three weeks was held to be more than a reasonable period of time in the first instance decision (on the very different facts of a defective motor car) in *Bernstein v Pamson Motors* (1987). We are not told what were the provisions of the contract regarding the time of payment. If a period of, say, one month was allowed for Marley to pay, then it may be that a reasonable period of time would be held to last at least until the deadline for payment (*Truk v Tokmakidis* (2000)).

Since **s35** was amended, there is now a right of partial rejection which would allow Marley to reject the desks which do not conform to the contract and to accept the rest (the other 260). However, it is clear from the facts that Marley would prefer to reject the lot. Thus, assuming that Marley has not 'accepted' the first consignment, he will have the right to reject that consignment (the whole of it). Whether that gives him the right to reject the later consignments also depends upon whether the contract is an entire contract or is a severable one. If it is not severable, then the breach of condition entitles Marley to reject all consignments. The test of whether a contract is severable is one of construction (interpretation) of the contract, that is, one is trying to discover from the words of the contract what was the intention of the parties. Was it their intention that a breach in relation to one consignment should entitle the purchaser to reject all? If not, then the contract is severable – see generally *Jackson v Rotax Motor and Cycle Co* (1910). The fact that the desks were to be delivered in instalments is some evidence that the contract was severable. We are not told, however, whether under the contract, the consignments were each to be paid for separately. If they were, then that would be strong evidence that the contract was severable. It may be argued that the parties had themselves clearly labelled the contract as not being severable but as being entire, because of the clause in the contract which read that the 'entire' contract was governed by English law. It is submitted, however, that this clause is nothing more than a choice of law clause and that the word 'entire', in the particular context of that clause, does not bear upon whether the contract was severable, but merely means that all of the contract, as opposed to part of it, was to be governed by English law.[3]

If Marley has not 'accepted' the first consignment and if the contract is *not* severable, then he is entitled to reject all the goods, including the later two consignments. If he has not 'accepted' the first consignment and the contract *is* severable, then he may still be able to regard the whole contract as repudiated and thus be able to reject the two later consignments. Whether the whole contract is repudiated depends upon the following two factors: (a) the ratio that the breach bore quantitatively to the whole contract; and (b) the likelihood of the breach being repeated in later instalments (*Maple Flock Co v Universal Furniture Products* (1934)). This is not so easy to determine. At the time that the

---

3 Showing an understanding of any subtleties demonstrates a deeper knowledge and understanding and will attract a higher mark.

breach occurs, one cannot tell anything about the second of these factors. As to the first, it could be said that the breach is fairly small in relation to the whole contract. First, it relates to only one consignment out of the three and, within that consignment, it affects only a small proportion of the total quantity of the desks.

Thus, based on the first defective delivery, one's advice to Marley would be cautious since: (a) he may have 'accepted' the goods; (b) the contract may be severable; and, if it is, the *Maple Flock* test may not be satisfied so as to allow him to regard the whole contract as repudiated.

THE SECOND DELIVERY

The breach in relation to the second delivery is simply a delivery of too small a quantity. The missing 50 desks would appear too many for the courts to be prepared to ignore the breach on the *de minimis non curat lex* principle. Thus, it is a breach of condition.

If the contract was not severable and Marley has not 'accepted' the first consignment, then he is entitled to reject all three consignments because of the breaches of condition in relation to the first two consignments. If the contract was not severable and Marley has 'accepted' the first consignment, then the position is clouded by the fact that the effect of s 11(4) and the new s 35A is not entirely clear. **Section 35A** introduced the concept of partial rejection, allowing the buyer to reject some or all of the non-conforming goods, provided he accepted all of the conforming goods. One thing which does seem clear is that **ss 11(4)** and **35A** do not allow the buyer to reject any goods (whether conforming or not) which he has actually accepted. Thus, if the contract is not severable and Marley has 'accepted' the first consignment, he cannot now reject any of the first consignment (though he may claim damages in respect of the breaches relating to the first consignment). As regards the second consignment, he is entitled to reject any non-conforming goods, but not conforming goods. However, there are no non-conforming goods, since the only breach relating to the second consignment is a shortfall in the number of desks. **Section 30(1)** entitles the buyer to reject all the goods if a quantity smaller than the contract quantity is tendered. The buyer appears, however, to be precluded from exercising this right by his acceptance of the first consignment. This is the effect of s 11(4) in the case of a non-severable agreement. Although s 11(4) is subject to s 35A, the latter is of no help to the buyer in this instance. **Section 35A(1)** applies only where it is non-conforming goods which are being rejected. **Section 35A(2)** also appears to be of no help, since it applies only where the buyer has a right to reject an instalment, and that is the very issue which we have to determine (that is, does the buyer have a right to reject the second instalment?). If this seems an odd result, it is explicable on the basis that the agreement is not severable. In the case of a non-severable agreement, acceptance by the buyer of any conforming goods precludes rejection of any goods. Perhaps this makes it more likely that the courts will regard contracts for delivery in instalments as severable contracts.

If the contract was severable, then Marley would certainly be entitled to reject the second consignment because of the breach of condition in relation to that consignment, and that is so even if he had 'accepted' the first consignment; s 11(4) does not apply to severable contracts.[4] In the event that the contract was severable, then the *Maple Flock* test again needs to be applied to determine whether Marley is entitled to reject the third instalment as well. This time, however, it seems much more likely that the test is satisfied. This is because, on two out of the three instalments, Kane has made a non-conforming delivery. Thus, the ratio that the breach(es) bear quantitatively to the whole contract is much higher and would also seem to suggest a higher probability that he will repeat this with the third and last delivery. On that interpretation, Marley is entitled, even if the contract is severable, to regard the whole contract as repudiated and thus to reject the third consignment as well as the second. Whether that entitles him also to reject the first consignment is debatable. Although on its wording **s11(4)** does not apply to severable contracts, it would seem unlikely that the law is such as to allow rejection of any goods which have actually been accepted. Of course, if Marley has not 'accepted' the first instalment, then the breaches relating to the first two instalments entitle him, for the reasons just given, to regard the whole contract as repudiated, to reject all the goods delivered under the first two instalments and to refuse to accept the third.

THE RIDER

Would it have made any difference if the second delivery had been made only on 3 February? This would affect the consideration of two issues discussed above. First, the time lapse between the first delivery and today would be longer (that is, from 20 January to 3 February) and that would increase the likelihood that Marley would be held to have accepted the first consignment and thus be precluded from rejecting that consignment or, if the contract was not severable, any of the consignments. Second, it would increase the seriousness of the breach in relation to the second consignment, which would suggest that there is a greater degree of breach compared to the contract as a whole, for there would be no doubt that the breach in relation to the second consignment did indeed affect the whole of that consignment. Thus, if the contract is severable, it would be much more likely that by the time the second delivery has come, several days late and with 50 desks short, Kane has committed a breach entitling Marley to regard the contract as repudiated and therefore to reject the third consignment immediately. After all, time is generally of the essence in commercial transactions (*The Mihalis Angelos* (1970)).

---

4 The consideration of different options ensures completeness of your analysis and attracts additional marks.

6 Making and Cancelling a Credit Agreement

INTRODUCTION

The landscape of consumer credit has changed dramatically. This chapter deals with the framework for the regulation of consumer credit under the **Financial Services and Markets Act 2000** ('**FSMA**') and **Financial Services and Markets Act (Regulated Activities) Order** ('**RAO**'), the **Consumer Credit Acts 1974–2006** ('**CCA**'), the **EU Consumer Credit Directive 2008/48/EC** and the common law. This chapter focuses on the law relating to the advertising and marketing of credit, the position of credit-brokers if they do not hold a valid licence, the making of a credit agreement, pre-contract disclosure and formalities, including coverage of the triangular scenario involving a customer, a garage and a finance company, and cancellation of credit agreements.

Checklist
The following topics should be prepared in advance of tackling the questions:

- definition of 'credit';
- definition of a 'regulated agreement' – **ss 8** and **9** of the **Consumer Credit Act 1974** (as amended by **ss 1–4** of the **Consumer Credit Act 2006**);
- definition of a regulated consumer hire agreement **s 15** of the **Consumer Credit Act 1974**;
- Financial Conduct Authority's ('**FCA**') powers to impose requirements on licensees and civil penalties;
- effects of unlicensed trading;
- criminal controls on false and misleading credit advertising;
- pre-contract disclosure requirements – **s 55** and **ss 55A–C 1974**;
- **ss 60–65** of the **Consumer Credit Act 1974** on the documentation formalities;
- **ss 66A–74** of the **Consumer Credit Act** on cancellation;
- **s 56** of the **Consumer Credit Act 1974** on the agency of the dealer and the position at common law.

QUESTION 15 `-----------------------------------------------`

Bert, in partnership with his two brothers, runs a sub-post office. Concerned about the continued viability of the business, the brothers agree that they need to offer added value services to entice customers in. Bert is approached by Reg, a self-employed sales-man, who acts for a variety of firms, including Stingray Photography, who specialise in placing photography booths in shops and other public areas. Reg is very experienced and has been dealing with Stingray Photography for over ten years. The booth is equipped with computerised printing facilities, which allow customers to produce prints of various sizes and to edit their photographs. Reg informs Bert that the hire is £300 per month, that the minimum duration of a hire agreement is 36 months and he must give three months' notice of termination. Reg assures Bert that based on his considerable experience, and taking into account the location of the sub-post office, annual takings are likely to be of the order of £10,000. The partnership enters into a hire contract and the booth is installed. After six months, Bert is extremely unhappy because takings from the machine are barely covering half the monthly hire fee, the computerised printing facilities are very temperamental and are continually jamming, and so he wants to terminate the hire contract, which Stingray Photography, the owners of the booth, are refusing to allow him to do.

(1) Advise the partnership; and
(2) would your advice differ if instead of hiring the machine, the partnership had licensed Stingray Photography to place the booth in their shop, agreeing to account for the takings on a monthly basis to Stingray Photography minus a 10% commission for doing this, dealing with customer queries and minor maintenance such as removing jams in the print facility?

How to Answer this Question

The question requires you to consider the scope of the **CCA 1974** in relation to hire agree-ments (and, in the second scenario, site licence agreements); the status of Reg and whether he is a principal in his own right or an agent, and, if the latter, whether **s 56** of the **CCA** applies; whether there is any liability for his misleading opinion about potential takings; whether there is a right to reject if the equipment is not working satisfactorily; and the position in relation to breach and termination if the equipment is found to be unsatisfactory.

Applying the Law

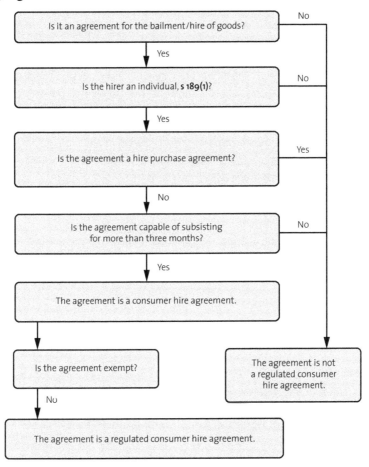

This diagram focuses on the status of the agreement in this scenario and how to determine whether it is a regulated consumer agreement. In addition to the issue, you will also have to consider the application of **s 56 CCA** *and whether any 'antecedent negotiations' are creating a statutory agency or liability for misrepresentation as well as the second scenario where there is an unregulated licensing arrangement.*

ANSWER

SCOPE

This is a hire agreement[1] with a business partnership requiring minimum payments of £10,800 over 36 months. The title of the **Consumer Credit Act 1974** was misleading, in that

....

1 Be careful here to remember when dealing with a pure hire agreement, which is not a hire purchase insurance agreement or a regulated consumer credit agreement, that you are dealing with a regulated consumer hire agreement. Always read questions carefully.

it protected all debtors other than corporate debtors (and even those might be partially protected if there was a joint credit agreement with individual debtors – **s185** of the **CCA 1974**). As part of an exercise in deregulation, the **CCA 2006** redefines 'individual' to include 'a partnership consisting of TWO or THREE persons not all of whom are bodies corporate and an unincorporated body of persons which does not consist entirely of bodies corporate and is not a partnership'.[2] The effect is that generally only small partnerships and not large-scale partnerships will benefit from the protections of the Act. The financial limit in **s15(1)(c)**, excluding hire agreements where the required hire payments would exceed £25,000, has been repealed (**ss1** and **2** of the **CCA 2006**). However, consumer hire agreements for wholly or predominantly business purposes where the required hire payments will exceed £25,000 are treated as exempt agreements under **RAO Art 60O**. The agreement here is therefore a regulated consumer hire agreement.[3]

AGENCY

The partnership may be able to take advantage of the statutory agency in relation to Reg's statements under **s56** of the **CCA 1974**. The statutory agency is very precisely defined and it is necessary to check whether the facts of a consumer credit or hire transaction fall within one of the three 'sub-categories of agency' in **s56(1)(a)–(c)** – see *Black Horse Ltd v Langford* (2007). The statutory agency does not apply to consumer hire agreements unless the statements are made by the creditor or owner himself (which can include his employees and agent) and not by third party credit-brokers or suppliers (*Moorgate Mercantile Leasing Ltd v Gell & Ugolini Dispensers* (1985) and *Lloyds Bowmaker Leasing Ltd v MacDonald* (1993)). It would be a question of fact whether at common law Reg is the agent of Stingray Photography, though the courts have been reluctant to create an agency in relation to intermediaries in credit transactions (*Branwhite v Worcester Works Finance* (1969)). If he were an agent,[4] then as principal, Stingray Photography would be held liable for the statements of Reg if they gave rise to any legal liability as either misrepresentations or terms of the contract. The statements by Reg would probably be regarded as 'antecedent negotiations' made in relation to a regulated agreement, even though not directly concerned with the hire payments element, and such liability would be non-excludable (**s56(1)(a)**, **(3)** and **(4)** – see *Forthright Finance Ltd v Ingate & Carlyle Finance* (1997)). If Reg were deemed to be not an agent but a freestanding principal, then **s56** of the **CCA 1974** would not apply.[5] The joint liability provisions in **s75** of the **CCA 1974** do not apply to consumer hire agreements.

MISREPRESENTATION

On the face of it, Reg's remarks as to likely revenue from the booth look to be a mere opinion, but given his status and experience, the courts would probably imply a statement

---

2 Showing an awareness of the development of the area of law in question demonstrates both knowledge and understanding.

3 Remember to draw conclusions from your analysis; this evidences your understanding of how to apply the law.

4 Outlining different possible conclusions demonstrates both understanding and knowledge of the legal area in question.

5 **Section 56** is a good illustration of the need to read sections of this Act carefully; it is very precisely drafted and there is need to be within the exact scope of the section for it to apply.

of fact that he had a reasonable basis for his opinion and, if this did not exist, then potential liability might arise for misrepresentation. If he is an agent of Stingray Photography, an action for statutory negligent misrepresentation would be available under **s 2(1)** of the **Misrepresentation Act 1967**, with the added advantage that the onus of proving a reasonable factual basis for Reg's opinion would lie on Stingray Photography (*Howard Marine & Dredging Co Ltd v A Ogden & Sons (Excavations) Ltd* (1978)).[6] If Reg is a free-standing principal **s 2(1)** would not apply, as the consumer hire contract would not be with him but with Stingray Photography; but here a common law tort action for negligent misstatement might lie, based on the principle in *Hedley Byrne v Heller & Partners* (1964), on the basis that Reg is aware that Bert is relying on his skill and judgment in relation to potential revenues and it is fair and just to impose liability on him.

IMPLIED TERM

If the computerised printing facilities keep breaking down and this is attributable to a defect in the equipment, there is the potential for the termination of the contract for breach of the implied term of satisfactory quality under **s 4** of the **Supply of Goods and Services Act 1982**,[7] even though Bert has had the booth for three months (see *UCB Leasing v Holtom* (1987) and *Farnworth Finance Facilities v Attryde* (1970)).

TERMINATION

Unfortunately for Bert, the statutory right of termination of consumer hire agreements provided in **s 101** of the **CCA 1974** will not apply as the annual payments exceed £1,500 and the agreement is for business purposes (**s 101(7)** of the **CCA 1974**).[8] In the absence of any contractual right of early termination, the partnership would be bound by the minimum hire period of 36 months.

BREACH AND DAMAGES

In the absence of any contractual right to reject for breach of the condition of satisfactory quality, or contractual right of early termination, then the partnership would be in breach of contract if they sought to terminate the hire before the 36-month minimum period had elapsed and could, assuming proper default procedures had been followed (**ss 87–89** of the **CCA 1974**), face an action for damages for breach of contract or face a demand for immediate payment of the hire charges under a valid acceleration clause (*Wadham Stringer Ltd v Meaney* (1981)), as well as of course the return of the photography booth to Stingray Photography. It is quite probable that as this is a business contract there will be a liquidated damages clause in the hire contract, and provided this is a reasonable pre-estimate of the owner's loss, will be upheld by the courts even if the amount payable

----

6 Always remember consumer and commercial law is built on foundations of contract law; do not forget basic law on the likes of terms and representations.

7 Bert is not a consumer for **Consumer Rights Act 2015** purposes, otherwise the corresponding implied terms are **ss 9** and **10**.

8 The explanation of why a particular legal principle is not applicable in relation to a question is as important as the explanation of why a particular legal rule is applicable: on the one hand, this is because it narrows your analysis down to what is relevant; on the other hand, it demonstrates understanding.

under the clause exceeds the actual loss on this occasion (*Robophone Facilities Ltd v Blank* (1966)). The statutory rebate provision in **s 94** of the **CCA 1974** does not apply to consumer hire agreements. It is unlikely on the facts that the hirer could claim relief under **s 132** of the **CCA 1974** on the grounds that it is just that he be relieved from some or all of his future hire payments and recover any part of instalments already made.

LICENSING AGREEMENT[9]

In the second scenario, the partnership merely licenses Stingray Photography to place the machine in their shop and to account for any proceeds received for use of the machine, minus a commission. It follows from this that if no one used the machine, they would not be required to pay any money to Stingray Photography. The question then arises whether it is still a regulated consumer hire agreement within **s 15** of the **CCA 1974**. The answer to that question appears to be no, as a result of the decision in *TRM Copy Centres (UK) v Lanwall* (2008),[10] where it was held that for a bailment to fall within the scope of the Act, there must be an element of payment involved, and where in that case, involving a photocopier in a post office, the owner of the shop only had to account for the proceeds of use of the copier minus a commission, it was held that as there were no mandatory hire charges, it was not a regulated consumer hire agreement.[11] The outcome here then is that in the second scenario it would be an unregulated credit agreement governed by the common law and it would depend on the terms of the licence whether and under what conditions the partnership could terminate the licence – presumably if the machine did not work they might, in the absence of any express provision, rely on an implied term to give business efficacy to the contract that the licensed equipment is required to work satisfactorily (*Liverpool City Council v Irwin* (1977)).

Aim Higher

A candidate looking to secure a first class mark will have picked up the more limited impact of the **Consumer Credit Act** regime on regulated hire agreements as opposed to regulated consumer credit agreements – in particular in relation to operation of **ss 56** and **101 CCA 1974**. Another key element in this question, and a number of other questions on consumer credit, is to be able to apply the known **CCA 1974** dimensions, but also 'think outside the box'. In this question, a candidate needs to include the scope and operation of the **Misrepresentation Act 1967** and the relevant common law provisions on breach and liquidated damages clauses in relation to hire agreements. In other words, not all the aspects of a question will be dealt with by the **Consumer Credit Act 1974** regime – examiners will give extra credit for this broadness of vision.

....

9 The proper application of the relevant legal principle to the requirements of the questions is what the examiner is looking for in an answer.

10 It is important to refer to relevant authorities to substantiate your argument – this might be case law or a statutory provision. Remember: it is the application of law upon which you are assessed.

11 This part illustrates the importance in the **CCA** regime of being on top of basic category definitions.

Common Pitfalls

Often marks may be lost by simple errors such as confusing pure hire agreements with hire purchase agreements and, for example, incorrectly applying the agency provisions in **s 56 CCA 1974** and the termination provisions in **ss 99** and **100 CCA** instead of the correct provision in **s 101 CCA 1974**. Another error is to fail to realise that the **CCA 1974** can apply to some business credit contracts, in particular with small partnerships – the weak candidate will not have taken on board the narrowed definition of an 'individual' in the amended **s 189(1) CCA 1974**. Another common oversight is failure to consider whether – which will commonly be the case – there is a valid liquidated damages clause in a business hire agreement. In relation to the second fact scenario, a weak student may not appreciate the parameters of the definition of a regulated hire agreement in **s 15 CCA 1974** and the impact of the House of Lords' decision in *TRM Copy Centres (UK) v Lanwall* (2008).

QUESTION 16

Pedro, who has no regular employment, but who has inherited subject to mortgage with a building society his late mother's house, earns small sums of money from part-time decorating. As a result of his small and intermittent earnings Pedro owes a variety of creditors some £30,000 unsecured debts. He sees an advertisement on the Internet by Access Finance which states 'We can provide you with peace and security from pressing creditors, easy to arrange and cheap consolidation loans; contact us straightaway, no delays. Mainstream lenders such as banks or credit card companies refusing you? Visit us.' The site goes on to give various examples of loans made to allegedly satisfied customers. It also states a £1,500 arrangement fee will be charged upfront or deducted from the amount of the loan.

The advertisement fails to state that Access Finance are credit-brokers and do not provide the loans themselves and that any loans they arrange will have to be secured by a first or subsequent charge on the debtor's property, if the debtor owns any property. The advertisement does not specify the name of any lenders with whom Access Finance deal, nor has it been approved by any of those lenders.

Pedro contacts Access Finance to try and arrange a loan for £35,000, which will pay off his existing creditors and leave him with some money left over to meet urgent house renovation expenses. Access Finance arrange a secured loan with sub-prime lenders Severn Finance at an APR of 40% per annum and secured by a second charge on Pedro's house. This is in fact a different credit contract from the one Access Finance initially sent him with Cymru Finance for a loan at 30% APR and which would be unsecured, but Pedro was later informed that this contract was not apparently available for 'reasons connected with the credit crunch'.

Pedro only gets £33,500 as Access Finance deduct a £1,500 arrangement fee and Pedro is further informed that his future repayments will include a brokerage fee of £2,500 payable to them – this is set out in the consolidation agreement but no mention was made in Access Finance's Internet advertisement.

Pedro has received no copy of either the unexecuted or executed consolidation loan agreement. Pedro is concerned about the transaction and, in particular, the way it was advertised and carried out.

▶ (a) Advise Pedro; and
▶ (b) would your advice differ if Pedro discovered that while Severn Finance are fully licensed under the Financial Services and Markets Act, Access Finance hold no licence under the Act at all.[12]

How to Answer this Question

You will:

❖ need to be aware of the extent to which **FSMA** applies to ancillary credit businesses such as credit-brokers;

❖ need to be aware of general controls on false and misleading advertising in the **Consumer Protection Unfair Trading Regulations 2008**;

❖ need to be aware of the advertising regime laid down by **Consumer Credit Act 1974**;

❖ need to be aware of the licensing regime in relation to ancillary credit businesses and also the impact of the introduction by an unlicensed credit-broker to a licensed creditor;

❖ need to be aware of the structure of the agreement, copies of agreements and regulations under **CCA**.

Applying the Law

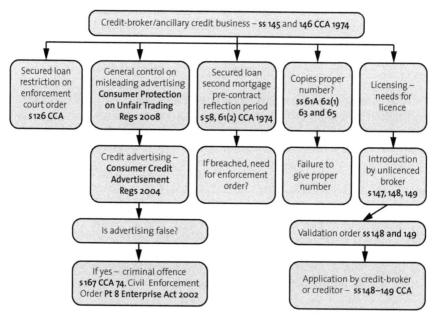

This flowchart shows the main factors to consider in this scenario in relation to the law around credit-brokers.

---

12 Read problem questions carefully. Candidates are advised to do a proper structure plan of the answer before writing – as many marks are lost by bad technique as by lack of knowledge. Do not waste time with repetition – you do not get double the marks by saying the same thing twice.

ANSWER

(A) ADVERTISING[13]

An initial point that might be made to Pedro is that as the agreement is secured by a land mortgage regulated by the consumer credit regime, it cannot be enforced by a court order and, at any such hearing, concerns about the procedure for entering into the loan and mortgage might be raised (**s 126**).[14]

Serious questions must be raised about the content of the advertising by Access Finance: they have failed to make clear they are brokers and also appear to be offering to arrange loans which they cannot in practice provide – is this an example of so-called 'bait and switch' advertising?[15] There is a strong possibility that they may be in breach of the **CPUTR**.[16] It is questionable whether the cheaper credit deal was ever on offer.

It is suggested that the advertising would influence an average consumer in the vulnerable section of sub-prime borrowers into making or potentially making a transactional decision to pursue a loan via the brokers (**CPUTR 2008 reg 2(2)**, **(3)** and **(5)**).

While Access Finance may face criminal prosecution (**CPUTR 2008 regs 9, 10** and **12**) or the possibility of a civil enforcement order under **Pt 8** of the **Enterprise Act 2002** to prevent the continuance of such conduct if adversely affecting the collective interest of consumers, at the moment Pedro has no direct civil right of action for breach of the **CPUTR 2008**.

However, it also appears that the brokers are guilty of breach of the relevant advertising regulations found in the **FCA Consumer Credit Sourcebook** ('**CONC**'). Key breaches of these regulations appear to be:

(a) **CONC 3.6.5** – failure to state that security will be required.

(b) **CONC 3.6.5** – does not seem to contain a 'typical APR' which is required in advertisements aimed at persons whose access to credit is restricted, which Pedro's appears to be. A typical APR is defined as: 'an APR at or below which the advertiser reasonably expects, at the date on which the advertisement is published, that credit would be provided under at least 66% of the agreements which will be entered into as a result of the advertisement'. The impression from the facts appears to be that vulnerable borrowers may be being lured on to the site with falsely optimistic APRs.

(c) **CONC 3.7.7** and **4.4.3** – failure to make clear the circumstances about the additional brokerage fee and that Access Finance are acting as brokers.

---

13 Always read questions carefully to check whether there is more than one part to answer; and, in terms of timing etc, get the balance right because of allocation of marks between parts.

14 In respect of advertising bear in mind the consumer credit regime is now less self-contained with the repeal of **s 46** and also to bear in mind the very expansive and all embracing **Consumer Protection from Unfair Trading Regulations 2008** (CPUTR).

15 Extra marks may be gained by putting in incidental points which are relevant to the answer in a wider sense; but be careful to stay within the bounds of relevance as no marks are given for irrelevant material.

16 **Consumer Protection Unfair Trading Regulations 2008 SI 1277: reg 5** (misleading advertising), **reg 6** (misleading omission) and **reg 3(4)(d) Sched I** (automatically unfair practices) paras 5 and 18.

An offence by the credit-broker may have criminal sanctions and may be punishable as a criminal offence, but does not render any agreement entered into void, voidable or unenforceable.

The deemed agency provisions in **s 56** do not appear to apply to these facts and, as the broker appears to act in relation to a range of lenders, it appears difficult to argue an agency relationship: rather, the broker is a free-standing stakeholder in the arrangements (*Branwhite v Worcester Works Finance* (1969)).

AGREEMENT

There appears to be nothing to suggest that the principal credit agreement has not been properly executed in compliance with **s 61**. We are not told the exact procedures relating to the entry into the agreement by Pedro. It is also worth noting that we are not told whether the lender has complied with the pre-contract reflection period provided for in **ss 58** and **61(2)** and **(3)** where certain land mortgage transactions are secured – this would be covered by these provisions and, in effect, if any approach had been made directly or indirectly by the creditor or the credit-broker in the seven-day reflection period, the subsequent credit agreement would be improperly executed and a court order, or the free, informed and voluntary consent of the debtor, would be required for the subsequent civil enforcement of the agreement.

COPIES[17]

However there appears to have been a breach of the statutory copy requirements. This is an excluded agreement as it is secured on land (**s 61A**) and, if the document was unexecuted at the time he signed it, he should have been given a copy of the unexecuted agreement (**s 62(1)**) and any other document referred to in the agreement, which would presumably include the mortgage agreement. Further, a copy of the executed agreement should have been sent to him within the prescribed period along with a copy of any document referred to in the credit agreement (**s 63(2)**).

The impact of this is to make the agreement 'improperly executed' under **s 65** and thus enforceable only with a court order, or the free and fully informed consent of the debtor given at the time enforcement is required (**s 65**). If Pedro refuses to pay, then Severn Finance will have to apply for an enforcement order under **s 127**, which the court can grant on a conditional or unconditional basis and subject to agreement to variation (**ss 135** and **136**). It might be in this case, because the subsequent brokerage fee is buried away in the agreement and his attention was not drawn to it previously, that an order might be granted enforcing the loan arrangements but subject to a reduction or removal of the subsequent brokerage fee.

....

17 This typifies what is in some ways a boring area, but failure to comply can have a major impact on the enforceability of the agreement so you need to know in broad terms the number of copies of executed and unexecuted agreements a debtor should normally have.

(B) LICENSING

Access Finance[18] are carrying on the business of credit brokerage, a regulated activity as defined by **RAO Art 36**, and an ancillary credit business under **CCA s 145(1)**, **(2)**, **(3)** – they are effecting introductions of individuals desiring to obtain credit to persons carrying on a consumer credit business. It is a criminal offence (**FSMA s 23**) to carry on this regulated activity unless one is an authorised person with authorisation to do so (**FSMA s 19**).

The credit brokerage agreement is not civilly enforceable unless the Financial Conduct Authority exercises its power under **s 28A FSMA** to issue a written notice requiring that the consumer comply with the agreement. Such a notice will only be issued where it is just and equitable to do so and in the circumstances set out in **s 28A FSMA**.

The same would apply if Severn Finance, who are authorised to carry on a regulated activity, sought to enforce the contract. **Section 28A FSMA** allows the Financial Conduct Authority to give notice that the agreement is enforceable but in addition to considering whether such enforcement is just and equitable will consider whether Severn Finance knew that Access Finance were in fact authorised.

---

18 Careful reading of the question is important as it is here all too easy to assume a credit-broker is licensed.

7 Default and Termination of Credit Agreements

INTRODUCTION

This chapter covers the termination of hire purchase agreements as well as other regulated agreements; challenges by the debtor to an allegedly unfair credit agreement; and the use of the Financial Ombudsman Service instead of the courts in the event of a dispute with the creditor.

Checklist
The following topics should be prepared in advance of tackling the questions:

- the need to issue arrears and default notices, and arrears and default information sheets under **ss 8–12** of the **Consumer Credit Act 2006**;
- the need for and effect of a default notice under **s 87** of the **Consumer Credit Act 1974**;
- non-default notice under **ss 76** and **98**;
- time orders under **s 129** of the **Consumer Credit Act**;
- liability of surety in relation to regulated agreements;
- protected goods provision in **s 90** of the **Consumer Credit Act**;
- accelerated payments clauses;
- hire purchase customers' right of termination under **s 99** of the **Consumer Credit Act**;
- claim by an owner against a third party to whom a hire purchase customer has sold or bailed the goods;
- the consumer credit jurisdiction of the Financial Services Ombudsman under **ss 59–61** of the **Consumer Credit Act 2006**;
- the jurisdiction to intervene in an 'unfair relationship' between the creditor and the debtor – **ss 19–22** of the **Consumer Credit Act 2006** replacing extortionate credit bargain provisions in **ss 137–140** of the **Consumer Credit Act 1974**;
- guidance on irresponsible lending set out in 'Irresponsible Lending' OFT Guidance for Creditors (OFT 1107, March 2010) and **Arts 8** and **9 EU Consumer Credit Directive 2008/48/EC**;
- the provisions of the **EU Consumer Credit Directive 2008/48/EC, 23 April 2008** and their implementation in the **Consumer Credit Act 1974**.

QUESTION 17 --

Just over five months ago, Fred traded in his old car in part-exchange for a new car which he acquired from XYZ Finance under a regulated hire purchase agreement. The hire purchase agreement showed the following details:

❖ a cash price of £21,000;
❖ a total hire purchase price of £24,000;
❖ a part-exchange allowance of £4,000.

Under the agreement, Fred agreed to make an initial cash payment of £2,000 and 36 monthly instalment payments of £500.[1]

Upon trading in his old car and taking delivery of the new one, Fred paid the initial payment of £2,000 and has since paid the first three of the £500 monthly instalments. However, he is now two months in arrears with his instalments and a week ago wrote to XYZ Finance, informing them that he was temporarily out of work and unable to keep up his payments.

▶ Advise Fred as to his legal position now that he has received a default notice which complies with the requirements of the Consumer Credit Act 1974 and states that unless he pays off his outstanding arrears within seven days, XYZ Finance will regard the agreement as terminated.

How to Answer this Question

This question demands a consideration of the area of termination of a hire purchase agreement. The plan is to consider the following:

❖ Have the procedures in relation to dealing with arrears been followed?
❖ Has a terminating event occurred?
❖ What are the consequences of termination arising from Fred's breach?
❖ Can Fred avoid those consequences, for example by paying off the debt before expiry of the default notice, or applying for a time order (and how in all of that does the fact that the goods are 'protected goods', if indeed that is what they are, help Fred)?
❖ Is it worthwhile for Fred to exercise his own right of termination?
❖ Is there any other way out of the mess for Fred, for example selling the car or refinancing the debt?

....

1 Where figures and limits are involved make sure you work out correctly the amounts involved in relation to the limit and, also, key in consumer credit questions in many areas, the law distinguishes 'credit' from 'total charge for credit'.

Applying the Law

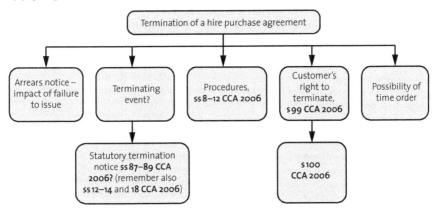

This diagram illustrates the factors to be considered in relation to a hire purchase agreement. When considering the agreement itself it is important to consider whether it is regulated or unregulated, and if they are protected goods.

ANSWER

The question states that the hire purchase agreement is a regulated one. It is assumed that the formalities and documentation requirements of the **Consumer Credit Act 1974** have been satisfied.

This problem requires a discussion of whether the agreement has been, or can be, terminated and the possible consequences for Fred.[2]

ARREARS INFORMATION AND ARREARS NOTICE

The creditor must first check whether a 'sums in arrears' notice must be served under **s 9** of the **CCA 2006**. This is required when the debtor is required to have made more than two payments under the agreement and the amount of the shortfall is no less than the sum of the last two payments that Fred is required to have made before the relevant time. This applies here. Within 14 days of these conditions being satisfied under a fixed-sum credit agreement, an arrears notice must be served with a copy of an FCA-issued 'arrears information sheet' which inform debtors who receive an arrears notice what steps they might take and the consequences of taking remedial action (**s 8** of the **CCA 2006**).[3] Failure to give such a notice will mean that while this default continues, the creditor may not enforce the agreement and the debtor will not be liable for interest or any default sum during the non-compliance period (**s 11** of the **CCA 2006**).

---

2   Providing a brief introduction which not only sets out the issues you are going to address but which also refers to the question set is a good way to demonstrate that you have understood what is relevant; relevancy is an important assessment factor.

3   The inclusion and consideration of material such as consultation papers demonstrates knowledge which goes beyond the normal textbooks and will attract additional marks.

TERMINATING EVENT – FRED'S BREACH

Fred is in breach of his agreement by becoming in arrears. There are three ways in which this could be argued to be a terminating event.[4] First, if it amounts to a repudiation by Fred. There is no outright refusal by Fred to honour the agreement and he has noted he is *temporarily* unemployed, hardly signifying a repudiation.

Second, if the agreement expressly gives XYZ Finance a right to terminate the agreement, if Fred falls into arrears. Third, if the agreement provides that the making of prompt payments is 'of the essence' of the contract (see *Lombard North Central v Butterworth* (1987)).[5]

Even if one of the last two possibilities proves to be the case, XYZ Finance could not treat the agreement as terminated until the expiry of the default notice (**s 87**). The default notice issued under **CCA 1974**, **ss 87–89** must comply with the requirements under **s 12** of the **CCA 2006**; default interest will not be payable until 28 days after the issue of the notice. Under **s 88(4A)**, to be a valid notice, a default information sheet must be included[6] (see www.fca.org.uk/firms/firm-types/consumer-credit/information-sheets).[7] If Fred remedies his default and pays off the arrears (plus default interest) before the expiry of the default notice (under **s 88** amended by **s 14** of the **CCA 2006**, Fred must be given at least 14 days from the service of the notice to rectify the breach – see *Brandon v American Express Services Ltd* (2011)), the breach will be treated as not having occurred (**s 89**) and XYZ Finance will have no right to terminate the contract.

There is no statutory sanction for failure to serve a compliant default notice but under **s 87** and/or **88** it can be used as a defence if the creditor seeks judicial enforcement of its claims.[8]

A non-compliant default notice might, therefore, jeopardise a creditor's claim. However, a bad default notice may be remedied by serving a 'good' default notice, as suggested in *Harrison v Link Financial* (2011).[9]

CONSEQUENCES OF TERMINATION UPON FRED'S BREACH

If Fred's breach is a terminating event, what will be the consequences of termination (that is, assuming also that Fred does not pay off his arrears before expiry of the default notice)?[10]

---

4 Considering different possibilities ensures that your analysis/advice is complete.

5 This question demonstrates that not all answers to consumer credit revolve around the statutory provisions. The common law on breach and assessment of damages in this area remains important.

6 In order to attract a good mark you need to ensure that you don't merely describe the law; you need to explain and apply it to the requirements of the question. This is a good example of how to achieve this aim.

7 Given the importance of FCA guidance and advice, good students will be able to show good knowledge of the extensive online materials available and be able to make specific reference to eg the **CONC**.

8 Always try and be aware of sanctions and penalties that flow from breach of provision and whether it will render agreement permanently or temporarily unenforceable.

9 Marks can be gained by mentioning relevant *obiter dicta* or suggestions by judges on what the position might be even if it is not central to the finding in the particular case, as in *Harrison*.

10 Proceeding from the previously drawn conclusions gives your answer a logical structure.

If the termination arose because XYZ Finance had a right of termination upon the debtor falling into arrears, the consequences would be as per *Financings v Baldock* (1963).[11] Fred would lose the right to keep the car and be liable for the arrears due up to termination; assuming that the agreement required him to take reasonable care of the vehicle, he would also be liable for any loss caused by his failure to do so.

If the termination arose because the agreement made Fred's prompt payment of instalments 'of the essence', XYZ Finance would be entitled to regard the termination as resulting from repudiation and be able to claim the return of the car and damages assessed on a *Waragowski* (1961) basis. XYZ Finance could claim the arrears already fallen due and all outstanding instalments, minus the value of the vehicle recovered and a deduction (calculated under **s 95**) to reflect the fact that XYZ Finance was getting early payment of some instalments.

In principle, however termination occurred, XYZ Finance would be entitled to recover the goods. At common law, an owner is entitled simply to take possession of his own goods if he can do so without trespassing (see *Bowmakers v Barnet Instruments* (1945)). However, this is not possible if the car is 'protected goods' under **s 90**.[12] The car will be 'protected goods' if Fred has made or tendered payments totalling one-third (that is, £8,000) or more of the total price (of £24,000). Fred has made payments totalling £7,500 (£2,000 deposit + £4,000 trade-in allowance + three instalments of £500). Were he to tender payment of one more instalment, the goods would become protected goods; XYZ Finance would then have to bring proceedings seeking a return order (under **s 133**) to recover the car.

As noted, even if the car is not 'protected goods', XYZ Finance could not trespass to recover it (see **s 92**) unless Fred waived the protection afforded by **ss 90** and **92** and consented to the recovery of the goods at the time of repossession (**s 173(3)**). His consent would not be effective had he not been informed of his rights if he refused that consent (*Chartered Trust v Pitcher* (1987)), although the default notice is likely to have provided that information.[13] Fred would be well advised not to give that consent as doing so would make it very difficult in later proceedings to keep Fred's hire purchase agreement 'alive'. If, on the other hand, XYZ Finance have to bring proceedings to recover the car, Fred will have the option to apply under **s 129** for a time order. The court could then allow Fred extra time to pay off his arrears (*Southern and District Finance v Barnes* (1995) and reorganise the future payment pattern (**s 130(2)**).

If the car does not fall within the definition of protected goods and is kept on the highway, then Fred should consider applying immediately for a time order, to pre-empt any attempt by XYZ Finance to recover the goods. As a default notice has been served on him, Fred has the right to apply for a time order under **s 129** without waiting for proceedings to be commenced against him.

....

11 The consideration of different options ensures completeness of your analysis and attracts additional marks.

12 Pointing out any potential limitations of the application of a particular legal principle is a good way to demonstrate that you have understood the complexities of the rule in question.

13 Showing an understanding of any subtleties/intricacies of a particular rule demonstrates a deeper knowledge and understanding and will attract a higher mark.

FRED'S RIGHT OF TERMINATION[14]

Alternatively, Fred could exercise his right of termination under **s99**, by serving written notice on XYZ Finance. The effects of doing so are laid down in **s100**. He would have to return the car and would be liable to pay the arrears which have already fallen due: £1,000. However, Fred may be liable to pay such further sums as would be required to bring his payments up to one-half of the total price, unless the loss suffered by the creditor is less than that amount. After payment of his arrears, his payments to date will be £8,500.[15] Thus, the final sum to be paid by Fred (in addition to the £1,000 arrears) could be up to £3,500, which would bring the £8,500 up to £12,000 (which is the total price of £24,000). This figure of £3,500 would be reduced to such sum, if any, stipulated in the agreement as payable upon termination. Normally, an agreement will state a formula which will produce exactly the same figure as, in this case, the £3,500; if the agreement fails to stipulate any sum as payable upon termination, the figure of £3,500 is reduced to zero. Assuming that the sum of £3,500 is stipulated in the agreement, the court still has discretion under **s100** to reduce the £3,500 to such lesser figure as it considers sufficient to compensate XYZ Finance.

CONCLUDING ADVICE[16]

Which is the better (or least negative) option outlined above largely depends on the likelihood of Fred getting back into work and the value of the car.[17] If he is able to return to work an application for a time order is an attractive option if XYZ Finance cannot otherwise take possession of the car. Exercising the **s99** right of termination is less attractive when he has already paid £7,500 towards it and would still be liable for the £1,000 arrears.

Alternatively, he could ask XYZ Finance for a settlement statement and seek to sell the car to pay off the remaining debt (getting the benefit of a rebate of charges under **s95**). If Fred could find a willing buyer, as soon as XYZ Finance is paid off, Fred will acquire title to the goods, which title would of course be 'fed' straight on to Fred's purchaser (*Butterworth v Kingsway Motors* (1954)).

QUESTION 18

Harley had longed for a motorcycle which he had seen in the window of Cycles Sellers Ltd. On his 17th birthday, Harley acquired the motorcycle under the terms of a regulated hire purchase agreement which he made with Davison Finance. Davison Finance had refused to make the agreement until Harley's father, Gullible, had provided a guarantee of Harley's liabilities under the hire purchase agreement. Davison Finance also has a recourse agreement with the dealer, Cycles Sellers Ltd. The hire purchase agreement provided for an initial payment of £3,000 and 36 monthly payments of £200 each. After making the

---

14 There is rarely one route to be followed in consumer credit problems: always think of possible alternative routes to gain extra marks for thinking around the issues.

15 Do not be frightened if figures are mentioned: in the vast majority of cases very simple calculations are involved.

16 Always try and tie up loose ends to a question in a good strong conclusion: go out on good exit velocity!

17 Explaining why a course of action might be preferable/more successful will attract additional marks.

initial payment and paying one of the monthly instalments, Harley stopped making payments. Davison served a default notice upon him at a time when he was two instalments in arrears and, upon expiry of the default notice without Harley having paid off his arrears, Davison Finance terminated the agreement and repossessed the motorcycle, taking it from outside Gullible's house where Harley had left it. That was yesterday. The motorcycle is now worth £3,000 and Harley has no assets.

▶ **Advise Davison Finance.**

What difference, if any, would it make, if at the time when Harley fell into arrears, he had already paid three of the monthly instalments and if the agreement which Gullible signed was expressed as an indemnity?

How to Answer this Question

This question tells us that Harley has no assets and thus it requires us to consider any claims Davison Finance may have against Harley's father and the dealer. The fact that the agreement signed by Gullible is a guarantee means that we cannot avoid examining what claims in law Davison Finance may have against Harley. Since we are not told of the terms of the recourse agreement, it seems sensible first to consider the claim against Gullible. It is assumed that the correct procedures have been followed in relation to the issuing of any required arrears notice and default notice (**s 9** of the **CCA 2006** and **s 87** of the **CCA 1974**).

Applying the Law

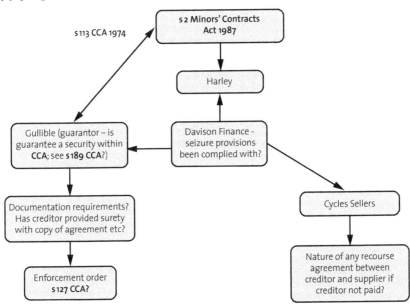

The application of the **Minors' Contracts Act** *in this answer is shown above. You will need to be clear about the position of a guarantor/surety under the* **CCA 1974**. *In addition, the impact of any non-compliance with document and copy requirements will have to be considered under* **ss 65** *and* **127** *of the* **CCA 1974**.

ANSWER

GULLIBLE'S LIABILITY[18]

Since Harley has no assets, Davison Finance would not be advised to consider any proceedings against Harley. It is nevertheless necessary to ask what is the legal liability of Harley, because the liability of Gullible, if not of the dealer, may well depend upon it. The most obvious issue is that Harley was, at the time of the making of the contract, a minor. This might well make the contract unenforceable against Harley. Even if that is so, however, that particular defence will not be available to someone, here Gullible, who has guaranteed Harley's liability. If the only reason that the principal debtor is not liable is that he was a minor at the time of the contract, then that will not prevent someone who has guaranteed that liability from being liable on his guarantee (**s 2** of the **Minors' Contracts Act 1987**).[19] Apart from that exception, Gullible, as Harley's guarantor, cannot be liable to any greater extent than Harley (**s 113** of the **CCA 1974**).[20]

Ignoring the fact that Harley was a minor, what is the extent of Harley's liability? The hire purchase agreement made by Harley was a regulated consumer credit agreement, providing for a total hire purchase price of £10,200. Upon termination, Harley had paid £3,200, which is less than one-third of the total price. The motorcycle was not 'protected goods' under **s 90** of the **Consumer Credit Act 1974**. Consequently, once the contract had been validly terminated, Davison Finance had a right to possession of its own goods irrespective of whether the contract stated so in express terms (*Bowmakers v Barnet Instruments* (1945)). We are told that the motorcycle was repossessed from outside Gullible's house: it is not clear if it was in the street or in Gullible's garden.[21] If the latter, despite the fact that Davison Finance was entitled to possession of the motorcycle, it was not entitled to trespass in order to retrieve it (**s 92**) and is liable to Gullible for breach of statutory duty (**s 92(3)**). As there is no other sanction, it will have no bearing upon Gullible's liability under his guarantee.[22]

Harley's liability, and hence Gullible's, would include a liability to pay off the arrears already due before termination occurred. Beyond that, liability depends upon the terms of the agreement.[23] If it provided that prompt payment of all instalments was 'of the

----

18 An easily overlooked area is the liability of sureties if the principal debtor does not pay. You need to know basic rules concerning giving of guarantees for a debtor.

19 It is important to refer to relevant authorities to substantiate your argument – this might be case law or a statutory provision. Remember: it is the application of law upon which you are assessed.

20 Key point: work out if debtor has any liability first because, apart from the case of infancy, surety has no greater liability under the **CCA** than the principal debtor.

21 Pointing out omissions in the information provided by the question and considering the impact these omissions might have on the outcome of your analysis will attract a higher mark as it demonstrates your understanding.

22 Remember to draw conclusions from your analysis: this evidences your understanding of how to apply the law.

23 Proceeding from the general to the specific is a good way to structure your answer in a logical manner; it also demonstrates your knowledge and understanding.

essence' of the agreement, that would result in liability for the whole outstanding balance of the hire purchase price (*Lombard North Central v Butterworth* (1987)) minus the value of the motorcycle when recovered (£3,000) and any rebate due for the consequent earlier payment of the outstanding instalments.

The mathematical process is thus as follows:[24]

1	Ascertain the total HP price	£10,200
2	Deduct from the total HP price all sums already paid	£3,200
3	Gives the outstanding balance	£7,000
4	Divide the outstanding balance into:	
	(a) arrears owing at termination	£400
	(b) future payments owing	£6,600
5	Deduct from future payments owing, both:	
	(i) value of vehicle repossessed	£3,000
	(ii) amount of rebate for early settlement	£X
6	The total due is then:	
	(a) arrears owing at termination	£400
	(b) future payments owing minus the items at 5(i) and (ii) above	£3,600 less £X
7	The total due thus is	£4,000 less £X

Note
£X is the statutory rebate for early payment of outstanding instalments.

If, however, the contract contained no provision for making prompt payment 'of the essence' there will be no liability beyond an obligation to pay off arrears due before termination, together with damages (if any) for any failure by Harley to take reasonable care of the motorcycle (*Financings v Baldock* (1963)). This is because, on the facts, there is no evidence of Harley having repudiated the contract. In this situation, there is no question of Gullible being held liable to any greater extent than Harley, for example, for the outstanding instalments, because a guarantor cannot be liable to any greater extent than the debtor whose debts or obligations he has guaranteed.

DOCUMENTATION

Can Gullible be held liable to the extent indicated above? Subject to documentation requirements which need first to be considered, he probably can.[25] The guarantee given by Gullible is 'security' within the meaning of the **Consumer Credit Act** (see **s189(1)**). Thus, it needs to be determined (the question does not tell us) whether the necessary documentation requirements were complied with in the making of both the hire purchase agreement between Harley and Davison Finance and the guarantee agreement. In respect of the hire purchase agreement, any defence available to Harley arising as a result of any

....

24 It is always sensible to set out clearly any calculations worth taking time on in your pre-answer plan.
25 Clear signposting of the issues discussed (eg by means of headings) enhances the readability of your answer and helps to achieve clarity of expression.

failure to observe documentation requirements is also available to Gullible. Such is the nature of a guarantee, reinforced by **s 113** of the **CCA**. The court has a discretion to grant an enforcement order even when the documentation requirements have been infringed (see **s 127**, **s 15** of the **CCA 2006** has repealed **s 127(3)–(5)** so there are no longer any cases where the infringement of the documentation requirements automatically renders the credit and/or security agreements permanently unenforceable and also reverses the effect of the House of Lords' decision in *Wilson v First County Trust (No 2)* (2003)).[26] There are documentation requirements which should have been observed in the making of the guarantee (see **s 105**), which include a requirement that Gullible receives a copy of Harley's hire purchase agreement. Again, however, the court has a discretion, under **s 127**, to grant an enforcement order against Gullible even if the requirements were not complied with (*Hurstanger Ltd v Wilson* (2007)).[27]

There is one further documentation requirement to be mentioned. It is that Gullible should have been (we are not told whether he was) served with a copy of the default notice served on Harley (**s 111**). If he was not, the court has a discretion (under **s 127**) nevertheless to grant an enforcement order against Gullible. Note, however, that in exercising its discretion, the court must take into account culpability (of Davison Finance) for the infringement and any prejudice caused by it. Failure to serve Gullible with a copy of the default notice, unless Harley informed Gullible about having received it, could have been severely prejudicial to Gullible. Had he been served with the default notice, then he might well have paid off the arrears owing, preventing the termination of the hire purchase agreement.

LIABILITY OF CYCLES SELLERS[28]

We are told that Davison Finance has a recourse agreement with Cycles Sellers but nothing of its terms. It is usual, however, for these agreements to be expressed as indemnities. Thus, Cycles Sellers will have taken on a primary liability and, unlike Gullible, will not automatically have available to it any defence available to Harley. Also, the recourse agreement will not be within the definition of 'security' in **s 189(1)**, since it is virtually certain that the recourse agreement was not entered by Cycles Sellers at the request (express or implied) of Gullible. It is highly likely that Harley and Gullible will have been unaware of the recourse agreement. Consequently, it is not subject to the documentation provisions, or **s 113**.[29] Furthermore, since the recourse agreement is not (we can be reasonably sure) a guarantee, it is possible for Cycles Sellers to be liable to a greater extent than Harley himself. For example, if Harley's hire purchase agreement did not make prompt

----

26 Showing that you are aware of the development of the relevant legal rules will set your answer apart from an average answer.

27 You will not normally be asked questions which involve transitional provisions, you can normally assume current law fully in force – but make clear if you are not assuming that or applying previous law and why.

28 The clarity of your answer is very important. Clearly separate the liability of the different parties involved to ensure you (and examiner) do not get lost in your answer.

29 By referring to a previously made explanation or discussion you link different stages of your analysis and thus present a more complete answer; it also saves valuable time.

payment of the instalments 'of the essence', and therefore Harley's liability was limited to *Financings v Baldock* damages, it is nevertheless possible for Cycles Sellers to be held liable for more than that if, by the terms of its recourse agreement, it had agreed to indemnify Davison Finance against any loss the latter might suffer as a result of Harley not paying the full hire purchase price (*Goulston Discount v Clark* (1967)).

THE RIDER[30]

If the agreement between Gullible and Davison Finance had been written as an indemnity instead of a guarantee that would make no difference at all to the answer above.[31] The agreement would still have been 'security' within the meaning of the Act (**s 189(1)**). However, it would have been subject to exactly the same documentation requirements as those already referred to. Furthermore, **s 113** would apply with the effect of rendering an indemnity (which is security within the meaning of the Act) of exactly the same effect as a guarantee. Thus, Gullible cannot be liable to any greater extent than Harley (ignoring for this purpose that Harley was a minor).

The fact that Harley had made three instalment payments before falling into arrears would alter the advice because Harley would have paid over one-third of the hire purchase price, meaning the motorcycle was protected goods within **s 90**. It does not appear that Harley gave his permission for the repossession at the time repossession took place or that Harley had disposed of or abandoned the motorcycle. Thus, the repossession of the goods was an infringement of the protected goods provisions and Harley (and therefore also Gullible) is relieved of any further liability under the agreement (**s 91**). For the same reason, Davison Finance is liable to repay to Harley all payments he has made under the agreement.

QUESTION 19

Consider what have been, so far, the most significant impacts on UK domestic consumer credit law brought about by the implementation of the **EU Consumer Credit Directive 2008/48/EC of 23 April 2008**.

How to Answer this Question

This is a question that requires the candidate to take an overview of the **EU Consumer Credit Directive 2008/48/EC** (**CCD**) and assess the main changes it will require in UK domestic law. The candidate will not be required to go into all the intricate detail of implementation but to focus on significant changes required and the relationship of the new law to the pre-existing domestic regime. Among the main points to consider:

❖ the **CCD** is only a partial harmonisation of consumer credit law, eg it does not deal with provisions relating to unfair credit transactions or regulated hire agreements;

❖ however, where it does apply, it follows the maximum harmonisation approach, not the traditional minimum harmonisation approach;

---

30 Don't miss out on marks by not discussing more minor issues raised by the question.

31 Don't be reluctant to use the wording of the question in the course of your analysis; this demonstrates that your answer is focused on the relevant issues and also helps you to structure your answer logically.

- ❖ the UK Government has retained much of the existing domestic law, particularly in areas where the **CCD** does not apply, eg to small business credit contracts and to hire agreements;
- ❖ outline the main areas of reform in relation to pre-contractual informational requirements;
- ❖ the information requirements in agreements, in particular the *Standard European Credit Information Sheet*;
- ❖ new unilateral right of withdrawal from credit agreements;
- ❖ new provisions in relation to credit intermediaries.

Applying the Law

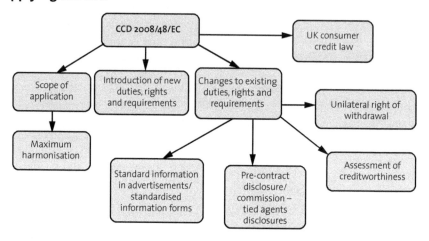

This diagram shows the main factors to consider in relation to the **CCD** *in this answer, and the relationship between these.*

ANSWER

The **EU Consumer Credit Directive 2008/48/EC of 23 April 2008** (CCD)[32] is a partial harmonisation of European consumer credit law in EU Member States,[33] for example, it does not apply to provisions relating to unfair credit transactions, deal with damages for breach of consumer credit contracts or apply, to certain categories of agreements, eg consumer hire agreements. However, where it does apply, the approach adopted is that of maximum harmonisation, leaving Member States with no element of discretion; unlike the traditional minimum harmonisation approach where Member States could adopt stricter rules for their own nationals, provided that credit agreements that complied with a Directive provided by nationals of other EU Member States were acceptable (**Art 22**

---

32 Note the complex way the UK has incorporated the Directive by amending existing law and a separate set of parallel provisions implementing the Directive insofar as it goes beyond current UK law – see **ss75** and **75A** as illustration.

33 The provision of background information to a particular legal rule shows deeper understanding of the area of law in question and can also help to frame the issues raised in an appropriate manner.

CCD). As is common with most EU consumer law protection, the protections cannot be waived or excluded and cannot be avoided by a choice of law clause nominating the law of a non-EU country (**Art 22(2)–(4) CCD**). One major area that is untouched is the regulation of creditors (**Art 20 CCD**) – so although creditors must be properly supervised, the UK can retain the current licensing system, now operated by the Financial Conduct Authority.

The UK has largely adopted a 'bolt-on approach' with the regime being created by the **CCA 1974** and **2006**[34] being largely retained and the new rights being added on or interwoven into current provisions – the retention of many parts of the latter following revisions by the **FSMA 2000** does nothing to change this. The result was to complicate further an already complex regime. So much so that that UK Government extended the time for compliance with the new hybrid regime to 1 February 2011, almost a year later than intended (**Art 27 CCD**).[35] The **CCD** does not apply to hire agreements (**Art 2(d) CCD**) but the UK chose to retain the provisions of pre-existing domestic legislation regulating hire agreements. The **CCD** only applies to agreements with 'a natural person, who in transactions covered by this Directive, is acting for purposes which are outside his trade, business or profession' (**Art 3(a) CCD**); however, UK law retained pre-existing protections for small business debtors and in some cases extended the new protections to these debtors even though not required to do so by the **CCD**. A good example of the marrying of a UK provision with a provision required by the **CCD** is the connected lender liability provision in **s75** of the **CCA 1974**[36] – the UK secured the right to retain this connected-lender liability provision (**Art 15(3) CCD**) but to comply with the linked liability provision in **Art 15(2) CCD** – adopting the approach commonly used in civil law in EU countries that you can only sue a creditor when an attempt to recover compensation from the supplier has failed. An additional, alternative linked liability action is provided for in **s75A** of the **CCA 1974**, which applies where the main provision in **s75** of the **CCA 1974** does not but, nevertheless, the agreement falls within the scope of the **CCD**. So, the linked liability provision does not apply where the cash price of the item is under £30,000, and so within the scope of the main **s75** of the **CCA 1974**, and also not where the amount of credit advanced exceeds £60,260 (75,000 euros), the upper limit in sterling of the application of the Directive. Small business debtors are able to take advantage of this additional form of protection, though this is not required by the **CCD**. In some cases, new definitional categories exist alongside pre-existing similar domestic categories, eg 'credit intermediaries' (**Art 3(f) CCD**), 'credit brokers' (**s145(2)** of the **CCA 1974**), 'linked credit agreements' (**Art 3(n) CCD**) and 'linked transactions' (**s19** of the **CCA 1974**). In some cases domestic rights have ceased to apply where new EU rights are introduced, eg the new unilateral right of withdrawal (**Art 14 CCD** implemented in **s66A** of the **CCA 1974**) has largely supplanted the existing cancellation right in **s67** of the **CCA 1974**, but the cancellation regime has continued to apply to those cases not falling within **s66A** of the **CCA 1974**.

....

34 In revising make sure you are looking at the most up to date version of the **Consumer Credit Act 1974** – amendments etc will largely be incorporated into the parent Act.

35 Showing that you are aware of the development of the relevant legal rules will set your answer apart from an average answer.

36 Considering concrete examples demonstrates your knowledge and understanding of the relevant legal rules and also substantiates your analysis/argument.

Many of the changes were matters of detail and the UK consumer has not seen significant changes in the essence of protection.

The main changes have been:[37, 38]

❖ standard information to be included in advertisements (**Art 4 CCD**);
❖ toughened pre-contractual information (**Arts 5** and **6 CDD**);
❖ an obligation to assess the creditworthiness of the consumer (**Art 8 CCD**);
❖ standardised information in relation to credit agreements and in particular the introduction of Standard European Credit Information (**Arts 10–12** and **Annex II CDD**);
❖ a unilateral right of withdrawal from a credit agreement (**Art 14 CCD**);
❖ a right to sue a creditor where action against a supplier has failed to produce compensation where the goods or services supplied are not in conformity, or only partially in conformity, with the contract (**Art 15(2) CCD**);
❖ standardised method for assessing early repayment rebate (**Art 16 CCD**);
❖ new standardised calculation of the annual percentage rate of charge (**Art 19** and **Annex I CCD**);
❖ new disclosure requirements in relation to receipts of commissions and whether tied to a particular creditor or independent imposed on credit intermediaries (**Art 21 CCD**);
❖ Member States to provide 'adequate and effective' out-of-court dispute resolution procedures (UK already complies with the consumer credit jurisdiction of the Financial Ombudsman Service (FOS)) and encourage those bodies to cooperate in order to resolve cross-border disputes (**Art 24 CCD**).

Given that many consumers do not take advantage of, or understand, informational requirements in credit advertisements, agreements or copies of agreements, in many ways the chief advantage which will flow from the **CCD** is the ability of the creditors to take advantage of more cross-border opportunities for the provision of credit, eg awareness that in advertisements the illustration of a 'representative example' (eg that he can reasonably expect to supply at least 51% of debtors on those terms) will be the same throughout the EU, making pan-European advertising campaigns easier – see **regs 1, 4** and **5 Consumer Credit (Advertisement) Regulations 2010/1012**.

From a debtor perspective it should make entering credit agreements with creditors in other EU countries easier.[39] In practical terms, the main improvements in relation to consumers will, first, be the stronger disclosure receipts of commissions and the nature of their relationship with the prospective creditor imposed on credit intermediaries – particularly in the

---

37 Remember to draw conclusions from your analysis; this evidences your understanding of how to apply the law.
38 Good marks can be gained by constructive use of bullet points and even the odd diagram if it helps to show you are aware of an area – particularly in essay questions which can degenerate into a dense stream of consciousness, with repetitions and contradictions even on the same page.
39 You should avoid making unsubstantiated arguments or premature conclusions when you are asked to 'critically consider/analyse' a statement. Remember that it is the application of the law upon which you are assessed – simply saying that eg you don't think something is fair is not good enough. This is a good example of how to achieve this aim.

sub-prime market, where brokers are often used. Second, the reforms increase the move-ment of consumer credit law towards a 'know-your-customer' approach that is common in such areas as the selling of investments and insurance. **Art 6 CCD**, for example, aug-ments **s 55** of the **CCA 1974** and **Consumer Credit (Disclosure of Information) Regulations 2004**, while new pre-contract disclosure requirements are also introduced by the **Consumer Credit (Disclosure of Information) Regulations 2010**.

Another major improvement is a movement to a unilateral 14-day withdrawal period (**Art 14 CCD** implemented by **s 66A** of the **CCA 1974**). This is a welcome move from the byzantinely complicated cancellation provisions in **ss 67–74** of the **CCA** – tied into the often irrelevant fact that the agreement was signed off trade premises and the need for 'antecedent negoti-ations' to be conducted in the presence of the debtor, so ruling out telephonic communica-tions. It will also bring consumer credit law more into line with other withdrawal rights.[40]

CONCLUSION[41]

Given that the UK had one of the most sophisticated consumer credit regimes in the EU, the changes being brought in by the **CCD** will not have a radical impact on the levels of protection. However, key changes in the pre-contract regime and the new right of with-drawal are welcome changes for consumers. For creditors, the third major set of legal reforms in six years means an unwelcome increase in compliance costs and the 'bolt-on approach' adopted by the UK increases the complexity of an already complex regime.

QUESTION 20

Steve acquires a car which has a cash price of £4,000 under a conditional sale agreement with Fleece You Finance (FYF) for a total price of £6,000 including interest and all other charges. He puts down a deposit of £1,500 and has made six further monthly payments of £100 when he is declared redundant and makes no further subsequent monthly pay-ments. He has missed three monthly payments so far. He then writes to FYF saying 'I am in trouble with this car contract, I want to pay but cannot. I will have to give it back.' Two days later FYF arrange for two mechanics from the garage which supplied the car to go to Steve's house where they go up his drive and proceed to drive away the car, using a duplicate set of keys, from Steve's open garage. FYF rely on a clause in the conditional sale agreement which states that the car can be repossessed at any time if the debtor defaults on a monthly instalment repayment. Steve, who is mowing his back garden lawn at the time, is very angry and that night he goes to the supplier's garage, where the car is temporarily parked on their forecourt pending a decision as to its future, and using his set of keys takes the car back. Steve then decides to sell the car to his friend Mike who agrees over a pint in their local pub to pay him £2,000 cash for the car 'no questions asked'. Steve intends to use this money to help pay off his debt to FYF. Unfortunately he is so drunk leaving the pub he loses the envelope with the £2,000 cash Mike has given him. When FYF demand Mike return 'their' car immediately he refuses saying that he bought the car in good faith.

▶ Advise FYF.

How to Answer this Question

❖ You will need to consider whether the agreement between Steve and Fleece You Finance (FYF) has been validly terminated, in particular whether the provisions of **ss 87–89** of the **CCA 1974** have been complied with.

❖ You will also need to look at whether the goods are 'protected goods' within **ss 90–92** of the **CCA** and, if they are, what is the impact of a wrongful seizure of them?

❖ You will also need to consider Steve's action in seizing his car back from the garage – who has title to the car at this point? Has Steve a right as bailee under an existing hire purchase agreement to take back the car?

❖ If Steve has no title to the car, what is the impact of his purported sale to Mike and, in particular, whether Mike can take advantage of **ss 27–29** of the **Hire Purchase Act 1964** and claim he is a *bona fide* purchaser for value from a person holding under an existing hire purchase or conditional sale agreement.

Applying the Law

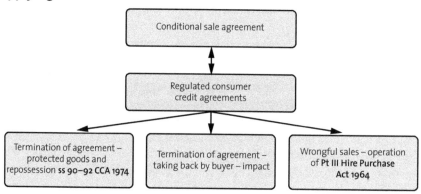

This diagram illustrates the key points to be covered in this answer.

ANSWER

DEFINITION

This agreement is a regulated fixed sum restricted-use debtor–creditor–supplier agreement (**ss 8**, **9**, **11(1)(a)** and **s 12(a)**). Under a conditional sale agreement, title to the car remains in the finance company until the instalments are paid (**ss 17** and **19** of the **Sale of Goods Act 1979**)[42] and it differs from a hire purchase agreement only in that the buyer has

---

42 Questions can involve more than one Act. **Sections 17** and **19** of the **SGA** are not affected by the **Consumer Rights Act 2015**.

irrevocably committed himself to the purchase at the outset of the contract. Steve will have permitted possession of the car under the contract and is in effect a bailee of it (it can be assumed that all the necessary formalities have been completed, and the statutory copies of the credit agreement provided to Steve and FYF are properly licensed under the **CCA 1974**).

BREACH

Steve is clearly in default by the non-payment of three successive monthly instalments[43] and, in addition to his letter to FYF saying he cannot go on with the agreement and that they better take the car back, would, it is suggested, amount to a repudiation of the contract. However, before FYF accept that repudiation and terminate the contract for breach, they must issue a statutory termination notice in the prescribed form under **ss 87–89**.[44] Under **s 88(1)** the notice must be in the prescribed form and set out the nature of the alleged breach; if the breach is capable of remedy, what action needs to be taken to remedy it and the date before which such action is to be taken, and, if not remediable, the amount of compensation which is payable (**s 88(1)**). Attached must also be a copy of the current default information sheet required under **s 86A**. Steve must be given at least 14 days from the date of the service of the notice – allowing two days for receipt if the notice is sent by first class post – to carry out these actions (**s 88(2)**) and if he can remedy the breaches within this period the breach is treated as never having taken place (**s 89**). No such notice appears to have been issued here – though no sanction appears to be provided for breach of the section, it is suggested any legal action against Steve will be stayed until a proper default notice is issued (*Brandon v American Express Services* (2011)). A further problem which might exist for FYF is that Steve is more than two payments in arrears and there is no reference to them having issued a notice of arrears as required by **s 86B** and, while this failure continues, the creditor or owner shall not be entitled to enforce the agreement (**s 86D**). Further, while this default continues, Steve is not liable for any default interest or to pay any default sum (**s 86D(4)**).

PROTECTED GOODS

Steve has paid a total of £2,100 out of a total price of £6,000 and, as this amounts to more than one-third of the total price, the car has become 'protected goods' under **s 90**. This means that the creditor is not entitled to recover possession of the goods without an order of court (*Bentinck Ltd v Cromwell Engineering Co Ltd* (1971)) or the free, informed and voluntary consent given at the time possession is sought (**ss 90(1)** and **173(3)**, *Mercantile Credit Co Ltd v Cross* (1965), *Chartered Trust plc v Pitcher* (1988)). Further, and even if the goods were not protected goods, the creditor is not entitled to enter the land of the debtor to repossess the goods without the debtor's consent and thus, here, a statutory trespass has occurred as Steve has obviously not consented to the repossession (**s 92**). The

---

43 Always read a problem question carefully and note material facts – the fact that Steve has not paid three successive instalments. Why is three mentioned? Does it have any relevance to your answer?

44 The consumer credit regime is quite strong on formalities and following proper procedures in making and terminating agreements. Whilst it is not necessary to put down all complex technical details, it is necessary to be aware of broad requirements in these areas.

consequence of this that is the regulated agreement, if not previously terminated, shall terminate and the debtor shall be released from all liability under the agreement, and shall be entitled to recover from the creditor all sums paid by the debtor under the agreement (**s 91**) and so, on the face of it, Steve is no longer required to make any future payments and can recover the £2,100 he has already paid. However, the restriction on creditor repossession does not apply if it is the debtor who has terminated the agreement (**s 90(5)**) and, here, Steve seems to have terminated by saying he cannot carry on with the agreement and asking FYF to take the car back.[45] However, under equivalent provisions in the **Hire Purchase Act 1965**, the courts have often interpreted such statements as a repudiation of the contract by the debtor which the creditor, by retaking possession of the car, has accepted so, in fact, it is the creditor, by accepting the debtor's repudiation, who terminates the contract (*United Dominions Trust (Commercial) Ltd v Ennis* (1968) *F.C. Finance v Francis* (1970)). Thus Steve may still be in a strong position.

PART III HIRE PURCHASE ACT 1964[46]

Title in the car never passed to Steve so he has no right to sell it and, arguably, is committing conversion for wrongful interference with goods by retaking possession of the car. If we regard the contract as terminated, he no longer has any legal right to possession of the car. In any event, even if he has a right to possession of the car, he has no property in it as title has not passed to him and, therefore, on the face of it he cannot pass any title to a *bona fide* purchaser for value who would be liable, in the strict liability tort of conversion for wrongful interference with goods, to FYF. However, there is a possibility that Mike might be able to take advantage of one of the exceptions to the *nemo dat non quod habet* rule (that you cannot pass better title than you have) contained in **ss 27–29** of the **Hire Purchase Act 1964**. Where a motor vehicle has been bailed under a hire purchase agreement or sold under a conditional sale agreement and, before property in the vehicle has become vested in the debtor, he disposes of the vehicle to a good faith private purchaser (though not to a trade purchaser – *Stevenson v Beverley Bentinck* (1976) and *GE Capital Bank Ltd v Rushton* (2005)), that private purchaser will obtain good title to the car as against the finance company. Good faith means having no actual notice of the prior agreement between the debtor and finance company (*Barker v Bell* (1971), **s 29(3)** of the **HPA 1964**) and onus of proving good faith and no notice is on the purchaser, that is, Mike (*Dodds v Yorkshire Bank Finance* (1992)). The major problem for Mike here is, first, at the time he acquired the car from Steve it appears that Steve is a trespasser and is no longer holding the car under a subsisting conditional sale agreement and thus **s 27(1)** is not satisfied (*Shogun Finance v Hudson* (2004))[47] and, second, given that he appears to be buying the car in a public house at a considerable discount to the recent cash valuation of the car,

45 It is important to consider carefully the legal impact of what is being done. It is all too easy to assume Steve has forfeited his rights here because he is terminating, but what does that mean in legal terms?
46 This question illustrates the importance of remembering a question can involve multiple issues – it is important to understand core implications of common credit agreements such as hire purchase agreements.
47 Always consider analogous cases. *Shogun* is not on this issue but shows the scope of **s 27** and the need for existence of a hire purchase or conditional sale agreement for the section to operate.

even allowing for the dramatic levels of depreciation which occur to cars as soon as they leave the forecourt, questions may be raised about whether he has actual notice of the facts and the dispute over the prior agreement between Steve and FYF. If that is the case Mike must either return the car or at least pay its equivalent value in damages to FYF, though he might be able to recover his price and consequential damages for breach of **s 12** of the **Sale of Goods Act 1979** (breach of the implied term as to title in contracts for sale of goods)[48] from Steve. However given Steve's current financial position that might be a forlorn hope!

CONCLUSION

The question highlights the need for finance companies to have proper systems in place to ensure the proper issue of notices of arrears under **s 86** and default notices under **ss 87–89**, and to act precipitately in repossession and seizure of goods where the debtor is in default and so falling foul of the draconian provision for breach of the protected goods provisions (**ss 90–92**). It is also worth noting that Steve could possibly have exercised his statutory right of termination by paying a maximum of an additional £900 to bring up his payments to a maximum of 50% of the total price under (**ss 99–100**), or sought a time order and presented a proposed re-scheduling of repayments of a lesser sum over a longer period of time (**ss 129** and **130**).

---

48 Since both Steve and Mike are consumers, the relevant implied term under **s 12** of the **Sale of Goods Act** remains. The **Consumer Rights Act 2015** only applies to sales by a trader to a consumer.

8   Connected Lender Liability

INTRODUCTION

This chapter covers the liability of the creditor for breaches of contract or misrepresentation by the dealer/supplier. The **Consumer Credit Act 2006** does not amend either **s 56** or **s 75** dealing with connected lender liability and deemed agency. The **EU Consumer Credit Directive 2008/48/EC** ('**CCD**') does not amend the deemed agency provision in **s 56**, leaves intact the connected lender liability provision in **s 75** (**Art 15(3) CCD**), but has required the introduction of an additional liability against creditors in relation to 'linked credit transactions' ('linked liability') in **Art 15(2) CCD**.

Checklist

The following topics should be prepared in advance of tackling the questions:

■ definitions in the **Consumer Credit Act 1974** and, in particular, that of debtor–creditor–supplier agreements;

■ **s 56** of the **Consumer Credit Act**;

■ **s 75** of the **Consumer Credit Act**;

■ **s 75A** of the **Consumer Credit Act**;

■ **Art 15** of the **EU Consumer Credit Directive 2008/48/EC** ('**CCD**');

■ rules on modifying agreements, **s 82** of the **Consumer Credit Act 1974**;

■ rules on provision of copies during currency of running account agreements, **s 78** of the **Consumer Credit Act 1974**.

QUESTION 21

Betty decided to have a new kitchen installed. At Kitch Kitchens Ltd, she contracted to have the work done according to an agreed specification. She needed to borrow money to finance the new kitchen and, at Kitch Kitchens Ltd, she also signed a proposal form for a loan from Flash Finance. This was a loan of £5,000 to be paid direct to Kitch Kitchens and to be repaid by Betty by monthly instalments spread over five years. All documentation and other formalities required under the provisions of the **Consumer Credit Act** were observed in the making of the loan agreement. It is now three months since the new kitchen was installed and Betty has found that the new waste disposal unit is defective, the new cupboards are falling off the walls and the turbo-charged oven will never work properly, since it needs an outlet to the outside. Therefore, it must be installed immediately in front of an outside wall, and Betty's kitchen has no outside wall.

It is going to cost £3,000 for Betty to get a substitute oven and to have the other matters put right. Kitch Kitchens Ltd is insolvent and has gone into liquidation.

▶ **(a)   Advise Betty.**
▶ **(b)   Would your advice differ if the kitchen had a cash price of £50,000 and Betty had borrowed the money from Flash Finance?**

How to Answer this Question

This question demands knowledge of the application of the rules in **s 75**. It must be established that there is legal liability on the part of the supplier and that the basic requirements for **s 75** and **s 75A** have been satisfied. Those two issues should be dealt with in that order followed by the consequences for Betty. It is also important in answering not to overlook the second part of the question which involves new law introduced by the **EU Consumer Credit Directive 2008/48/EC** and implemented in the UK by **s 75A** of the **Consumer Credit Act 1974**.

Applying the Law

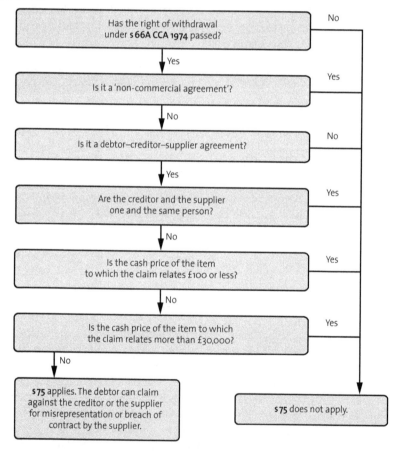

This diagram focuses on the debtor's right to claim under the **CCA** in this scenario. In addition to connected lender liability under **s 75** set out below you will also have to consider 'secondary liability' under **s 75A** where **s 75** does not apply.

ANSWER

(A)

It seems reasonably clear that Betty has a good claim in law against Kitch Kitchens for breach of implied (or express) terms of the contract. Because the contract is for goods and services, the implied terms as to satisfactory quality and fitness for purpose under the **Consumer Rights Act 2015**[1] will apply to Betty's contract with Kitch Kitchens. In the case of the waste disposal unit, it appears that there is a breach of **s9** as to satisfactory quality and, in the case of the oven, a breach of **s10** as to fitness for purpose, since she must have indicated to Kitch Kitchens the particular purpose (installing it in her kitchen) for which she wanted the oven. So far as the cupboards are concerned, it appears that there has been a breach of the term in **s49** of the same Act, that the work will be carried out with reasonable care and skill (see *Jones v Callagher t/a Gallery Kitchens and Bathrooms* (2004)).[2] The problem in this case is that it is of no use to Betty that she has a good claim in law against Kitch Kitchens Ltd, because the latter is insolvent.

The issue is what remedies Betty may have against Flash Finance by virtue of the **Consumer Credit Act**. **Section 75** provides that in certain circumstances, the debtor (here, Betty) may bring a claim against the creditor (here, Flash Finance) for breach of contract or misrepresentation by the supplier (here, Kitch Kitchens Ltd). For **s75** to apply, the credit contract must be a regulated debtor–creditor–supplier agreement within **s12(b)** or **(c)**. It seems highly likely that the loan agreement satisfies this requirement and falls within **s12(b)**. It does not fall within **s12(c)** since it appears to be an agreement for restricted-use credit, because the loan was to be paid not to Betty, but direct to Kitch Kitchens. The agreement will fall within **s12(b)**, however, only if it was made under 'arrangements' between Kitch Kitchens and Flash Finance. Since it appears that Kitch Kitchens had a stock of Flash Finance loan proposal forms, it would seem quite likely that there were such arrangements. If there were a commission paid by Flash Finance to Kitch Kitchens (or indeed vice versa), that would be conclusive. Assuming such arrangements exist, Betty has a like claim against Flash Finance as she has against Kitch Kitchens (a like claim means that in circumstances where the debtor has a right to rescind the supply contract, the 'like' claim under **s75** is to rescind the loan contract). As confirmed by the Supreme Court in *Durkin v DSG Retail Ltd* (2014), both the supply contract and linked loan contract could be rescinded simultaneously (as posited by Macqueen in 'Faulty goods, rejection and connected lender liablity' (2011) Edin LR 15(1) 111–115).[3] Since the service provided by Kitch Kitchens was not provided with reasonable care and skill, Betty could have demanded repeat performance (**s55** of the **CRA 2015**). However, since three months have now elapsed, repeat performance is no longer possible (particularly as Kitch Kitchens is insolvent), leaving Betty with a remedy of price reduction (**s56** of the **CRA 2015**). This

---

1 Remember, consumer credit questions involving goods and services will often require some knowledge of the implied terms in the **CRA 2015**. **CRA** applies whenever a trader supplies goods or services to a consumer. See Chapter 1, Question 3 and Chapter 2, Question 7.

2 Don't state all you know about the area of law in question; remember to focus on the relevant issues – it is as much your ability to apply the relevant legal rules to the question as your knowledge that is assessed.

3 The reference to academic literature rather than the 'mere' consideration of case law shows not only that you have researched and read more widely but also adds to the criticality of your analysis.

could be up to the full amount of £5,000, although that sum may be reduced to take into account that Betty has had some benefit from the use of the kitchen. Furthermore, since the supply of the waste disposal unit and oven are clearly in not of satisfactory quality nor fit for purpose under **ss 9** and **10** of the **CRA**, Betty could have demanded Kitch Kitchens repair or replace both these items. Since Kitch Kitchens is insolvent, this is also no longer possible. Nevertheless, Betty may be entitled to rescind the supply contract and obtain a full refund if she exercises her final right to reject within six months of the kitchen being installed. That claim being a valid legal claim against Kitch Kitchens, Betty is entitled to succeed with it against Flash Finance.

In this sort of situation, it is quite common for the finance company still to expect the debtor to maintain monthly payments under the loan agreement while the other claim is still being contested and, if the debtor ceases to maintain those payments, the finance company will keep sending reminders; and of course there will be default interest, which the finance company will show on each successive statement, though the pressure is less with the bringing into force of **s 13** of the **CCA 2006**, which stipulates that only simple interest can be charged on default sums under regulated consumer credit agreements and not compound interest, which of course involves charging interest on interest. This operates as a clear pressure upon the debtor, who may doubt the likelihood of success with her claim under **s 75**. Cautious advice to Betty is, therefore, to maintain her loan repayments while also pursuing her claim against Flash Finance.

(B)

Most European Union states did not have the equivalent connected lender liability provisions that the UK had but, rather, a substituted liability in relation to contracts financed by a credit company where the consumer had failed to get redress from the supplier. If action to get redress from the supplier had failed, action for redress could be taken against the creditor but the debtor always had to take reasonable steps against the supplier first. **Article 15(2)** of the **CCD** provides for this type of liability. The UK has provided for such an action in those cases falling outside the connected lender liability provision in **s 75** of the **CCA 1974** but within the scope of the **CCD**. This is done in **s 75A** of the **CCA 1974**.[4] This can be described as the 'linked liability' provision and would only kick in if Betty had failed to get redress from Kitch Kitchens. There are four situations where the section can apply:

❖ the supplier cannot be traced;
❖ the debtor has contacted the supplier but the supplier has not responded;
❖ the supplier is insolvent;
❖ the debtor has taken reasonable steps, which need not include litigation, to pursue the claim against the supplier but has not obtained satisfaction of his claim – satisfaction includes accepting a replacement product or service or other compensation from the supplier in settlement of the claim.[5]

....

4 It is all too easy to overlook recent reforms; many students would have assumed that **s 75** not applying meant the end of the story and would have lost marks by not discussing **s 75A**. You get extra merit for being up to date.

5 This shows where a statute book is useful in an exam. It is helpful for those detailed qualifications to a general liability proposition: in an area like this if you can take a statute book into an exam it may be a good investment.

However, this provision will only apply where the cash value of the goods or services is in excess of £30,000 and the linked credit agreement is for credit which does not exceed £60,260 (the upper limit of the Directive converted from euros to sterling at the date of the UK's adoption of the Directive).[6] Betty is covered here as the cash value of the kitchen is £50,000 and the linked credit agreement for less than £60,260. Neither has Betty seemingly acquired the kitchen 'wholly or predominantly' for business purposes carried on by her – if she had, the protection would not have applied (s 75A(6) of the **CCA 1974**).

The sole issue that might cause problems is whether the provision of a loan for the acquisition of the kitchen and its fitting is a 'linked credit agreement'. A 'linked credit agreement' means a regulated consumer credit agreement that serves 'exclusively' to finance an agreement for the supply of specific goods or the provision of a specific service, and where:

(a) the creditor uses the service of the supplier in connection with the preparation or making of the credit agreement; *or*
(b) the specific goods or provision of a specific service are explicitly specified in the credit agreement (s 75A(5) of the **CCA 1974**).

The question says Betty signed the Flash Finance loan form at Kitch Kitchen's premises, which suggests that condition (a) is satisfied and probably condition (b) as well.[7] If this is the case and she has failed to secure compensation from Kitch Kitchens, and on the facts she seems to have taken reasonable steps to do so, she can then pursue her claim for £3,000 against Flash Finance under **s 75A** of the **CCA 1974**.

QUESTION 22

Andrew works as a debt adviser in a debt advice centre and has been approached by several clients in connection with disputes with their credit card company, the Excess Credit Card Company ('Excess'):

(a) Iain has used his Excess credit card to buy a Persian carpet from a dealer in Morocco while on holiday there. He has discovered a number of moth holes in the carpet and wishes to reject it on the grounds that it is not of satisfactory quality and recover his price and consequential damages. Excess have rejected his claim on the grounds that he was abroad when he used the card and has not attempted to pursue his claim against the retailer in the first instance. Further, as the Moroccan retailer has now gone out of business they will not be able to indemnify themselves if they have to compensate Iain.
(b) Mark is refusing to pay his outstanding balance of £12,000 on his Excess credit card because Excess cannot supply him with a copy of the original agreement that Mark

6 Considering any potential limitation after outlining and applying the general legal rule to the requirements of the question ensures that your analysis proceeds in a logical way.
7 Remember to relate your analysis to the issues raised/facts outlined by the question; it is the proper application of the relevant legal rules to the requirements of the question upon which you are assessed, not the abstract discussion of the law.

entered into in 1996. Mark has been sent by Excess copies of the standard terms and conditions in operation at the time instead.

(c)   David has purchased a vintage car for a cash price of £100,000, paying part of the price, £58,000, using his Excess platinum super credit card. The car has frequently broken down and David wishes to reject for breach of **s 9 and s 10** of the **Consumer Rights Act 2015** and recover his price. The vintage car firm have gone into liquidation and were not insured and Excess say that as the cash price of the card exceeds £30,000, **s 75** of the **CCA 1974** is inapplicable and they have no joint liability with the retailer under the section.

(d)   Suzannah bought a kettle for £60 which was described on the box as 'super efficient and safe to use' with her Excess credit card. Due to faulty wiring the kettle causes a fire and Suzannah's kitchen is severely damaged and will cost an estimated £50,000 to restore. Suzannah has no property insurance and is claiming the money from Excess.

How to Answer this Question

You will:

❖   need to consider the operation of connected lender liability provisions under **s 75** of the **CCA**;[8]

❖   need to consider new 'secondary liability' under **s 75A** of the **CCA**;

❖   need to consider the 'deemed agency' provisions in **s 56** of the **CCA**;

❖   need to consider the documentation requirements during currency of a credit card running account agreement in **s 78**.

Applying the Law

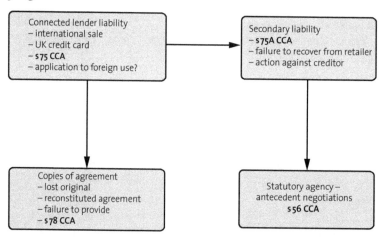

This diagram shows the connection between key points discussed in the answer.

8   For general criticism of the policy behind **s 75**, see: A Campbell, 'Credit cards and section 75: time for a change in the law?' (1996) 11 JIBL 527–532 and C Bisping, 'The case against s 75 of the Consumer Credit Act 1974 in credit card transactions' (2011) 5 JIBL 457–474.

ANSWER

(A)

Does the **Consumer Credit Act** apply to cards used abroad? It has been decided that the Act does apply to regulated agreements governed by English law,[9] as Iain appears to be, where the card is used to purchase goods abroad (*Financial Conduct Authority v Lloyds TSB plc* (2007)). A credit card agreement contains what amounts to a standing offer, that is, an offer to supply credit on the terms of the credit card agreement. The offer is accepted *pro tanto* each time an authorised user uses the card to finance a transaction. Liability, however, is derivative. Iain must have a claim either for misrepresentation or breach of contract against the retailer. That would appear to be the case here, even if the contract were governed by Moroccan law. If there is such a claim Iain has a 'like claim' against Excess. There is no requirement on Iain to seek to pursue his claim with the Moroccan retailer before seeking compensation from Excess. The liability of the credit card company is primary and not secondary under **s 75**. The credit card company has a statutory right to be indemnified, subject to any agreement to the contrary, under **s 75(2)**. The fact that this right cannot be effectively exercised here is irrelevant to Iain's claim. Excess will either have to bear the loss or possibly claim against any insurance they have taken out to meet such a contingency. Excess cannot exclude this liability to Iain by virtue of **s 173(1)** of the **CCA 1974**.

(B)

Mark's refusal to pay may at least be temporarily justified.[10]

The failure to provide him, after payment of a small fee, with a copy of a regulated running-account agreement along with such details as are practicable to provide of the current state of the account, means that while the default continues the creditor is not entitled to enforce the agreement (**s 78(1)** and **(6)**). In *Phoenix Recoveries (UK) v Kulechna* (2011) a creditor had failed to satisfy a debtor's request under **s 78(1)** for a copy of a credit agreement as it had not, on the evidence, included the original terms and conditions in respect of interest rates then in force. The creditor was accordingly not entitled to proceed to enforce the debt, though enforcement does not prevent a notice indicating the debtor has defaulted to a credit reference agency (*McGuffick v Royal Bank of Scotland* (2009)). This has become a major problem for some companies with records of original agreements being discarded or lost on mergers of companies etc. There is also no dispensing provision allowing a court either wholly or partially to disregard any breach of the provision, unlike the case where the original agreement is improperly executed. A large number of claims, often instigated by claims management companies, have been launched though the courts and have not always been sympathetic to debtors seeking to use 'technical defences' to avoid payments clearly due. In *HSBC Bank plc v Brophy* (2011), the Court of Appeal rejected the argument that a signed and returned credit card application was not a contractual document and, therefore, there had been a failure of the credit card agreement regulations.

---

9 Always remember **CCA** only applies to credit agreements regulated by English law but can apply where sales or services contract is governed by foreign law.

10 Remember questions may well involve separate areas. You cannot always expect a question to focus on a single issue or section.

In *Carey v HSBC Bank plc* (2009) it was common ground that the **s 78** copy did not need to be a photocopy or other form of literal copy of the executed agreement. However, a creditor also did not need to prove execution of the agreement by reference to the document itself. It could instead satisfy its duty under **s 78** by providing a reconstituted version of the executed agreement which might be from sources other than the actual signed agreement. The debtor's name and address at the date of the executed agreement had to be provided in the copy but could be provided within the reconstituted copy from whatever source the creditor had of those details. It did not have to take them from the executed agreement itself. A reconstituted copy agreement had to include a heading, names and addresses of the debtor and creditor and any cancellation clause which was applicable to the executed agreement. That information could be provided on a sheet which was separate from the full statement of terms and conditions that also formed part of the reconstituted agreement. Its format should not be such as to mislead the debtor as to what he agreed to. Thus, provided Excess can do this, they should be able to enforce the credit card agreement.

(C)

Excess are correct in asserting that **s 75** is inapplicable because the cash price of the vintage car exceeds £30,000 (**s 75(3)(b)**).[11] However, they have overlooked that, as result of the implementation of the **EU Consumer Credit Directive 2008/48/EC**, David may have an alternative claim under **s 75A**. Assuming that the purchase was made with the card after 1 February 2011 when **s 75A** came into force, David may be able to recover his price from Excess. The liability of Excess under **s 75A** is secondary; that is, in the first instance David must pursue his claim against the retailer but, if one of four conditions in **s 75A(2)** is satisfied, David may make a claim against Excess:

  (i) that the supplier cannot be traced;
 (ii) that the debtor has contacted the supplier but the supplier has not responded;
(iii) that the supplier is insolvent; or
(iv) that the debtor has taken reasonable steps to pursue his claim against the supplier but has not obtained satisfaction for his claim.

It should be noted that under **s 75A(3)** 'reasonable steps' need not include litigation.

The vintage car must have been purchased under a 'linked agreement', which is defined in **s 75A(5)** as a regulated consumer credit agreement that serves exclusively to finance an agreement for the supply of specific goods or the provision of a specific service and where:

 (i) the creditor uses the services of the supplier in connection with the preparation or making of the credit agreement; or
(ii) the specific goods or provision of a specific service are explicitly specified in the credit agreement.

....

11 Here, poor students would stop and move on but it is important to consider whether any other options are open to the claimant and you would get credit for being up to date with alternative forms of secondary liability.

Under **s75(A)(6)** if the cash price of the car exceeds £30,000 and the amount of credit advanced is under £60,260, and the vintage car appears not to be purchased wholly or predominantly for business purposes, David will be able to make a claim against Excess only providing he has not been able to secure satisfaction of his claim from the retailer.

(D)

As the cash price of the kettle purchased by Suzannah has a cash price of less than £100, **s75** does not apply (**s75(3)(b)**). However, she may have an alternative claim under the 'deemed agency' provision in **s56**.[12] The argument would be that the statement on the box constituted 'antecedent negotiations' within **s56(1)(c)**. 'Antecedent negotiations' under **s56(4)** shall begin when the negotiator and the debtor or hirer first enter into communication (including communication by advertisement) and to include any representations made by the negotiator to the debtor and any other dealings between them. It is suggested that the statement on the box, although placed there by the manufacturer, has been adopted by the retailer and can therefore be deemed to be a 'communication' in the wide sense used in **s56**. It is suggested the retailer is a 'negotiator' within **s56(1)(c)**, in that he is a 'supplier' in relation to a transaction financed or proposed to be financed by a debtor–creditor–supplier agreement within **s12(b)** or **(c)**. A credit card agreement is a debtor–creditor–supplier agreement under either of one of these sections given the wide concept of 'arrangements' adopted by the House of Lords in *OFT v Lloyds TSB plc* (2007). The supplier would therefore be deemed to be the agent of Excess and this statutory agency cannot be excluded (**s56(3)**). This would mean that, as the kettle is unsafe, this is an actionable misrepresentation under the section and Excess would be liable for reasonably foreseeable loss flowing from the breach which, it is suggested, would include damage to Suzannah's kitchen and damages to restore it to its original condition.

---

12 A common pitfall when answering questions on connected lender liability is to forget the provisions in relation to deemed agency – examiners will often give credit for identifying alternative claims that may be available.

9 General Principles of Agency

INTRODUCTION

The doctrine of privity in contract law normally prevents a person acquiring rights under a contract unless he is a party to it. The long-established exception to that rule is the concept of agency. The most important feature of the relationship created by an agency agreement is that where a contract is concluded by an agent on behalf of a principal, the agent's acts are treated as if they were the acts of the principal and the principal becomes a party to the contract through the agreement. Examiners often set questions dealing with the general concept of agency contracts, either in the form of whole-essay questions or part-essay questions.

A contract of agency is governed by the general law of contract and is subject to the same rules as other contracts. However, unlike other types of contract, there are special terms which are implied into agency contracts, such as the fiduciary relationship between the principal and the agent as a result of which a number of duties are cast on the agent and, similarly, the agent has rights as against the principal. In addition, in relation to one type of agent – the 'commercial agent' – the relationship will be at least partially governed by the **Commercial Agents (Council Directive) Regulations 1993**. These Regulations, deriving from a European Directive, are particularly important in relation to the rights of the agent on termination of the agreement. They apply only to self-employed agents engaged to arrange contracts for the sale or purchase of goods.

The questions in this chapter concentrate on the general principles of agency contracts, and those in Chapter 10 deal with the scope of an agent's authority to bind the principal.

Students should be familiar with the following areas:

❖ general concept of agency and its relationship to the doctrine of privity;
❖ rights and duties of an agent vis-à-vis the principal;
❖ ratification – when can it be used and what are its effects;
❖ termination of an agency contract;
❖ the **Commercial Agents (Council Directive) Regulations 1993**.

QUESTION 23

The duties owed by agents to their principals may or may not be dictated by the express terms of the contracts between them.

▶ **Explain the duties of an agent in the context of this statement.**

How to Answer this Question

As with any other contract, the express terms of a contract of agency primarily determine the obligations of the parties to it. However, by the very nature of the relationship, the agent stands in a position of trust vis-à-vis the principal. A fiduciary relationship therefore exists between them and other important duties are implied into the contract, based on the notion of good faith, save insofar as these are not excluded or modified by the express terms of the contract.

In relation to commercial agents falling within the **Commercial Agents (Council Directive) Regulations 1993**, there is a duty to act 'dutifully and in good faith' which cannot be modified by the contract between principal and agent. Even where an agent acts gratuitously (and therefore there is no question of contractual obligations arising), the agent still owes fiduciary duties and the lack of consideration per se is no bar to these arising, and the possibility of a general liability in tort arises.

The following points need to be considered:

❖ express contractual duties determined by the terms of the contract;
❖ fiduciary duties which, if not expressly provided for in the contract, are either implied or enforceable per se;
❖ in the case of a gratuitous agent, a general duty of care in tort.

Applying the Law

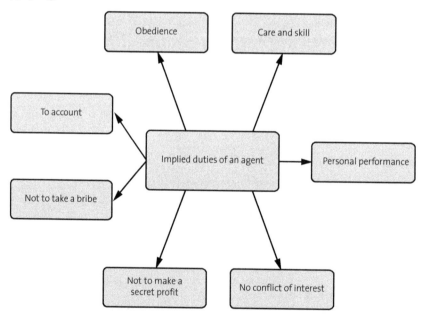

This diagram shows the main points to consider in your answer, illustrating the way these relate to the commercial agent.

ANSWER

Any contract between a principal and an agent may expressly impose duties on the agent and, in the absence of any relevant express duties, the obligations of the agent are regulated by a number of duties as a matter of law. Even in the absence of a contract, an agent who acts gratuitously owes fiduciary duties to the principal in the law of tort.

Where there is an agency contract, the terms of that contract will generally dictate the internal obligations between the principal and the agent. In relation to commercial agents falling within the **Commercial Agents (Council Directive) Regulations 1993**, however, there is a non-derogable duty on the agent to look after the principal's interests and to act dutifully and in good faith. Subject to this, an agent's duties will include the following.

OBEDIENCE[1]

An agent must obey the principal's lawful instructions and must not exceed his authority. This applies to both paid and gratuitous agents. Where the agent's instructions are ambiguous, however, he will not be liable if he acts on a reasonable interpretation of them (*Weigall v Runciman* (1916); *The Tzelepi* (1991)), although a duty will be imposed on the agent to seek clarification of the instructions.

A paid agent must act according to the terms of the contract and is liable for loss caused either by a failure to act or acts in excess of the authority. In *Turpin v Bilton* (1843), for example, an agent who was instructed to insure his principal's ship but failed to do so was liable in damages to his principal when the ship was lost.

A gratuitous agent is generally under no duty to act so that, albeit liable for exceeding his authority, he cannot be liable for a complete failure to act. There is generally no liability in tort for negligent omissions. However, some academic authorities maintain that liability could arise if the agent does not warn the principal that he has not or does not intend to perform the agency.[2] On this basis, a gratuitous agent acting in *Turpin* above would still have been liable to the principal.

CARE AND SKILL

All agents owe a duty of care to their principals to exercise reasonable care and skill in the execution of their authority. A paid agent is expected to exercise care and skill which is usual and proper in the type of business or work for which the agent is employed. An unpaid agent's duty of care arises in tort, and his actions are judged against the skill actually possessed. Whether or not an agent has fulfilled this duty is a question of fact in each

---

1   Dealing with the points raised in an essay question on a one-by-one basis adds structure and clarity to your analysis.

2   *Hedley Byrne & Co Ltd v Heller & Partners Ltd* (1964) suggests that liability will be imposed for loss caused by a failure to warn the principal where the agent had voluntarily assumed such a responsibility, although the point remains undecided in English law.

case. Any attempt by an agent to exclude or limit liability for failure to exercise care and skill is subject to the **Unfair Contract Terms Act 1977**.

The standard of care required is whatever is reasonable in the circumstances of each case. Where the agent holds himself out as being a member of a profession, the standard of care and skill expected of him is that of a reasonably competent member of that profession, irrespective of the degree of skill he may personally possess. In deciding what care is reasonable, the court will take into account whether or not the agent is paid.

In *Chaudry v Prabhakar* (1988), P, who had recently passed her driving test, asked a friend, A, to buy a car on her behalf, stipulating that the car must not have been involved in an accident.[3] A, who was not a mechanic and acted gratuitously, bought a one-year-old car for P. When P discovered that the car had been badly damaged in an accident, P sued A. The Court of Appeal, taking into account that A acted gratuitously, held that, on the facts, A had failed to exercise reasonable skill and was liable to P.

PERSONAL PERFORMANCE

As a general rule, an agent must personally perform the task because, in every case, the principal places trust in the agent: 'confidence in the particular person employed is at the root of the contract of agency', *per* Thesiger LJ in *De Bussche v Alt* (1878). This is often expressed in the Latin maxim *delegatus non potest delegare*. There are exceptions to the rule, but if the agent delegates duties without authority to do so, the agent is liable to the principal for breach of duty. The principal is not bound by an unauthorised sub-agent's acts unless the agent had apparent authority to delegate and the principal is thereby estopped from denying the want of authority. There are some exceptions to this rule.

First, where the agent is expressly authorised to delegate. In *De Bussche v Alt*, for example, an agent employed to sell a ship at a specified price at one of a number of specified places was unable to do so and obtained the principal's authority to appoint a sub-agent who subsequently sold the ship according to the principal's instructions. This was held to be a permissible delegation by the agent of his authority. Second, where the agent has implied authority to do so in the circumstances because of a custom in a particular trade or profession. For example, a solicitor practising outside London generally has authority to appoint a London-based solicitor to conduct litigation on his behalf in London courts (*Solley v Wood* (1852)). Third, where the principal is aware, at the time of making the contract of agency, that the agent intends to delegate part or all of his authority and the principal does not raise objections. Fourth, where the circumstances necessitate delegation, for example, where a company is appointed as an agent, it must delegate performance to its employees since it must act through human agents. Finally, where the task delegated does not require the exercise of discretion, for example, signing documents or sending notices. In *Allam v Europa Poster Services* (1968), for example, it was held that an agent

---

3 Outlining the facts of a relevant case is a good way to illustrate the relevant legal rules and thus strengthens your argument/conclusion.

who was instructed to revoke certain licences could delegate to his solicitor the task of actually sending the notices of revocation. Estate agents provide a common example where authority cannot normally be delegated. Selling the principal's property is not a purely ministerial act and, should they delegate their task to sub-agents without authority, they are not entitled to commission on a sale effected by the sub-agents.

NO CONFLICT OF INTEREST

This fiduciary duty of good faith is paramount. This is because the agent has the power to affect the legal relations between a principal and third parties; the agent is placed in a position of trust and confidence. So equity will intervene and place fiduciary duties on the agent to protect the principal from an abuse of trust, and applies whether or not the agent receives payment. The duty is very strict and applies even where it can be proved that there was no actual conflict of interest. It is enough that there is the possibility of conflict. In *Boardman v Phipps* (1966), for example, where the duty was strictly applied, a solicitor, while acting as agent, acquired information relating to the value of certain shares.[4] Acting in good faith, he used this information for his own benefit after the principal had declined to use it for his. The House of Lords held that the agent was accountable to his principal for the profit made, because the information that he had acquired and used for his own benefit belonged to his principal. This is true even if the principal suffers no loss as a result of the agent's breach of duty.

More generally, this duty is reflected in the principles that an agent should not purchase the principal's property or act for both parties in a transaction. Where, for instance, an agent is instructed to buy property on behalf of the principal and the agent sells his own property to the principal, the agreement reached will be a breach of the duty owed to his principal. This is true even if it is a custom of a particular market (for example, the London tallow market) that agents in that market could sell their own goods to the principal (*Robinson v Mollett* (1875)). In such a situation, the potential for conflict is clear, since a seller's interest is to get the best price, whereas the buyer's is to pay as little as possible. Even if the agent acts fairly and pays a reasonable price, he will be in breach of duty unless there is full disclosure to the principal and the principal consents to the transaction.[5]

NOT TO MAKE A SECRET PROFIT

An agent must not make a secret profit over and above the agreed commission. Again, this rule is strictly applied and it is irrelevant that the agent acted in good faith or that the principal suffered no loss (see *Boardman v Phipps*). If a secret profit is made and discovered, it may be claimed by the principal (*Imageview v Kelvin Jack* (2009)).[6] The duty

....

4   Stating the facts of a particular case can be helpful in explaining a legal principle.
5   Where an agent deals with the principal in breach of his duty, the principal may rescind the contract. His right to rescission subsists until the breach is actually discovered. In *Oliver v Court* (1820), the principal was able to rescind 13 years after the transaction.
6   *Imageview Management v Kelvin Jack*, per Jacob, LJ: 'An agent's own personal interests came … entirely second to the interest of his client. If you undertake to act for a man you must act 100% body and soul, for him. You must act as if you were him. You must not allow your own interests to get in the way without telling him.'

applies equally to unpaid agents. In *Turnbull v Garden* (1869), for example, an agent was employed without payment to purchase clothes for his principal's son. He was allowed a trade discount on the transaction by the seller, but sought to charge his principal the full price. The court held that the agent had to account to his principal for the discount that he had received.[7]

NOT TO TAKE A BRIBE

A bribe is a particular form of secret profit and arises where a payment between a third party and an agent is kept secret from the principal. If an agent takes a bribe, the principal is entitled to claim the amount of the bribe as money had and received (*Logicrose v Southend United Football Club* (1988)) or to damages against either the agent or the third party. The principal can also refuse to pay commission to the agent on that transaction (or recover any commission already paid) and summarily dismiss the agent, and can set aside the transaction with the third party. The principal's remedies are cumulative save that, in *Mahesan v Malaysia Government Officers' Co-operative Housing Society Ltd* (1979), the Privy Council held that the principal must choose between recovering the bribe or an action for damages (to prevent the principal receiving a windfall profit). If, however, property constituting or representing the bribe has increased in value, the principal can claim the full value (*Attorney General of Hong Kong v Reid* (1994)).

Furthermore, both parties to the bribe may be liable to prosecution under the **Bribery Act 2010**.

TO ACCOUNT

An agent must keep his principal's property strictly separate from his own and is treated in equity as though he was a trustee of the property. On the termination of the agency, an agent must account for all such property. For example, in *Lupton v White* (1808), it was held that where an agent fails to keep the principal's property separate, the principal is entitled to a charge on the entire mixed property unless the agent is able to establish who owns what.

An agent is also required to keep proper accounts and present these to his principal.

Common Pitfalls

Students need to focus on the question asked. Those who use this question as an excuse to write all they know about the fiduciary duties of agents will not score well.

QUESTION 24

(a)   When is an agent entitled to claim commission?

---

7   See also *Hippisley v Knee Bros* (1905), where the court found that although the agent, acting in good faith, was in breach of duty, he was allowed to keep his commission on the transaction. Similarly, in *Boardman v Phipps* (1966), the agent was allowed some reimbursement for his expenses.

(b) Jessop engages Penny to sell Jessop's 'Supaclean' industrial carpet-cleaning service. The terms of the contract specify that Penny may only give 14 days' credit to purchasers, and provide for Penny to be paid 2% commission on all sales arranged by her. Penny negotiates contracts with Hamish and Timothy, incurring considerable travelling and subsistence expenses in order to do so. In her negotiations, Penny discloses her agency to Hamish, but not to Timothy. In addition, Penny agrees that Timothy can have 30 days' credit. Penny communicates her dealings to Jessop and Jessop agrees to allow Timothy 30 days' credit. Contracts are entered into between Jessop and Hamish, and Penny and Timothy, Jessop subsequently confirming the latter contract directly with Timothy. Subsequently, a dispute arises between Penny and Jessop, and Jessop refuses to supply the Supaclean service to Hamish and Timothy. Jessop also refuses to have any further dealings with Penny. Discuss the legal position of the parties involved.

How to Answer this Question

The first part of the question concerns the right of an agent to claim commission. The conditions for such payment at common law are as follows:

❖ the agent is acting with the principal's authority;
❖ the contract expressly or impliedly provides for commission to be paid;
❖ the event has happened on which payment was made conditional;
❖ the acts of the agent were the effective cause of that event happening.

The provisions of the **Commercial Agents (Council Directive) Regulations 1993** in relation to the payment of commission to commercial agents will also need to be noted.

The second part of the question deals with an agent's right to claim remuneration and expenses necessarily incurred in the course of her agency. The question also involves a discussion of an agent's rights and liabilities under a contract which she makes on behalf of an undisclosed principal. Finally, we need to consider whether an undisclosed principal may ratify a contract.

Applying the Law

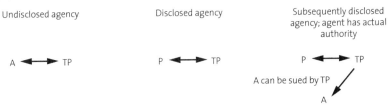

This diagram focuses on how to determine the nature of agency in this scenario. Issues of ratification and breach of warranty of authority will also have to be considered.

ANSWER

(A)

The general rule is that an agent is only entitled to commission if that has been agreed with the principal. There are, however, instances where the court will imply a term giving the agent a right to be paid for his services even if there is no express agreement.

If the contract is silent as to *when* commission is payable, the normal intention of the parties is that the agent can claim commission when the contract of sale is concluded, particularly where the agent is acting in the course of a profession or business. As regards commercial agents falling within the **Commercial Agents (Council Directive) Regulations 1993**, the time for payment of commission is dealt with by **reg 10**. In the absence of any more favourable agreement, commission will be payable when either the principal or the third party has 'executed the transaction', and at the latest when the third party has executed his part of the transaction (or should have done if the principal had executed his part as he should have). At common law, it is only rarely, however, that a court will interfere where to do so varies or is contrary to the express terms of the agency contract. For example, in *Kofi Sunkersete Obu v Strauss & Co Ltd* (1951), the contract provided for the agent to receive £50 per month as expenses but that the scale of commission was solely at the company's discretion.[8] The Privy Council in that case was not prepared to intervene to determine the rate and basis of the commission that the agent claimed he had earned.

The principal's duty to pay commission only arises where the agent has earned it. If the agent acts contrary to instructions, therefore, under common law, no right to commission will arise. For example, in *Marsh v Jelf* (1862), an auctioneer was employed to sell property by auction and was held not to be entitled to commission when he sold the property by private contract. If the agent is in breach of instructions under the contract of agency, but a contract of sale has been concluded between the principal and a third party, the agent may still be entitled to commission if her breach was done honestly and in good faith (but she does forfeit her commission if she acted in bad faith).[9] As regards a commercial agent payable by commission, the right will only be lost if a contract concluded between the principal and a third party is not executed for a reason for which the principal is not to blame (for example frustration, or where the third party withdraws) (**reg 11** of the **Commercial Agents (Council Directive) Regulations 1993**). The **Regulations** make no provision for the right to commission to be lost as a result of the agent acting contrary to instructions, even where this is in bad faith. The agent will of course be in breach of the duty of good faith, and if this has resulted in loss to the principal, compensation could be sought, but commission cannot be withheld on this basis.

....

8 Providing details of relevant cases demonstrates deeper knowledge and substantiates your argument.

9 See also *Hippisley v Knee Bros* (1905), where the court found that although the agent, acting in good faith, was in breach of duty, he was allowed to keep his commission on the transaction. Similarly, in *Boardman v Phipps* (1966), the agent was allowed some reimbursement for their expenses.

An agent will only earn her commission when she has been the direct or effective cause of the event upon which the principal has agreed to pay commission. The relevant phrase in the **Commercial Agents (Council Directive) Regulations** is where a contract 'has been concluded as a result of [the agent's] action' (**reg 7**). It is to be assumed that this will be interpreted in the same way as 'effective cause'. The question of causation is ultimately a question of fact in the absence of judicial definition of 'effective cause'. If some event breaks the chain of causation between the agent and the event on which payment of commission depends, then the agent will not be entitled to commission. Thus, in *Coles v Enoch* (1939), A was employed to find a tenant for P's property. T overheard a conversation between A and an interested party and, although A only gave T a general description of the location, T found the property himself and made an offer directly to P which was accepted. The court held that A was not entitled to commission since his actions had not been the direct cause of T's agreement with P.[10]

A commercial agent may also be able to claim commission in relation to contracts between the principal and a customer previously introduced by the agent, even though the agent has not taken any action in relation to the later contracts (**reg 7(1)(b)** of the **Commercial Agents (Council Directive) Regulations 1993**).

In some cases, an agent will be entitled to commission where the principal wilfully breaks his contract with a third party whom the agent has introduced and whom the principal has accepted. In *Alpha Trading Ltd v Dunnshaw-Patten Ltd* (1981), a principal was introduced to a buyer for a quantity of cement. The principal accepted the introduction and contracted with the buyer accordingly. In order to take advantage of a rising market, the principal decided not to perform the contract of sale (preferring instead to pay damages for breach of contract). The agent claimed damages for lost commission. The Court of Appeal held that the agent was entitled to commission because it was an implied term of the agency contract that the principal would not deprive the agent of his commission by breaking the contract with the third party. As noted above, this common law principle also operates under **reg 11** of the **Commercial Agents (Council Directive) Regulations 1993**. If a contract is not performed for a reason for which the principal is to blame, the commercial agent is nevertheless entitled to commission.

Where a person is appointed 'sole agent', he is entitled to be paid even if the sale is not effected by him but by some other agent.[11]

(B)
PENNY'S POSITION VIS-À-VIS JESSOP
Penny's position here depends on applying the rules relating to an agent's rights against her principal. These are: the right to be remunerated; the right to be indemnified for expenses properly incurred; and the right to a lien over items of the principal's property in her possession.

....

10 The inclusion of a concrete example is a good way to substantiate your argument by showing the practical implications; as such, it demonstrates understanding.
11 This takes the form of damages for breach of the term that he should be the 'sole' agent.

Because the contracts negotiated by Penny are for the supply of a service rather than the sale of goods, the **Commercial Agents (Council Directive) Regulations 1993** will not apply to this situation. The precise conditions to the right of remuneration will therefore depend on the terms of the agency contract but, in essence, the agent must have acted within the scope of her authority and her acts must have been the effective cause of the event she was employed to bring about. Whether or not the agent's acts were the 'effective cause' will be a question of fact in each case.

In the case of the contract with Hamish, Penny has fulfilled the criteria for payment and is entitled to her commission.

Unless excluded from doing so by her contract with Jessop (of which there is no evidence), Penny can also claim her expenses from Jessop in relation to the contract with Hamish, since these have been properly incurred in the performance of the agency. The right to indemnity covers all expenses and liabilities necessarily incurred by the agent while acting within her actual authority. Furthermore, should Penny be in lawful possession of property or documents of title belonging to Jessop, she may protect her rights by exercising a lien over them for unpaid commission and expenses.

The position in relation to the contract with Timothy is more problematic. Penny exceeded her authority by giving Timothy 30 days' credit. Where an agent acts outside her authority, she is generally not entitled to commission, even though her principal may be bound by the transaction. Although Jessop purported to ratify the contract, at law, an undisclosed principal cannot do so (*Keighley Maxsted & Co v Durant* (1901)). In that case, the agent entered into a contract for the purchase of wheat in his own name at a price in excess of the limit agreed with his principal.[12] The agent did not disclose to the seller of the wheat his intention to contract on the principal's behalf as well as his own. Later, the principal purported to ratify the agent's act. The House of Lords unanimously held that an undisclosed principal cannot ratify. It seems therefore that whatever the position as between Timothy and Jessop or Timothy and Penny, Penny is not entitled to commission on the contract made with Timothy.[13]

As for Penny's expenses, in order to render Jessop liable to indemnify her, she must have acted within the scope of her authority. For the same reasons as above, Penny will not be entitled to claim for her expenses because she has acted in breach of her instructions.

PENNY'S POSITION VIS-À-VIS HAMISH AND TIMOTHY
Where an agent acts with authority and names or sufficiently identifies the principal in such a way that it is clear to the third party that the agent is acting as such, the contract is made between the principal and the third party, and the agent drops out of the

....

12 It is a good idea to provide details of the cases you cite as it supports your argument by illustrating the points you have just made.
13 Remember to draw conclusions from your analysis; this evidences your understanding of how to apply the law.

transaction entirely. This is Penny's position with regard to Hamish – she incurs neither rights nor liabilities on the contract made between Hamish and Jessop.

In relation to Timothy, Jessop's purported ratification of Penny's actions is without legal effect, because a principal can only ratify if he was identified at the time the contract was made (*Keighley Maxsted & Co v Durant* (1901)). Thus, the position is exactly the same as it was when the contract was made – Timothy thought the contract was made with Penny and, therefore, Penny is contractually liable to Timothy. No question of breach of warranty of authority arises here, because Penny was, at law, the principal when the contract was entered into. It is clear that an agent is personally liable on a contract where it has been negotiated on behalf of an undisclosed principal. If the agent is unable to supply the Supaclean service under the contract made personally with Timothy, Penny will be liable to pay damages for breach of that contract.

JESSOP'S POSITION VIS-À-VIS HAMISH AND TIMOTHY
Once again, the position in relation to Hamish is straightforward. Penny acted within her authority and identified Jessop as her principal; the contract was therefore solely between Jessop and Hamish. Thus, if Jessop refuses to supply the Supaclean service to Hamish, Jessop is in breach of this contract and Hamish has a right of action against Jessop alone. In relation to Timothy, Jessop is able to rely on the rule in *Keighley Maxsted & Co v Durant* (1901) that an undisclosed principal cannot ratify. Jessop therefore has no rights nor liabilities under the contract between Timothy and Penny.

QUESTION 25
To what extent is it true to say that, once an agent has brought his principal and a third party into a contractual relationship, the agent drops out, and has no rights or liabilities as against the third party?

How to Answer this Question
This question requires you to know, and to explain, the exceptions to the general rule that an agent is neither liable under, nor entitled to enforce, a contract he makes on behalf of his principal. It goes a little further than that, however, in that there are some actions which may be taken by the third party against the agent which are not strictly speaking based on the contract. Examples are liability on a collateral contract, or liability for breach of the implied warranty of authority. The issues to be discussed are:

- ❖ intention to contract personally;
- ❖ custom;
- ❖ undisclosed principal;
- ❖ principal non-existent;
- ❖ collateral contract;
- ❖ implied warranty of authority.

It may also be useful to say a little about the power of the third party to choose whom to sue in a situation where both principal and agent may be potentially liable.

Applying the Law

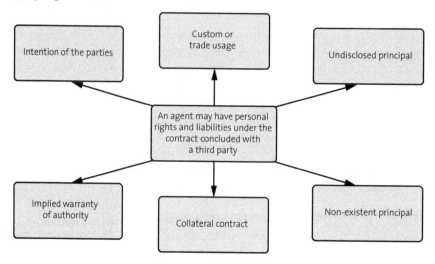

```
Intention of the parties        Custom or              Undisclosed principal
                                trade usage

                    An agent may have personal
                    rights and liabilities under the
                    contract concluded with
                    a third party

Implied warranty                                        Non-existent principal
of authority                    Collateral contract
```

ANSWER

There is no doubt that it is true to say that, in the normal course of events, once the principal and the third party have made a binding contract, the agent has no further rights or liabilities against the third party.[14] The agent may, of course, have outstanding claims on, or obligations towards, the principal, but that is a separate issue, arising from their continuing relationship rather than the specific contract which has resulted from the agent's activities. It is also true, however, that, in certain situations, the agent will have rights and liabilities either alongside or in place of the principal, and it is to those exceptions which we now turn. Some of them relate to rights and liabilities on the contract itself; some are independent of the contract.

The first exception which must be considered is where the parties themselves intend that the agent should have personal rights or liabilities. At one time, much stress seemed to be placed on the exact form in which the contract was signed, for example, to sign 'as solicitors' left the agent liable (*Burrell v Jones* (1819)), whereas to sign 'on behalf of' or 'per pro' was taken to indicate an intention that the agent should not be liable. The more recent approach, set out by Brandon, J in *The Swan* (1968), suggests that it is a question of looking carefully at the contract and the surrounding circumstances to try to determine the intention of the parties.[15] *The Swan* involved a one man company, JD Rodger Ltd,

---

14 'The contract is that of the principal, not that of the agent, and *prima facie* at common law the only person who can sue is the principal and the only person who can be sued is the principal' (*per* Wright, J in *Montgomerie v United Kingdom Mutual Steamship Association* (1891)).

15 The test is, as in most other areas of contract law, objective, that is, the question is not what the two individuals actually intended but what 'two reasonable businessmen making a contract of that nature, in those terms, and in those surrounding circumstances, must be taken to have intended' (*per* Brandon, J in *The Swan* (1968)).

which had hired a boat belonging to JD Rodger himself, who was a director of the company. The company gave instructions, through JD Rodger, for repairs to be carried out. It was held that, in all the circumstances, although the order for the work had been signed simply as 'Director' (which carried no implication of personal liability),[16] JD Rodger, the agent, was personally liable. It was natural for the ship repairers to assume that the ship-owner would accept personal liability.[17]

By way of contrast, in *The Santa Caterina* (1977), the defendants requested the claimants to supply bunkers to the ship, *Santa Caterina*.[18] The claimants forwarded the invoice to the defendants who denied liability on the basis that they had requested the bunkers as agents of the time charterers of the ship. The Court of Appeal held that, since on the facts the claimants *knew* the defendants were agents, the onus was on the claimants to intro-duce evidence to enable an inference to be drawn that the defendants were personally liable. In the absence of such evidence, the court held the agents not personally bound by the contract.

It is also clear that, if there is a custom or trade usage (for example, in the tallow trade: *Thornton v Fehr* (1935)) that agents are personally liable or entitled, the courts will give effect to it, provided that it is consistent with the express terms of the contract, and the surrounding circumstances.

The rights and liabilities of the principal and agent against third parties may differ accord-ing to whether the agency is disclosed or undisclosed. Agency is disclosed where the agent reveals that he is acting as an agent.[19] Agency is undisclosed where the agent does not reveal the fact of agency at all and appears to be acting on his own behalf. Where the principal is undisclosed and the agent acts in accordance to his actual authority, then it is only fair that the third party, who thinks that the agent is the other party, should be able to take action against the agent (*Sims v Bond* (1833)). Once this is established, it must also be fair to allow the reciprocal right to the agent (*Siu Yin Kwan v Eastern Insurance* (1994)).

There may also be rights and liabilities where there is, in fact, no principal standing behind the agent. This might occur in two ways. It may be that the agent is, in fact, the principal and is simply pretending to act as an agent. Second, the principal may not be in existence at the time the contract is made.

If the agent is simply pretending to be acting for a principal (real or imaginary), while really acting on his own behalf, then there is no doubt that he will be liable on the

---

16 Though it did nothing to avoid liability either.
17 The court thought relevant that the repairs were extensive and greatly increased the value of the ship, such that it was reasonable for the repairers to assume JD Rodger acted as both agent and in a personal capacity.
18 The consideration of possible alternative arguments makes your answer stand out from the rest and demonstrates both deeper knowledge and understanding.
19 It is sufficient that the fact of agency is revealed without the need for the principal to be named.

contract. He will also be able to enforce the contract provided that he gives due notice of the fact that he was acting on his own behalf, and the contract is not one where the personal characteristics the other party are important, as they would be, for example in an employment contract, or an underwriting contract (*Collins v Associated Greyhound Racecourses Ltd* (1930)).[20]

More difficulty can arise where the principal was not in existence at the time of the contract. This can happen in relation to contracts made on behalf of a company which has yet to be incorporated. The common law approach was demonstrated by *Kelner v Baxter* (1866) where it was held that the promoters were personally liable for the contract. This has now been given statutory force by **s 51** of the **Companies Act 2006**. The section deals with liability, rather than ability to enforce. At common law, the only authority in this area was *Newborne v Sensolid* (1954) where the decision against allowing the agent to enforce turned on a very pedantic argument about the precise form of the signature on the contract.[21] This kind of technical argument has been disapproved in later cases, and in particular by the Court of Appeal in *Phonogram v Lane* (1982). The balance of opinion seems to be that, following the statutory intervention noted above, the agent should be able to sue as well as being liable, where a contract is made on behalf of a company not yet incorporated.

The situations we have looked at so far have involved the agent being liable on the contract itself. There are two situations, however, in which the agent may have a separate type of liability to the third party. The first is where there is a collateral contract between the agent and the third party. The kind of situation where this could arise is exemplified by the case of *Andrews v Hopkinson* (1957). The claimant wanted to acquire a car on hire purchase. The dealer said 'It's a good little bus. I would stake my life on it'. The claimant entered into a hire purchase contract with a finance company for the car, arranged through the dealer. When the car turned out to be defective, it was held that the claimant, although, at first sight, having no contractual remedy against the dealer, could in fact sue him on the basis of a collateral contract. At the time, the dealer was in fact held not to be the agent of the finance company, but that has now been changed by statute. The case illustrates how a statement made by an agent that encouraged the third party to enter into the contract could make the agent liable for breach of a collateral contract.

The final way in which the agent may be liable to the third party is for breach of the implied warranty of authority. This will occur where the agent has held himself out as having authority from the principal, when in fact he does not. Of course, in some circumstances, the principal may nevertheless be liable for the contract on the basis of usual or apparent authority. If the principal is not liable, however, the agent will be liable for breach of this implied warranty. The remedies that the third party will be able to recover,

---

20 In this case, the problem was that an undisclosed principal wanted to take over the contract, but there is no reason why it should not also apply where the agent is wanting to step into the shoes of the supposed principal. See, also, *Schmalz v Avery* (1851).

21 It was taken to have been signed in the name of the company, that is, 'Leopold Newborne (London) Ltd'.

however, are limited to what could in practice have been recovered from the principal. Thus, if the principal is insolvent, it may not be worth suing the agent for breach of the implied warranty.

The existence of the warranty does not depend on the agent's awareness of the lack of authority. This was established in *Collen v Wright* (1857) and taken to its logical extreme in *Yonge v Toynbee* (1910). In the latter case, the warranty was held to operate against a solicitor who had continued to act for a client who, unknown to the solicitor, had become mentally incapacitated (which had the automatic effect of terminating the solicitor's authority). The fact that the solicitor had acted in good faith throughout was regarded as irrelevant.

A final issue which may need consideration is the position where the third party has the possibility of suing either the agent or the principal. Judgment cannot, of course, be enforced against both, but supposing judgment has been obtained against the principal, who turns out to be unable to pay. Can the third party then sue the agent in respect of the same loss? Or does he have to make a choice at an earlier stage? The rules are not very clear. The test is whether the third party has 'elected' to sue one party. If so, this will bar any action against the other. The problem is in deciding what amounts to an 'election'. In *Clarkson Booker Ltd v Andjel* (1964), it was held that what was required was a 'truly unequivocal act'. It might have been thought that the institution of proceedings was such an act, but the Court of Appeal thought that this was only *prima facie* so. The election to be binding must be made with knowledge of all relevant facts. In the case before them, the third party had issued a writ against the principal, but had subsequently discovered that the principal was insolvent. It was held that, because they were not in possession of the full facts, the issue of the writ against the principal was not a binding election. Proceedings could be started against the agent. The question of the precise requirements for an election remains unclear.

As we have seen, there is a variety of ways in which the agent may have rights against, and liabilities towards, a third party. Most of the rules seem to operate in a reasonably satisfactory way. Some criticism might be made, however, of the rather strict approach to the implied warranty of authority. Moreover, as has just been pointed out, the rules relating to 'election' are in considerable need of clarification.

10 Relationship with Third Parties

INTRODUCTION

This chapter is concerned with the scope of an agent's authority and when a principal will be liable, or be able to sue, on a contract made by the agent without authority. The different types of authority must be understood, in particular, apparent authority (sometimes known as 'ostensible' authority) and usual authority. Furthermore, students must pay sufficient attention to the important concept of the doctrine of the undisclosed principal. The general rule is that an undisclosed principal can sue and be sued on the contract made by the agent on his behalf, if it was within the scope of the agent's actual authority. The justification for the doctrine of the undisclosed principal has been the subject of much discussion by academic writers. It is generally accepted that, although it runs against the fundamental principles of privity of contract (that is, there must be agreement between the parties), the doctrine is justified on grounds of commercial convenience.

QUESTION 26

Homes Ltd appoints Juliet to act as its agent in the sale and purchase of furniture for sale through its shops in England. Juliet is instructed to obtain the consent of the company's board of directors before making any purchase above £15,000. Juliet has undertaken various actions.

(a) SilentNite, a bed manufacturer, contacts Juliet offering to sell a consignment of beds. SilentNite is in financial difficulties and, therefore, offers the beds for £20,000, which represents a substantial discount on the normal price, but SilentNite requires an immediate decision. Juliet says, 'I need to check with the company's board for such a large transaction, but they usually back my opinion on such matters, especially in an emergency like this.' Juliet, therefore, agrees to buy on behalf of Homes Ltd. The next day, SilentNite receives a better offer for the beds from another furniture retailer. SilentNite telephones Juliet and says it is withdrawing from the deal. That afternoon, the board of directors of Homes decides it wishes to go ahead with the purchase from SilentNite.

(b) Juliet is offered, by Heritage Ltd, wardrobes for £10,000, which is the normal price. During negotiations, the sales manager of Heritage says to Juliet, 'Once this deal goes through, you'll be on the top of the list for a Christmas hamper which contains a voucher for a one-week all expenses paid caravan holiday.' Juliet agrees to buy the wardrobes, but manages to persuade Heritage to agree to a price of £9,500. Later, she receives a Christmas hamper containing the holiday voucher from Heritage. When asked about this by the board of directors, Juliet strongly denies that she was influenced by the promise of a Christmas hamper. Juliet points out that Heritage wardrobes have always been popular with customers.

(c)   Juliet contracts to buy table lamps from a manufacturer in Estonia for £5,000. The lamps do not conform to safety standards and cannot be sold in England.

▶ Advise Homes Ltd.

How to Answer this Question

This question concerns the extent to which a principal can be bound by contracts which the agent has made without authority. Part (i) involves the principal's attempt to ratify its agent's act. The general requirements of ratification need to be stated. SilentNite is aware that Juliet has no authority to accept its offer. Since ratification requires an agent to purport to act for the principal, there is simply no agreement for the board of directors to ratify. In Part (ii), Juliet may be in breach of her fiduciary duties not to make a secret profit or take a bribe. An agent is required to perform with honesty and good faith for the benefit of the principal. The consequences of such a breach need to be discussed. Part (iii) requires a discussion of the Estonian manufacturer's possible breaches of the **Sale of Goods Act 1979**, namely, under **s 14**.

Applying the Law

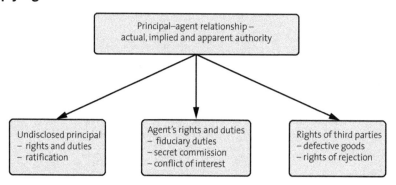

This diagram shows key points to be discussed in the answer.

ANSWER

Homes want to know whether they are bound by the transactions carried out by Juliet. In order for Homes to be bound, Juliet, as their agent, must have had some form of authority from Homes to enter into the transactions. If Juliet had no authority, then Homes cannot be bound to the contracts made with the third parties. We will look at the individual situations to see if Homes are bound.[1]

....

1   Providing a brief introduction which not only sets out the issues you are going to address but which also refers to the question set is a good way to demonstrate that you have understood what is relevant; relevancy is an important assessment factor.

(A) SILENTNITE

An agent has actual authority when what is done was previously authorised either expressly or impliedly by the principal. Homes instruct Juliet to obtain the consent of the company's board of directors before making any purchases above £15,000. There is nothing vague or ambiguous about these instructions (*Weigall v Runciman* (1916)). So Juliet does not have actual authority to conclude the contract to purchase beds for £20,000. Although this was what Juliet explained to SilentNite, Juliet agreed to buy the beds anyway, in the belief that the board would approve the transaction. Indeed, she is correct, because the board of directors in fact does wish to go ahead with the deal.

Although a principal may ratify an agent's unauthorised act, there are limitations to this rule.[2] The right to ratify depends on whether the agent purported to act on behalf of the principal at the time of agreeing to the transaction (*Keighley, Maxsted v Durant* (1901)). SilentNite knew Juliet did not have authority, because Juliet specifically told SilentNite this. Even though Juliet believed that the Homes board would approve the transaction, when she agreed to purchase the beds from SilentNite, Juliet did not purport to act on behalf of Homes. Thus, there was no unauthorised transaction which Homes' board of directors could ratify. This is unlike the situation in *Bolton Partners v Lambert* (1889), where the managing director of a company accepted the offer to purchase a property on behalf of the company without its authority.[3] When the third party wanted to withdraw from the contract, the court held that it was too late, because when the company ratified the agent's unauthorised act, ratification related back to the time when the unauthorised act was concluded. It was thus too late for the third party to withdraw. Here, Juliet did not conclude the unauthorised act on behalf of Homes. She specifically told SilentNite that she did not have the company's authority. So, there is no concluded transaction which Homes' directors could ratify. The effect of ratification is that an unauthorised contract made by an agent becomes an authorised one from when it was made. Here, Homes cannot ratify because there was no unauthorised contract to which they were a party. Thus, there is no binding contract with SilentNite and SilentNite can withdraw their offer at any time up to the point of acceptance (*Payne v Cave* (1789); *Byrne v Van Tienhoven* (1880)).

Homes have no action against Juliet, since she had followed her instructions and had acted within the limits of her purchasing power on behalf of Homes. She has not acted in excess of her actual authority.

(B) HERITAGE LTD

Juliet has express authority to purchase furniture. So, *prima facie*, Homes is bound by contract to purchase wardrobes with Heritage. But as Homes' agent, Juliet owes a fiduciary duty and is in a position of trust and confidence. So equity will intervene and place fiduciary duties on an agent to protect the principal from an abuse of trust. A major

---

2 Pointing out any potential limitations to the application of a particular legal principle is a good way to demonstrate that you have understood the complexities of the rule in question.

3 Outlining a relevant contrasting case shows your understanding and supports your argument.

consequence of this is that an agent must not put herself in a situation where there might be a conflict of interest and duty. The fiduciary duty of good faith has been applied very strictly (*Boardman v Phipps* (1966)) and it appears that Juliet is in breach of this paramount duty. Furthermore, Juliet must not make a secret profit or take a bribe. She cannot accept commission from a third party.

It seems clear that Heritage is aware that Juliet is an agent. Nevertheless, they offer her a Christmas hamper containing a holiday voucher. This constitutes a bribe. It is conclusively presumed against Heritage that their motive was corrupt and that Juliet was affected and influenced by the offer of the hamper and holiday. It is irrelevant that Juliet managed to persuade Heritage to reduce the price to £9,500. In this situation, Juliet may be summarily dismissed, even if appointed for a fixed period. We are not told what Juliet's remuneration package was, but certainly Juliet would lose her right to commission on this transaction.[4] If Juliet has already consumed the contents of the hamper and used the holiday voucher, Homes could claim damages from Juliet and Heritage for any loss it suffers as a result of the bribe. Homes can, if it wishes to do so, set aside the transaction with Heritage (*Logicrose v Southend UFC* (1988)). Furthermore, Juliet and Heritage may incur criminal liability under the **Bribery Act 2010**.

It is not clear whether Juliet is a commercial agent within the **Commercial Agents (Council Directive) Regulations 1993**.[5] The **Regulations** would apply if she is a self-employed intermediary with continuing authority to negotiate the sale and/or purchase of goods (**reg 2**). If Juliet is a commercial agent, she is certainly in breach of her duties to look after the interests of Homes and to act 'dutifully and in good faith' (**reg 3**). Although the **Regulations** state that an agent is entitled to commission where a transaction is concluded as a result of an agent's action (**reg 7**), the **Regulations** are silent as to whether an agent loses the right to commission if the agent acts contrary to instructions – even if the agent acts in bad faith. Certainly, Juliet is in breach of her duty of good faith under **reg 3** and, if this resulted in loss to Homes, compensation could be sought, but it seems that her commission on this transaction cannot be withheld. Although an agent has the right to an indemnity or compensation on termination of the agency agreement (**reg 17**), if Homes terminates Juliet's agency contract as a result of her taking a bribe, **reg 18** will preclude her from making such a claim.

(C) ESTONIAN MANUFACTURER

Juliet has actual authority to purchase furniture on behalf of Homes, so Homes is bound in contract with the Estonian manufacturer. However, the table lamps cannot be sold in England. Homes has two possible actions: first against the Estonian manufacturer and, second, against Juliet.

---

4 Pointing out omissions in the information provided by the question and considering the impact these omissions might have on the outcome of your analysis will attract a higher mark as it demonstrates your understanding.

5 Considering ambiguities in the question ensures completeness of your answer and demonstrates your understanding.

Assuming the sales contract is governed by English law, the **Sale of Goods Act 1979** requires goods sold by a seller in the course of business to be of satisfactory quality (**s14(2)**) and fit for their purpose (**s14(3)**). Since Homes resells the goods in the course of their business, the sales contract is not a consumer transaction.[6] This means that the court has a discretion where it is just to do so to treat the implied terms under **s14** as giving the buyer a right to warranty damages only (**s15A**).

By **s14(2)**, goods are required to be of satisfactory quality. We are told that the table lamps do not conform to safety standards. If these standards were applicable worldwide, it is likely that the Estonian manufacturer would be in breach of **s14(2)**, since no reasonable person would regard table lamps to be of satisfactory quality if they are not safe and do not meet a general level of safety.

It may be, however, that although the table lamps supplied by the Estonian manufacturer are in general satisfactory but merely do not meet the standards for resale in England, then whether or not Homes has an action against the manufacturer would depend on whether there is a breach of **s14(3)**. Certainly, if the Estonian manufacturer knows that Juliet is contracting on behalf of an English company and that the goods are to be delivered to England, this will be sufficient to impliedly make it known to the Estonian manufacturer that the goods are required to be fit for resale in England. However, there will be no breach of **s14(3)** if either the buyer does not rely on the skill and judgment of the seller, or it is unreasonable to rely on the seller to supply suitable goods. In *ST Belton v Teheran Europe* (1968), air compressors were sold to a Persian buyer. The Persian buyer complained that the goods were unfit for their purpose because the air compressors did not meet the safety regulations and could not be resold in Persia. The court held that there was no breach of **s14(3)**, since it was unreasonable for the buyer to rely on the seller's knowledge of the safety regulations in Persia.[7] Following this case, therefore, it may be that Homes has no action against the Estonian manufacturer. If the court finds otherwise, and Homes has an action for breach of **s14(3)**, this would normally entitle Homes to reject the entire consignment of lamps and claim damages under the *Hadley v Baxendale* (1854) principles. However, as discussed, since Homes is a business buyer, the court has a discretion under **s15A** to make an award of damages only.[8]

Homes' second possible action would be against Juliet.[9] Although she has carried out her instructions in purchasing furniture within her credit limit, she is under a duty to act with due care and skill. If she is being paid for special skills as a purchasing agent, a greater

----

6 The **Consumer Rights Act 2015** only applies to consumer contracts. A consumer is defined as an 'individual' who acts for purposes that are wholly or mainly outside that individual's trade, business, craft or profession. Homes Ltd is therefore not a consumer.

7 A good answer does not merely refer to the provision of a particular Act; where possible, it substantiates and illustrates the application of an Act with case law examples.

8 And might do so if, for instance, it was simply a matter of making minor adjustments to remedy the safety issue to make it comply with British standards.

9 The consideration of different options ensures completeness of your analysis and attracts additional marks.

degree of care and skill is expected of her. If she has failed in purchasing suitable furniture and this results in loss to Homes, she is in breach of her agency contract, entitling Homes to claim an indemnity from her for their loss either under the common law or under the **Commercial Agents (Council Directive) Regulations 1993**.

QUESTION 27

On 1 April, Xavier, an art dealer in Manchester, appoints Rosalind as his agent in Liverpool and that same day, he sends a letter to FineArt Ltd, a company dealing in paintings in Liverpool, confirming Rosalind's appointment and her authority to buy and sell pictures on his behalf. In fact, Rosalind is under an express instruction not to deal with any pictures alleged to have been painted by Lowry, because of the risk of forgery. On 10 May, Rosalind, purporting to act on behalf of Xavier, contracts with FineArt to buy from it *The Floating Bridge*, a genuine Lowry painting, for £470,000. On 12 May, Rosalind visits the office of Princeton Galleries and, without mentioning Xavier, contracts to sell it for £530,000. Rosalind intends to keep the profit from this transaction for herself. On 16 May, FineArt discovers what Rosalind is trying to do, and tells Xavier that it intends to withdraw from the contract and keep *The Floating Bridge*. On 17 May, Xavier purports to ratify Rosalind's actions of 10 and 12 May.

▶ Consider the rights and liabilities of all parties.

How to Answer this Question

Part of this problem is concerned with an agent's authority and, in particular, apparent authority. This relates to the effect of Rosalind's actions on 10 and 12 May, and whether they can be regarded as falling within the scope of her authority so as to bind Xavier.

The second issue that should be looked at is Rosalind's attempt to make a secret profit out of her position as Xavier's agent. The duty of the agent to act in good faith and account for any secret profit (for example *De Bussche v Alt* (1878)) needs to be noted here. Rosalind may also be said to have broken another duty of an agent in her failure to follow instructions.

Finally, there is Xavier's attempt to ratify what Rosalind has done. The general requirements of ratification should be stated, that is:

- ❖ the agent must purport to act for the principal (*Keighley Maxsted and Co v Durant* (1901));
- ❖ the principal must be in existence at the time of the contract (*Kelner v Baxter* (1866)); and
- ❖ the principal must have capacity at the time of contract and at the time of ratification (*Grover and Grover v Matthews* (1910)).

These should be applied to the problem, and you should also note the effects of ratification, in particular its retrospective nature (*Bolton Partners v Lambert* (1889)).

The answer could well conclude with a summary of the position of each of the parties.

Applying the Law

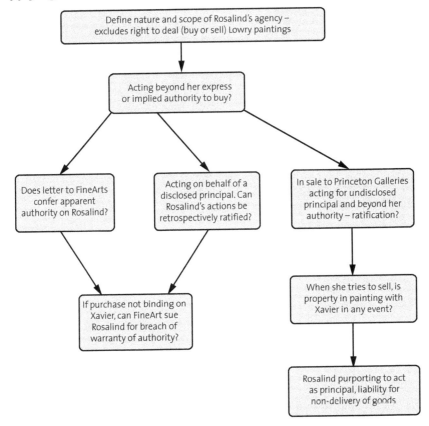

This diagram illustrates the development of key points that will be covered in this answer.

ANSWER

This question raises issues relating to the extent of an agent's authority, the duties of an agent and the power of a principal to ratify an agent's unauthorised acts. These will be looked at in turn in discussing the rights and liabilities of all the parties.[10]

In making the contracts of 10 and 12 May, Rosalind is acting outside the actual authority given to her by Xavier, in that she has been forbidden to deal in pictures by Lowry. This does not necessarily mean, however, that her actions cannot bind Xavier. This is because she may have 'apparent' authority (also known as 'ostensible' authority or 'agency by estoppel'). The requirements for this, as set out by Slade, J in *Rama Corp Ltd v Proved Tin and General Investment* (1952), are: (a) that there is a representation of authority by the

....

10 In your introduction, you should clearly identify the legal issues raised by the question. This is a good way to convince the examiner that you have understood what is relevant and will make him to be positively inclined towards your answer.

principal to the third party;[11] (b) that the third party relies on that representation; and (c) that the third party alters his position in reliance on the representation. This approach was followed by the Court of Appeal in *Freeman and Lockyer v Buckhurst Park Properties (Mangal) Ltd* (1964), which made it clear that the representation could be by conduct, rather than by a statement. Here, however, as far as FineArt is concerned, there was a clear and apparently unequivocal representation as to Rosalind's authority in Xavier's letter of 1 April. Provided that FineArt could show that it was important to it that Rosalind was Xavier's agent (in other words, that it was relying on Xavier's representation), then the apparent authority would seem to operate. This would mean that if, on 10 May, FineArt had sought the £470,000 from Xavier, it would have had every chance of success. This does not mean, however, that Xavier can necessarily enforce the contract against FineArt. The doctrine of apparent authority has developed to protect third parties. It is unlikely that the courts would allow it to be used against a third party in a situation such as this. That is why it will become important to look later at Xavier's power to ratify Rosalind's actions.[12]

In relation to the contract with Princeton Galleries, the position is different. We are not told of any letter being sent to it about Rosalind's authority. Moreover, Rosalind apparently purports to contract on her own behalf. Even if she had been acting for Xavier, so that Xavier was an undisclosed principal, this would not affect the position. There can be no apparent authority without a representation from the principal to the third party, and it is difficult to see how this could occur if the third party is unaware of the existence of the principal. The possibility of Xavier ratifying what Rosalind has done will be considered later.

Turning to Rosalind, what is her position? Her actions have involved breaches of two of the duties which an agent owes to a principal. First, she has disobeyed an instruction not to deal with Lowry pictures.[13] She will be liable for any loss flowing from this. This rule has been applied strictly, even in cases where there was some doubt as to whether, even if the agent had carried out his instructions, the principal would have avoided the loss. An example of this is *Fraser v Furman* (1967),[14] where the agent failed to take out an insurance policy on the principal's behalf, but argued that even if he had taken it out, the insurer would have been

....

11 In *Armagas v Mundogas* (1986), the House of Lords emphasised that for apparent authority to exist, the representation must come from the principal, not from the agent. In this case, the vice president of a company had indicated that he had authority to agree a deal for the sale and charter-back of a ship. His plan was to make a secret profit out of the transactions. When his deceit came to light, the third party argued that the shipowners were bound by the agent's apparent authority. The House of Lords disagreed, holding that there was no representation of authority from the principal as opposed to the agent, and that therefore apparent authority could not arise.

12 Pointing out that you are going to discuss/analyse something at a later stage in your answer is a good idea for two reasons: first, it gives you more time to focus on the relevant issues rather than having to constantly repeat yourself and thus waste valuable time; second, it might also enhance the readability of your argument and shows a certain degree of planning ahead on your part.

13 This assumes that Rosalind has a contractual relationship with Xavier.

14 Referring to examples supports and strengthens your analysis; it also demonstrates your knowledge.

able to avoid paying out because of a minor omission on the part of the principal. The Court of Appeal refused to get involved in that argument, and held the agent liable.

Second, Rosalind is in the process of breaching one of her fiduciary duties, that is, the duty not to make a secret profit out of her position as agent. If she does, she will be liable to account to the principal for the profit. This is what happened in *De Bussche v Alt* (1878), where an agent, engaged to sell a ship, bought it himself at the minimum price specified by the principal and shortly afterwards sold it at a substantial profit. This profit had to be handed over to the principal. Here, if Rosalind completed her transactions as she planned, the £60,000 profit on the resale of the picture would have to be handed over to Xavier. There is no suggestion in the facts that Rosalind has taken any bribe. This type of secret profit is dealt with even more severely, with the principal being entitled to dismiss the agent, and sue both the agent and the third party for any losses resulting (*Logicrose v Southend United Football Club* (1988)), but it does not appear to be relevant on these facts.

Although Rosalind has been acting beyond her instructions, and has been trying to make a profit for herself, Xavier has now apparently recognised that the contracts which Rosalind has negotiated in relation to *The Floating Bridge* amount to a good bargain. He is therefore trying to take the benefit of them himself by ratifying Rosalind's actions of 10 and 12 March. Can he do this?

The power of a principal to ratify the unauthorised acts of an agent is well established. There are, however, certain limitations.[15] First, the agent must have purported to act for a principal. This was established in *Keighley Maxsted & Co v Durant* (1901). The agent was authorised by the principal to buy wheat for their joint account at a certain price. He made a contract with the third party (Durant) at a higher price. He intended this to be for the joint account, but did not tell Durant this. The next day, the principal ratified what the agent had done, but subsequently refused to take delivery. An action by Durant against the principal failed because the agent had not purported to act for the principal, and ratification was therefore impossible.[16] Provided that the agent says that the contract is on behalf of a principal, however, it does not matter that in fact the agent is acting on his own account. In *Re Tiedemann and Ledermann Freres* (1899), it was held that in these circumstances, the principal could still ratify.

The second limitation on the power to ratify is that the principal must have been in existence at the time of the contract between the agent and the third party. This problem arises where contracts are made on behalf of companies which have not yet been incorporated. In *Kelner v Baxter* (1866), the promoters of a company which had not yet been incorporated made a contract to buy stock for it. When the company was incorporated, there was an attempt to ratify this contract. It was held that this was ineffective, and the promoters remained personally liable.

---

15 Pointing out any potential limitations of the application of a particular legal principle is a good way to demonstrate that you have understood the complexities of the rule in question.

16 The lower courts disagreed on the result, but this was the unanimous decision of an eight-person House of Lords.

The third requirement is that the principal must have been able to make the contract at the time of the contract and at the time of ratification. The first part of this will be a problem where, for example, a minor attempts to ratify a contract which the minor would not have had capacity to make. The second part will also apply where at the time of ratification the contract would simply not have been possible. In *Grover and Grover v Matthews* (1910), for example, there was an attempt to ratify a contract of fire insurance after a fire had destroyed the property that was the subject of the insurance. It was held that ratification was impossible because, at that stage, the principal would not have been able to make the insurance contract.

How does all this apply to the facts of the problem and to Xavier's attempts to ratify Rosalind's actions? The second two requirements appear not to create a problem, so we must concentrate on the first – that is, that the agent must purport to act for a principal. In relation to the contract made on 10 May, this is no problem. Rosalind clearly says that she is acting for Xavier, and we have seen that the fact that she is in reality acting for her own benefit is irrelevant (*Re Tiedemann and Ledermann Freres*). When Rosalind makes the contract with Princeton Galleries on 12 May, however, she makes no mention of Xavier or any other principal. This contract cannot therefore be ratified by Xavier. So, it seems that Xavier can take over the contract to buy *The Floating Bridge*, but not the contract to sell. What about FineArt's attempt to withdraw, which comes before the ratification? This does not matter, because ratification is retrospective; it was so held in *Bolton Partners v Lambert* (1889), where it was said that the contract, once ratified, had to be treated as if it had been made with proper authority from the start. Similarly, in *Re Tiedemann and Ledermann Freres*, the third party had tried to withdraw on the basis of the false pretence about whom he was contracting with (which is similar to the situation here), but was prevented from doing so by the subsequent ratification of the contract.

Where does all this leave the various parties?[17]

Xavier has a contract to buy *The Floating Bridge* at £470,000, but no contract for resale. He may also be able to take action against Rosalind for her various breaches of duty.

Rosalind has a contract with Princeton Galleries to sell *The Floating Bridge* at £530,000. She will have difficulties fulfilling this contract, since *The Floating Bridge* now belongs to Xavier. She is also likely to face action by Xavier, as noted above.

FineArt is obliged to sell *The Floating Bridge* at £470,000 to Xavier, and seems to have no possibility of any action against anyone else. Xavier's ratification of Rosalind's actions prevents it from pursuing her. Princeton Galleries has a contract to purchase *The Floating Bridge* from Rosalind which, as we have noted, Rosalind will have difficulty fulfilling. It will

---

17 Finishing your essay with a conclusion ensures completeness of your analysis; this should summarise your findings in a clear and succinct manner. Don't introduce new arguments here.

be able to sue her for breach of contract. Finally, the best outcome for all concerned, apart from FineArt, might be for Xavier to get together with Princeton Galleries, and see if they can come to a similar arrangement to that negotiated by Rosalind.

QUESTION 28

Lillian, who owned a shop named 'Lillian Fruits and Flowers', sold the business earlier this year to Wilmslow, which appointed Lillian as manager and renamed the business 'Lillian Flower Specialists'. A sign was put up stating 'Under new management, part of the Wilmslow group'. Lillian knows that Wilmslow does not sell fruit at any of its business outlets.

Lillian, however, continues to sell at the shop fruit grown in her own garden. Robert, who bought some strawberries from her, is claiming that the fruit was infected, causing him severe stomach pains which prevented him from working for two weeks. Robert is an architect and lost the opportunity to bid for a lucrative contract during that period. He is threatening to sue Wilmslow.

Thomas, Lillian's former landlord, accepts five bouquets of flowers in part-settlement of Lillian's unpaid rent.

Lillian is persuaded by Joanna on one occasion to sell some fairy cakes which she has baked. Joanna gives Lillian £10 for doing this.

▶ **Advise Wilmslow.**

How to Answer this Question

Part of this question is concerned with the types of authority, in particular usual or apparent authority, and the extent to which a principal can be bound by contracts that the agent has made without authority. This relates to Lillian selling fruit and the fact that it is unclear whether Wilmslow had given her any instructions in this respect. If Robert does not have a claim against Wilmslow, Lillian may be personally liable (*The Swan* (1968)). The amount of damages Robert may recover will also need to be discussed.

As for Thomas, Lillian has used her position as manager to satisfy a personal debt. If Wilmslow sues Thomas for the value of the five bouquets of flowers, set-off may offer a partial defence to such a claim. This will depend on whether Wilmslow is held to be a disclosed or undisclosed principal.

In accepting £10 from Joanna, Lillian is in breach of one of her fiduciary duties, that is, the duty not to make a secret profit out of her position as agent. The consequences of such a breach need to be discussed.

Applying the Law

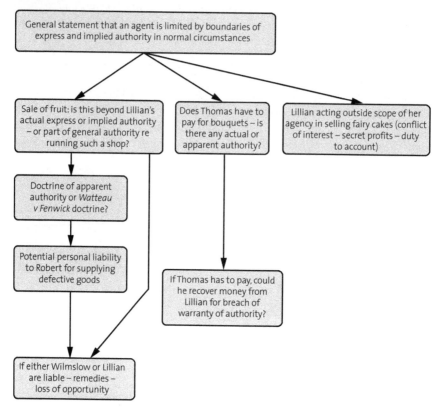

This diagram illustrates the progression of the main points that are covered in the answer.

ANSWER

This question concerns the issue of an agent's authority and, in particular, the extent to which a principal can be bound by contracts which the agent has made without authority.

As far as selling fruit is concerned, Wilmslow did not give any express instructions to Lillian. The general rule is that where an agent is expressly appointed, the scope of his authority depends on the construction of the agreement.[18] If the terms of the agreement are ambiguous, the court will generally construe them in a way which is most favourable to the agent as long as the agent construes his instructions reasonably (*Weigall v Runciman* (1916)). Therefore, it could be argued that Lillian was entitled to continue to sell fruit. The more likely view, however, is that Lillian should have known that Wilmslow would not permit the selling of fruit, partly because of the renaming of the business to 'Lillian Flower Specialists' with no mention of 'fruit', and partly because Lillian knew that Wilmslow did

---

18 Use the general rule as a starting point for your analysis, then proceed to more specific points; this helps to structure your answer in a logical manner.

not sell fruit at any of its outlets. Furthermore, it would be reasonable to expect Lillian, faced with an ambiguity in her agency agreement, to seek clarification from Wilmslow (*European Asian Bank v Punjab and Sind Bank (No 2)* (1983)). Therefore, not only did Lillian have no actual express authority to sell fruit, but it could be said that Lillian should have known of the restriction not to sell fruit.

However, if it is usual for a flower shop manager such as Lillian to have certain authority, then Wilmslow will be liable to a third party even if Lillian knows that she is prohibited or restricted from acting in the way she did unless the third party had notice of the limitation (see *Watteau v Fenwick* (1893)). This doctrine of usual authority, however, may only be relied on by a third party where the agent makes a contract within the scope of the usual authority of an agent in that position.[19] Wilmslow may rely on the fact that a business named 'Lillian Flower Specialists' does not imply that anything other than flowers would be sold in that shop, and a manager of such a shop would not have the authority to sell fruit. Wilmslow may thus escape liability on this basis.

The other possibility is that Robert could argue for the existence of apparent authority (also known as 'ostensible' authority or 'agency by estoppel'). From the decisions in *Rama Corp v Proved Tin and General Investment Ltd* (1952) and *Freeman and Lockyer v Buckhurst Park Properties (Mangal) Ltd* (1964), the factors that must be present to create apparent authority include a representation that the agent has authority, which must be made by the principal. Such a representation must have been relied on by the third party claiming apparent authority.

The essence of a principal's representation is that the agent is authorised to act on his behalf. It is an authority which 'apparently' exists, having regard to the conduct of the parties. The principal's representation need not depend on previous course of dealings, as in *Summers v Solomon* (1857), but could it be argued that simply by employing Lillian as the manager, Wilmslow is representing that Lillian has authority to do all the things that a flower shop manager would normally do, including selling fruit? The answer on the facts is likely to be in the negative, on the ground that a third party such as Robert would not expect the manager of a well-known flower shop chain to have the authority to sell anything but flowers. Since the sign that was put up clearly states that 'Lillian Flower Specialists' is part of the Wilmslow group, it is unreasonable for Robert to believe that he is dealing with a manager who possesses the necessary authority to sell fruit.

Robert does not seem to be on strong ground against Wilmslow. This does not mean, however, that Robert has no claim at all. Lillian may be personally liable to Robert if the intention was that Lillian should be personally liable. The intention is to be gathered from the nature and terms of the contract and the surrounding circumstances. An objective test is applied so that if Lillian sells strawberries to Robert in circumstances that make it reasonable to assume that Lillian was contracting personally, Robert will have an action against Lillian.

19 Showing an awareness of limitations to the rule is a good way to attract additional marks as it demonstrates knowledge.

In *The Swan* (1968), the defendant owned a boat called *The Swan* which was hired to a company of which he was a director. The company, on company notepaper, which was signed by the defendant as director of the company, instructed the claimant to repair the boat. The company could not pay, and the question was whether the defendant was personally liable on the contract to repair the boat. The court held that the defendant contracted as agent for the company, but since it was reasonable for the repairer, who knew that the defendant owned the boat, to assume that the owner would accept personal liability for such repair, the defendant was personally liable on the contract. Applying this case to the question, if Lillian sold the strawberries in such a way that Robert reasonably assumed that Lillian was selling in her personal capacity, then Lillian will be personally liable to Robert in damages.

If, as is more likely, Lillian is held not to have contracted personally but to have contracted as an agent, Lillian cannot be made personally liable on the contract. However, since Lillian had no authority to sell fruit, Lillian will be liable to Robert who has contracted with her on the faith of her representation of authority. The nature of her liability depends on whether Lillian had knowledge that she had no authority to sell fruit,[20] or whether she merely acted negligently or in good faith and under the honest but mistaken belief that she was contracting with Wilmslow's authority. The latter is the more likely, rendering Lillian liable to Robert for breach of the implied warranty of authority.

The amount of damages recoverable depends on the nature of the wrong committed. Essentially, the measure of damages will be either the loss that flowed directly as a natural or probable consequence, or the loss that was foreseeable by the parties as a probable consequence, of the breach of warranty. It seems, therefore, that Robert will be able to sue Lillian for damages. Whether or not Robert can recover for the lost opportunity to bid for the 'lucrative' contract will depend on whether this opportunity was made known to Lillian at the time the contract was made. This seems unlikely, in which event, Robert will not be able to recover damages on the basis that the damage was too remote (*Victoria Laundry (Windsor) Ltd v Newman Industries Ltd* (1949)).

As far as Thomas is concerned, can Wilmslow recover from Thomas the price for the bouquets of flowers?[21] The right of a third party to set off a liability against a principal will only apply where the principal has induced the third party to believe that the agent is acting as a principal and not as an agent, that is, where the principal is undisclosed. Did Thomas know of the existence of Wilmslow? Clearly, Thomas knew that Lillian had owned the business, but the question is really whether Thomas had actual notice[22] of the existence of Wilmslow. This will depend on whether Thomas noticed the sign which had been

---

20 In which event, Lillian acted fraudulently and will be liable in the tort of deceit (*Polhill v Walter* (1832)). This will be the case if Lillian knew Wilmslow's policy of restricting the types of goods sold at its outlets.

21 Don't miss out on marks by not discussing more minor issues raised by the question.

22 It is clear from *Greer v Downs Supply Co* (1927) that in respect of the existence of an undisclosed principal, the kind of notice that is required in order to be effective is actual notice, and constructive notice will be insufficient to affect the position of the third party.

put up – that the business was now part of the Wilmslow group. If Thomas had actual notice, then Thomas has no right of set-off and Wilmslow is entitled to recover the price of the bouquets of flowers from Thomas.

As far as accepting £10 for selling Joanna's fairy cakes is concerned, Lillian is in breach of one of her fiduciary duties, that is, the duty not to make a secret profit out of her position as agent.[23] Unless Lillian has revealed all the circumstances to Wilmslow and Wilmslow has consented to her retaining the profit, she will be liable to account to Wilmslow for the profit. If an agent takes a bribe, the principal is entitled to claim the amount of the bribe as money had and received (*Regier v Campbell-Stuart* (1939)).[24]

QUESTION 29

Edward, the owner of a shop selling antique British goods, has several red telephone boxes for sale. Edward is an eccentric and is well known for his dislike of Americans. Regan, an American, knows that Edward is unlikely to sell a telephone box to him and therefore asks his friend, Nancy, to visit Edward's shop and to purchase one of the telephone boxes on his behalf, promising to buy it from Nancy for 10% more than she paid for it. Nancy takes Edward out for lunch (the bill for which came to £30) and buys from him a telephone box for £300. She also agrees to buy an old chimney pot for £100. Regan is delighted with the telephone box and also wants to take up Nancy's offer to sell the chimney pot for £120. Edward learns of Nancy's association with Regan and purports to cancel both agreements.

▶ **Consider the rights and liabilities of all parties.**

How to Answer this Question

Part of this question is concerned with the problem of 'who is an agent?' It is not always easy to recognise an agent. It is the effect in *law* of the conduct of the parties that must be considered in order to determine whether the agency relationship has come into existence. This question requires you to analyse the nature of the relationship between Regan and Nancy, and to consider whether Nancy is acting as an agent or buying in her own name and reselling to Regan. If it is the latter, then the agreement is not one of agency (*Lamb v Goring Brick Co* (1932); *AMB Imballaggi Plastici SRL v Pacflex Ltd* (1999)).

If Nancy is an agent, she has acted on behalf of Regan in such a way that the agency is wholly undisclosed. Many of the cases dealing with the effects of undisclosed agency are old, but will need to be discussed. There is a general right for the undisclosed principal to intervene on and enforce the contract made on his behalf, but there are restrictions on that right, as in *Said v Butt* (1920).

---

23 The facts do not suggest that the £10 was a bribe. This type of secret profit is dealt with more severely, with the principal being entitled to summarily dismiss the agent and sue both the agent and the third party for any losses resulting.

24 Lillian holds the £10 on constructive trust (*Boardman v Phipps* (1966)). See also Question 23 on the duties owed by an agent.

Applying the Law

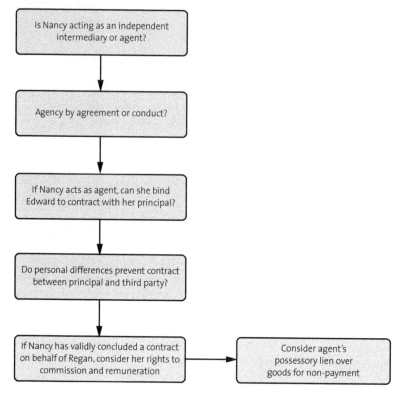

```
┌─────────────────────────────┐
│ Is Nancy acting as an       │
│ independent                 │
│ intermediary or agent?      │
└─────────────────────────────┘
              │
              ▼
┌─────────────────────────────┐
│ Agency by agreement or      │
│ conduct?                    │
└─────────────────────────────┘
              │
              ▼
┌─────────────────────────────┐
│ If Nancy acts as agent, can │
│ she bind Edward to contract │
│ with her principal?         │
└─────────────────────────────┘
              │
              ▼
┌─────────────────────────────┐
│ Do personal differences     │
│ prevent contract between    │
│ principal and third party?  │
└─────────────────────────────┘
              │
              ▼
┌─────────────────────────────┐      ┌─────────────────────┐
│ If Nancy has validly        │      │ Consider agent's    │
│ concluded a contract on     │─────▶│ possessory lien over│
│ behalf of Regan, consider   │      │ goods for non-      │
│ her rights to commission    │      │ payment             │
│ and remuneration            │      └─────────────────────┘
└─────────────────────────────┘
```

This diagram shows the progression of key points in the answer.

ANSWER

This question raises issues relating to the nature of the relationship between a principal and his agent, the concept of the undisclosed principal and the right of an agent to be remunerated and indemnified for expenses in the performance of an agency agreement. These will be looked at in turn in discussing the rights and liabilities of Regan, Nancy and Edward.[25]

Regan asks Nancy to buy a telephone box which Nancy does not own or possess at the time of the contract. It is a difficult question of fact whether this agreement between them involves Nancy as the 'seller' of goods acting for Regan as the 'buyer', or as an agent acting for Regan as the 'principal'.

If Nancy is held to be buying and reselling on her own account, then she is not a true agent in law (*Lamb v Goring Brick Company* (1932); *AMB Imballaggi Plastici SRL v Pacflex Ltd*

25 A good introduction clearly identifies those legal rules which are raised by the question; this ensures a logical structure to your answer right from the start and puts your examiner in a positive frame of mind.

(1999)). Accordingly, Edward would be in breach of his agreement if he were to refuse subsequently to sell the telephone box to her. If the opposite is true, that is, Nancy is procuring the telephone box for Regan as Regan's true agent and Nancy is authorised to create privity between Regan as principal and Edward as the third party, Regan may intervene and enforce the contract made on his behalf, subject to certain restrictions which will be discussed.

On the facts, it is likely that Nancy is acting as an agent. A particularly important factor in favour of this is the fact that Nancy's remuneration in carrying out Regan's instructions has been fixed at 10% of the purchase price. Further, Nancy's duty to buy a telephone box on Regan's behalf is not absolute, in the sense that she will not be liable to Regan if she does not obtain the telephone box: her duty is to use her care and skill as an agent to endeavour to obtain what Regan wants (*Anglo-African Shipping Co of New York Inc v J Mortner Ltd* (1962)).

The essence of an agency agreement is the agent's power to affect the principal's legal position vis-à-vis third parties. Nancy has been authorised by Regan to buy a telephone box, but does not reveal the fact of agency to Edward at all and purports to be acting on her own behalf. The general rule is that there is no need for an agent to identify his principal. Provided that an agent has his principal's actual authority for his actions, the undisclosed principal may enforce a contract made by his agent with a third party.[26] This rule may appear harsh, since its effect on this question is that Edward deals with Nancy in ignorance of the presence of an American being interested in the contract. The doctrine does, however, carry certain restrictions to protect the position of the third party and, in some cases, the undisclosed principal is entirely prohibited from intervening on the contract.[27]

In *Said v Butt* (1920), the principal was a theatre critic who had been banned from a particular theatre after he had written an unfavourable review on a previous occasion. He wanted to obtain a ticket for the opening night of a new play and, knowing that the theatre manager would not let him have one, employed an agent to obtain one for him. When he arrived at the theatre, he was refused entry. He then sued for breach of contract. The court held that he was not entitled to enforce the contract, on the basis that if the identity of the person with whom the third party is contracting is material to the making of the contract, the failure to disclose the fact that the agent is acting on behalf of a principal will deprive the principal of the right to sue on the contract. Applying this case to the question here, it would appear that Regan will not be able to sue Edward on the contract if Edward refuses to sell the telephone box. Certainly, courts are likely to favour the interpretation of the situation which best protects the third party where third-party rights in goods are in issue.

....

26 Similarly, the third party may enforce the contract made by an agent against his principal.

27 Proceeding from the general rule to any existing limitations is a good way to structure your answer in a logical manner; it also demonstrates your knowledge and understanding.

However, there have been criticisms of the decision in *Said v Butt* on the basis that personal dislike of the undisclosed principal should not normally prevent him intervening on a contract. In *Dyster v Randall & Sons* (1926), the agent, without revealing the fact that he was acting on behalf of a principal, entered into a contract for the purchase of land. The court held that the identity of the person contracting with the third party was not material and, therefore, a valid contract was made with the principal who could sue for specific performance. Again, in *Nash v Dix* (1898), although the third party would not have sold the property concerned to the undisclosed principal had he known of the identity of the principal, the court held that the identity of the contracting party was immaterial. Since Edward's objection to the contract for the sale of the telephone box is not based on a particular dislike of Regan, but on his dislike of Americans generally, this would not amount to personal reasons. Regan will be entitled to intervene on the contract and sue Edward for specific performance.

As far as the chimney pot is concerned, Regan will be able to enforce the contract on the basis that Nancy was not acting as his agent at the time of her agreement to purchase it from Edward (and is thus free to resell to whoever she wishes).[28]

We are also told that Nancy takes Edward out for lunch, presumably to conduct her negotiations for the purchase of the goods. The general rule is that all agents are entitled to be reimbursed expenses necessarily incurred in the course of performing their duties. This is so whether or not the agent is acting under a contract of agency. Nancy thus has the right to be indemnified for the expenses of lunch, such expenses having been incurred while acting within her actual authority to persuade Edward to sell goods to her on Regan's behalf.

If Nancy has taken possession of the goods, she is entitled to protect her rights to remuneration and indemnity by retaining the telephone box and the chimney pot until the amounts outstanding relating to the goods are discharged.[29]

To summarise the positions of the parties: Edward has a contract with Regan to sell him the telephone box and a contract with Nancy to sell her the chimney pot. If Edward cancels either contract, he will be liable to damages to Regan and Nancy, respectively. Nancy is entitled to her 10% commission vis-à-vis the telephone box, has agreed to resell the chimney pot to Regan for a profit of £20 and has a lien over the goods in her possession until she is paid. Nancy is further entitled to be indemnified for the cost of lunch.[30]

....

28 Ratification does not apply here, since one of the requirements is that an agent must purport to act for the principal at the time the contract was made (*Keighley Maxsted and Co v Durant* (1901)). We are told that Nancy did not disclose the agency at the time she agreed to buy the goods from Edward.
29 Nancy is entitled to a particular lien, that is, she may retain Regan's property in her possession until debts relating to that property are discharged (cf a general lien exercised by certain types of agents, for example, bankers and solicitors).
30 Ending your answer with a conclusion, that is, a summary of the results of your analysis, ensures that you present a complete picture to the examiner.

Aim Higher

Before discussing the issues identified, a good answer needs to consider the question of whether Nancy is in fact an agent or just a reseller.

QUESTION 30

In January, Pedro appoints Karen as the manager of his restaurant. He tells her not to buy dairy products from a new company, Celebrate & Co, because he has heard that its products are of poor quality. In February, Barnaby, a representative of Celebrate & Co, visits the restaurant and as a result, Karen orders £100 worth of dairy products. Barnaby is unaware of Pedro's instructions to Karen. When, later in the day, Pedro discovers what Karen has done, they have an argument and Karen resigns. The following day, Karen goes to Magestic Ltd, Pedro's regular supplier of wines and spirits, and purchases three cases of whisky on credit in Pedro's name. She then absconds with the whisky.

▶ **Advise Pedro as to his liability to Celebrate & Co and Magestic Ltd.**

How to Answer this Question

This question is concerned with the issue of an agent's authority, and in particular the extent to which a principal can be bound by contracts which the agent has made without authority.

The two contracts concerned here raise different points, though there is some possibility of overlap. In relation to the contract with Celebrate & Co, there is the possibility of Pedro being liable on the basis of 'usual' authority, as in *Watteau v Fenwick* (1893). This will involve looking at what is the usual authority of a restaurant manager.

The contract with Magestic Ltd, on the other hand, will only be binding on Pedro if Karen can be said to have 'apparent' authority. This is sometimes referred to as 'ostensible' authority or 'agency by estoppel'. It involves the principal having made a representation of the agent's authority which is then acted on by the third party. *Freeman and Lockyer v Buckhurst Park Properties (Mangal) Ltd* (1964), which is one of the leading authorities on this area, will need discussion, though the case of *Summers v Solomon* (1857) is closer to the facts in the problem.

The overlap arises from the fact that it might also be possible to treat the contract with Celebrate as being binding on the basis of apparent authority, if it can be established that there was some representation of authority by Pedro on which Celebrate could rely.

Applying the Law

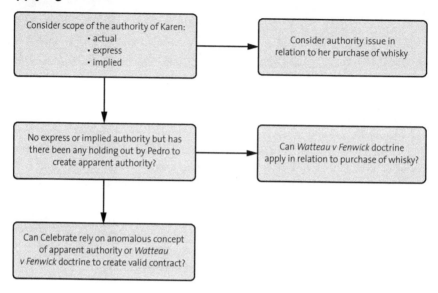

This diagram shows the progression of key points in the answer.

ANSWER ---

An agent frequently has the power to make contracts which are binding on his principal. Problems arise, however, where the agent exceeds the authority given. In what circumstances can the principal still be liable? There are two main ways. First, if it is customary for an agent of a particular type to have certain authority, then restrictions on that authority will be ineffective unless the third party knows about them. This is also referred to as 'usual' authority, or sometimes 'implied' authority.[31] An example of this type of authority which will be discussed below is the case of *Watteau v Fenwick* (1893). The second type of extended authority that we will need to consider is 'apparent' authority, which arises where the principal has made some representation of the agent's authority on which the third party has relied.[32] An example of this is the case of *Freeman and Lockyer v Buckhurst Park Properties (Mangal) Ltd* (1964). We will need to examine whether either type of authority will lead to Pedro being bound to either of the two contracts made by Karen.

In relation to the contract with Celebrate & Co, the most obvious type of authority to consider is usual authority. In *Watteau v Fenwick* (1893), the defendants owned a public house

....

31 Though it is probably preferable to restrict 'implied' authority to filling out the relationship between principal and agent, as in *Waugh v Clifford* (1982), rather than as indicating the extent to which the agent may bind the principal to a third party despite a clear breach of the authority given by the principal.

32 Pointing out that you are going to discuss/analyse something at a later stage in your answer is a good idea for two reasons: first, it gives you more time to focus on the relevant issues rather than having to constantly repeat yourself and thus wasting valuable time; second, it also enhances the readability of your argument and shows a certain degree of planning ahead on your part.

which was managed by a man named Humble.[33] Humble was under instructions not to buy cigars for the business from anyone other than the defendants. In breach of this instruction, Humble bought cigars on credit from the claimant. At the time of the contract, the claimant thought that Humble was the owner of the public house. When he discovered the truth, however, he sought payment from the defendants. The defendants resisted on the basis that Humble had no authority to bind them to this contract. On the contrary, he was acting in breach of express instructions not to act in this way. The court nevertheless found the defendants liable. They said that it was within the usual authority of the manager of a public house to be able to buy cigars from any source. The fact that Humble had been instructed not to do so was irrelevant, since the claimant was unaware of this restriction. He was entitled to rely on Humble's usual authority, and thus the defendants were obliged to pay for the cigars. The issue of what constitutes usual authority is a question of fact, which will have to be decided in each case. The decision in *Watteau v Fenwick* can, for example, be contrasted with the earlier case of *Daun v Simmins* (1879), where it was held that where a public house was 'tied' to a particular brewer, the third party should have realised that the freedom of the manager to purchase would be restricted.

Watteau v Fenwick has been the subject of considerable criticism, in that it applied this approach to a situation where the third party was unaware that he was dealing with an agent. This, however, does not detract from the general principle. Even if it only applies where the principal is disclosed, it is still a type of authority that can bind the principal even where the agent has exceeded his actual authority.

Applying this to the problem, we find that Karen, the manager of a restaurant, has, like Humble in *Watteau v Fenwick*, failed to follow an express limitation on the contracts she is entitled to make. It is not clear whether Barnaby knew that he was dealing with an agent. If he did not, it is possible that the court would refuse to apply *Watteau v Fenwick* on the basis that, despite what happened in the case itself, the concept of usual authority should not be applied to situations involving an undisclosed principal. It seems more likely, however, that Barnaby would have realised that he was dealing with a manager rather than the owner of the restaurant. In that case, the next issue to decide concerns the limits of the usual authority of the manager of a restaurant.

As indicated above, this is a question of fact, not of law. In other words, it would be necessary to look at evidence as to what was normally accepted as being within the scope of the authority of someone like Karen. If it was found that such managers usually had authority to purchase goods from suppliers chosen at their own discretion, then Pedro is likely to be liable for this contract. If the opposite is found, or if it is not possible to determine any particular usual authority for such managers, then Celebrate will probably have to pursue Karen rather than Pedro. The only other possibility is if Celebrate could argue for the existence of apparent authority. Consideration of this point, however, will be left until after the discussion of the position as regards Magestic Ltd.

---

33 Humble had in fact previously been the owner of the public house.

In respect of the contract for the whisky, there is no possibility of using usual authority, because Karen is no longer an agent when she makes the contract. The only possibility here will be for Magestic to argue that Karen had apparent authority to make this contract (the phrases 'ostensible authority' and 'agency by estoppel' are also used to describe this concept). As defined by Diplock, LJ in *Freeman and Lockyer v Buckhurst Park Properties (Mangal) Ltd* (1964), this requires a representation by the principal[34] intended to be acted on by the third party, and in fact acted on, that the agent does have authority to make the contract.[35] The representation need not be in the form of words: conduct will be sufficient. In *Freeman and Lockyer v Buckhurst*, a person had been allowed to act as managing director of a company by the other directors, although he had never been appointed as such in the manner required by the company's Articles of Association. It was held that the directors' actions in allowing him to act in this way amounted to a representation to the outside world that he had authority to do so. The company was therefore bound by his actions. The case which is closest to the facts of the problem, however, is *Summers v Solomon* (1857). Solomon owned a jeweller's shop and employed a manager to run it. Solomon regularly paid for jewellery that had been ordered by the manager from Summers. After the manager had left Solomon's employment, he ordered jewellery in Solomon's name from Summers and then absconded with it. It was held that Solomon was bound to pay for the jewellery. His previous conduct in paying for the jewellery had amounted to a representation of the manager's authority. That representation had not been contradicted or withdrawn, and so Summers was still entitled to rely on it.

At first sight, this decision would mean that Pedro will have to pay Magestic for the whisky. There are, however, two questions that need to be asked. We are told that Magestic is Pedro's regular supplier. What we do not know, however, is what the usual ordering procedures were. In particular, was it usual for goods to be ordered on credit? If so, did Karen follow the usual procedures in placing this order and immediately taking the goods away? If the answer to either of these questions is no, Pedro may escape liability. If it was not usual for goods to be ordered on credit, then there is less in the way of a representation of authority for what Karen has done in this case. Second, if Karen has not followed the normal procedures, should Magestic not have been put on notice that something unusual was happening, and therefore made some attempt to confirm that Karen was acting with authority? If, however, these issues are not resolved in Pedro's favour, then it seems certain that he will be bound by Karen's apparent authority and will have to pay for the whisky.

The final point to consider is whether the contract with Celebrate could fall under the heading of apparent authority as well. The problem here is that of finding a representation.

....

34 It was confirmed in *Armagas v Mundogas* (1986) that the representation must be by the principal. A representation by the agent will not be sufficient. But cf *First Energy (UK) Ltd v Hungarian International Bank* (1993), discussed in Question 31.

35 Note also *Rama Corp Ltd v Proved Tin and General Investment* (1952), where Slade J identified the need for: (i) a representation; (ii) reliance on the representation by the third party; (iii) an alteration of position resulting from such reliance.

We are told that Celebrate is a new company, and therefore there will have been no previous dealings. It might be argued, however, that simply by employing Karen as a manager, Pedro is representing that she has authority to do all the things that a restaurant manager would normally do, including, perhaps, making contracts to buy dairy products. This was the approach adopted in *United Bank of Kuwait v Hamoud; City Trust v Levy* (1988), where it was held that a firm that employed X as a solicitor was representing to the world that X had authority to engage in all transactions on the firm's behalf which came within the normal scope of a solicitor's responsibilities.[36] If this was followed here, it would be another argument for making Pedro responsible for Karen's contract with Celebrate.

The advice to Pedro in relation to these two contracts must be that he is on fairly weak ground. The doctrines of usual and apparent authority taken together mean that it is very likely that he will have to meet the obligations under the contracts with both Celebrate & Co and Magestic Ltd. His only remedy then will be to try to trace Karen, and attempt to recover his losses from her.

Common Pitfalls

If the difference between usual authority and apparent authority is not appreciated, it is impossible to answer this question correctly or to put forward a sensible argument for or against usual authority.

QUESTION 31

In October 2015, Greene approached Elizabeth, New Business Manager of Experian Bank plc, seeking a loan of £200,000 to start up a business selling sportswear. Elizabeth told Greene that approval was needed from Head Office for loans over £100,000. She sought approval for him, but Greene's application was rejected.

In January 2016, Greene, together with his wife, Anne, again approach Elizabeth, this time seeking a loan of £150,000 to set up an Internet business selling sportswear. On 10 January 2016, Greene and Anne receive a letter from Elizabeth, addressed to them both, stating 'I am pleased to inform you that your loan can proceed' and asking them to call in to deal with the paperwork. In fact, the papers are made out in Greene's name alone, since the loan is secured on property which is in his sole ownership. Anne resigns from her well-paid job as a lawyer so that she can devote her time to the new business.

Before the money is paid, however, Experian Bank informs Greene that Elizabeth has agreed the loan without authorisation. Although they have in the recent past ratified

---

36 Cf also *Gurtner v Beaton* (1993). This approach if used widely would, of course, render the concept of usual authority virtually redundant.

some loans of more than £100,000 arranged by Elizabeth without authorisation, in this case they are not prepared to do so because of the risks involved in Internet businesses.

▶ **Advise Greene and Anne.**

How to Answer this Question

There are two main issues to discuss in this question:

❖   Did Elizabeth have apparent authority to make the loan to Greene?
❖   If she did not, what remedies might Greene and Anne have against Elizabeth?

The first issue requires consideration of whether any representation has been made by Experian Bank plc to Greene as to Elizabeth's authority, as required by *Freeman and Lockyer v Buckhurst Park Properties (Mangal) Ltd* (1964) and *Armagas v Mundogas* (1986). The case of *First Energy (UK) Ltd v Hungarian International Bank Ltd* (1993) on the extent to which an agent can represent his own authority will also need to be considered.

As regards the second issue, since there is no basis for making Elizabeth liable on the loan contract, this will involve consideration of the remedies available against her in tort, or for breach of the implied warranty of authority. As far as Anne's reliance on the implied warranty is concerned, the effect of the decision in *Penn v Bristol and West Building Society* (1997) will need to be considered.

Applying the Law

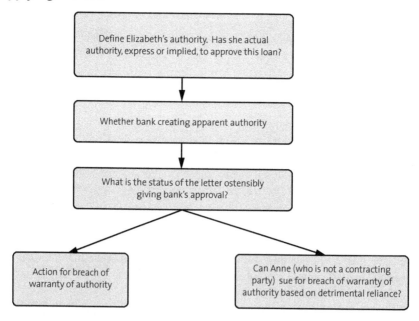

This diagram shows the progression of the key points in this answer.

ANSWER

This question concerns the extent to which agents may bind their principals even when acting outside their actual authority. It also raises the question of what remedies a third party will have if the agent has acted without authority, and this has led to loss.

The best outcome for Greene and Anne in this situation would be for it to be found that Experian Bank plc was obliged to make Greene the loan for the business, despite the fact that Elizabeth had not sought approval for it. If that is not possible, however, they may well wish to seek a remedy against Elizabeth personally.

There is no doubt that Elizabeth has acted beyond her actual authority in arranging the loan to Greene. She did not have authority to approve loans of over £100,000, and Greene was aware of this as a result of their previous dealings. Although Experian Bank has ratified some loans of over £100,000 made recently by Elizabeth, there is no suggestion that her actual authority has changed. Experian Bank is not obliged to ratify any contract, and is quite entitled to 'pick and choose' which ones it is prepared to accept. The fact that it does not wish to become involved in Greene's Internet business is therefore a decision which it is free to take.

Greene may argue, however, that Elizabeth has bound Experian Bank to the loan agreement on the basis of apparent authority. The requirements for apparent authority were established by *Freeman and Lockyer v Buckhurst Park Properties (Mangal) Ltd* (1964). There must be a representation (by words or conduct) from the principal to the third party, which is relied on by the third party and which leads to an alteration of position by the third party.[37] There is no doubt here that Greene has relied on an assumption that Elizabeth had authority, and changed his position by entering into the loan contract. The more difficult question is whether the assumption has been created by any representation from Experian Bank to him. In some situations, it can be argued that by placing a person in a particular position (for example, New Business Manager) this in itself amounts to a representation of authority or, alternatively, that agents in such a position might be argued to have the 'usual' authority attaching to that position. That cannot apply here, however, since Greene is aware of the limitation on Elizabeth's authority as a result of their dealings in October 2015. Nor can it be said that the ratification by Experian Bank of other loans of over £100,000 amounts to a representation, since there is no evidence that Greene is aware of these.

Could it be argued that the letter that Elizabeth wrote to Greene is a representation that she has authority to agree the loan? It may well have this implication, but the problem is that it emanates from Elizabeth, rather than from Experian Bank. In *Armagas v Mundogas* (1986), the House of Lords emphasised that, for apparent authority to exist, the representation must come from the principal, not from the agent. In this case, the finance

---

37 Dissecting the relevant legal principle into its constituent parts and considering these parts on a point-by-point basis ensures that your answer is structured logically.

manager of a company had indicated that he had authority to agree a deal for the sale and charter-back of a ship. His plan was to make a secret profit out of the transactions. When his deceit came to light, the third party argued that the shipowners were bound by the agent's apparent authority. The House of Lords disagreed, holding that there was no representation of authority from the principal as opposed to the agent, and that therefore apparent authority could not arise.

This case would suggest that Greene will not be able to rely on apparent authority, since he has only had dealings with Elizabeth, and there has been no direct representation from Experian Bank. The subsequent decision of the Court of Appeal in *First Energy (UK) Ltd v Hungarian International Bank Ltd* (1993) must, however, also be considered. The facts of this case bear some similarity to those of the problem. A senior branch manager of a bank had, in contravention of limitations on his actual authority, agreed arrangements with a third party for the provision of credit facilities to customers of the third party's business. The third party knew that the senior manager had no personal authority to enter into such arrangements on behalf of his principal, but assumed from a letter written by the senior manager that the appropriate approvals had been obtained. Although this appeared to amount to a representation by the agent, and therefore to fall foul of the decision in *Armagas v Mundogas*, the Court of Appeal felt able to distinguish the earlier case. It held that an agent who does not have apparent authority to enter into a particular transaction may nevertheless have apparent authority to communicate to a third party that such a transaction has been approved. Part of the reason for this was a feeling that it would be unreasonable to expect a third party to have to check in such situations whether the Board, or whatever other body within the principal company was appropriate, had in fact given approval to the transaction. It may well be, therefore, that it would be held here that Elizabeth did have apparent authority to communicate to Greene that the necessary approval for his loan had been obtained. If that is the case, then Greene will be able to insist that the loan goes ahead, or claim compensation if it does not.[38]

What is the position, on the other hand, if the strict requirements as laid down in *Armagas v Mundogas* are held to apply in this situation, so that Elizabeth did not have apparent authority, even to the limited extent found to exist in *First Energy (UK) Ltd v Hungarian International Bank Ltd* (1993)? Greene will then have to seek a remedy from Elizabeth herself. This is not a situation where Elizabeth would be liable for the loan contract itself. Greene will rather be looking for compensation for any losses he may have suffered. There are two ways in which this might be possible.[39] First, there is the possibility of an action in tort for deceit or negligent misstatement under the *Hedley Byrne v Heller* (1964) principle. If Elizabeth is found to have made a statement as to the fact that the transaction had been authorised, which she knew was false, or which she made without proper care, this could give an action for damages.

----

38 Drawing an interim conclusion is another way of signposting the relevant issues and also helps you to structure your answer logically.

39 The consideration of more than one possible legal argument or an opposing view demonstrates wider knowledge and deeper understanding.

Alternatively, and this is particularly applicable if Elizabeth's misrepresentation was innocent (that is, neither deliberately deceitful nor negligent), Greene may be able to sue for breach of the implied warranty of authority which is held to be given by agents (see, for example, *Collen v Wright* (1857)). This may enable him to recover all losses which have resulted from the fact that Elizabeth was in fact acting without authority.[40] It is possible to obtain either expectation or reliance damages under this action.

Finally, what is Anne's position? She was not a party to the purported contract with Experian Bank, but this does not necessarily mean that she would have no action against Elizabeth. In reliance on Elizabeth's letter, she has given up her job, and can therefore claim to have suffered loss. It is clear that she could bring an action in deceit, if it is clear that Elizabeth's misrepresentation was made to her and she acted on it. Similarly, an action for negligent misstatement would also be possible, provided that Anne could be said to be owed a duty of care by Elizabeth. This would not seem to be too difficult on the facts. Elizabeth's letter was addressed to both Greene and Anne; Anne was therefore within the group whom Elizabeth could have expected to rely on the statements in the letter. The type of action she took (giving up her job) was reasonably foreseeable, and she could therefore claim for damages consequent upon this.

What about a claim under the breach of the implied warranty of authority? It might be thought that this would not be applicable, since Elizabeth was not in the end someone whom Anne was purporting to bring into a contractual relationship with her principal. The decision in *Penn v Bristol and West Building Society* (1997), however, suggests that this may not be an obstacle. In this case, a solicitor agent's innocent misrepresentation of authority to a building society was held to give rise to liability for breach of the implied warranty, even though the building society's loss resulted not from attempting to contract with the solicitor's principal, but from lending money to someone who was entering into such a contract. It was held to be sufficient that the representation of authority had been made to the building society and that it had acted on it to its detriment. Applying that to the situation in the problem, the representation of authority was clearly made to Anne, and she has acted on it to her detriment by giving up her job. On this basis, Anne, like Greene, could also seek damages for breach of the implied warranty from Elizabeth.

In conclusion, therefore, it seems that either Elizabeth will be found to have apparent authority, so that the loan agreement with Experian Bank will be enforceable or, if she did not have such authority, both Greene and Anne will be able to recover compensation from her on the basis of an action in tort or for breach of the implied warranty of authority.

....

40 The existence of the warranty does not depend on the agent's awareness of the lack of authority. This was established in *Collen v Wright* (1857) and taken to its logical extreme in *Yonge v Toynbee* (1910). In the latter case, the warranty was held to operate against a solicitor who had continued to act for a client who, unknown to the solicitor, had become mentally incapacitated (which had the automatic effect of terminating the solicitor's authority). The fact that the solicitor had acted in good faith throughout was regarded as irrelevant.

11

Fob Contracts

INTRODUCTION

The central feature of an fob (free on board) contract is that the seller fulfils his obligations when he delivers goods conforming to the contract on board the ship. He must bear all the costs up to that point. Although he is not under a duty to insure the goods once he has delivered them, the seller is under a statutory duty to give notice to the buyer so that the buyer has an opportunity to insure. Examiners often set questions dealing with this duty under **s 32(3)** of the **Sale of Goods Act 1979**.

The primary duty of the fob buyer is to nominate an effective ship to carry the goods. Unless and until he does so, the seller is not obliged to deliver the goods. Examination questions often involve the buyer's inability to nominate an effective ship and the related problem of where there is a delay in the arrival of a ship which the buyer has nominated to carry the goods.

Questions on international sale of goods contracts invariably involve the financing arrangements between the parties, and the rules in relation to documentary credits are important. It should be remembered that the buyer in such transactions has two distinct rights of rejection: first, the right to reject documents arises when the documents are tendered; and, second, the right to reject the goods arises when they are landed and when, after examination, they are not found to be in conformity with the contract.

This chapter deals mainly with fob contracts, although it is usual to have parts of questions involving other types of international sale contracts (**Questions 34, 37** and **38**, for instance, deals with both an fob as well as a cif contract).

Chapter 12 deals mainly with cif contracts.

The following topics should be prepared in advance of tackling the questions:

❖ the duties of the parties to an fob contract;
❖ the requirements of proper shipping documents;
❖ the strict rules in relation to documentary finance.

QUESTION 32

Aurelia enters into three separate contracts for the sale of 4,000 tons of pinto beans to Augustus, 5,000 tons of kidney beans to Marcus and 1,500 tons of mung beans to Caesar.

Each contract calls for shipment in May, fob Southampton, and contains a clause permitting the buyer, on giving reasonable notice, to call for delivery at any time within the shipment period.

On 5 May, Augustus informs Aurelia that he has nominated *The Cavalry* to take delivery of the consignment, ready to load on 11 May. Aurelia protests at the length of notice, and since she is not able to have the consignment packed in time, she purchases 4,000 tons of already-packed pinto beans from a third party at 5% above the normal market price. Aurelia is able to send the pinto beans to the docks at Southampton on 11 May. *The Cavalry* is not ready to load and Augustus nominates *The Commius* to take the consignment on 28 May. By this time, the pinto beans have deteriorated due to rain seeping through the packaging. Augustus refuses to load the consignment.

On 8 May, Marcus nominates *The Gaul* and asks Aurelia to have the consignment ready to load on 20 May. The general market price of kidney beans has unexpectedly dropped by half since the contract was made. Owing to a strike at the farm, Aurelia is not able to send the kidney beans to the docks at Southampton until 23 May, and Marcus uses this as a reason for refusing to load the consignment.

On 25 May, Caesar informs Aurelia that *The Eurymedon* will be ready to load on 30 May. When Aurelia tries to load the goods, she is informed that recent regulations require an export licence for the supply of mung beans in excess of 1,000 tons. Caesar refuses to accept a smaller quantity when asked by Aurelia.

The contracts are governed by English law.
▶ **Advise Aurelia.**

How to Answer this Question
This question requires a review of the duties of both parties to an fob contract. In particular, the part of the question regarding the pinto beans involves the buyer's duty to nominate an effective ship and the seller's duty to ensure compliance with the implied terms as to quality under the **Sale of Goods Act 1979**. The situation with the kidney beans concerns a seller's failure to load within time.

The part of the question dealing with the mung beans is a little unusual, since it involves a partial prohibition on the export of goods imposed *after* the contract of sale was concluded. The issue is whether the contract is brought to an end because of frustration or whether the contract subsists for that part of the contract where performance was possible. Please note that frustration and prohibition of export have separate origins and consequences.

Since there are three parts to the question, the amount of detail required will be restricted to the time available for answering all the parts.

Applying the Law

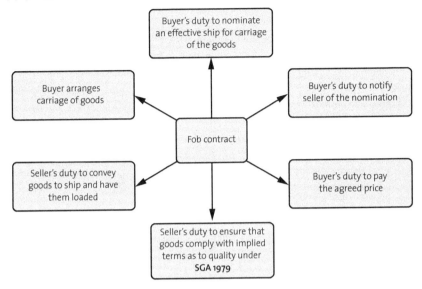

This diagram shows the main factors to consider in relation to fob obligations when writing your answer. It will also be important to consider definitions and how the specific circumstances of this scenario affect the contract.

ANSWER

In the absence of further information regarding express terms in the contract, the basic duties of the parties depend on commercial practice as recognised by English law. Under a 'classic' fob contract, the primary duties of the buyer are to nominate an effective ship to carry the goods, to notify the seller of such nomination in time for him to load the goods and to pay the agreed price (*Pyrene & Co v Scindia Navigation Co Ltd* (1954); *The El Amria and El Minia* (1982)). Once the buyer has nominated a ship, the seller is required to deliver goods which comply with the terms of the contract to the port in time for loading to take place during the contract period.

PINTO BEANS

Augustus informs Aurelia on 5 May that *The Cavalry* has been nominated to take delivery of the consignment on 11 May. Although Aurelia protests at the short notice, this is normally irrelevant since the buyer in an fob contract has the option of when to ship during the contract period. More particularly, there is an express term in the contract allowing the buyer to call for delivery at any time. It is clear, however, that if the buyer nominates a ship in such a way that the seller is not given reasonable time to have the goods ready for loading, the seller is entitled to claim damages[1] for the failure

---

1   The seller cannot claim the purchase price if the goods have not been shipped, even if non-shipment is the result of the buyer's failure to give effective shipment instruction: *Colley v Overseas Exporters* (1921).

of the buyer to nominate a suitable ship. The question of whether Augustus has given Aurelia adequate notice is one of fact.

In an fob contract, the timing of the nomination of an effective ship is normally of the essence, that is, it is a condition of the contract. If Augustus' notice of nomination is unreasonable, Aurelia is entitled to treat the contract as repudiated and will be entitled to damages (*Bunge & Co Ltd v Tradax England Ltd* (1975)).[2] However, by delivering to the docks on 11 May, Aurelia has probably waived her right to treat the contract as repudiated.

Aurelia has had to purchase the pinto beans at 5% above the normal market price. This additional cost cannot be recovered from Augustus since, under a 'classic' fob contract, the seller is responsible for all the expenses of getting the goods over the ship's rail (*AG v Leopold Walford (London) Ltd* (1923)).

Augustus subsequently nominates *The Commius*. A buyer is entitled to substitute a fresh nomination provided there is time to do so in accordance with the contract. Augustus' first nomination is not irrevocable (*Agricultores Federados Argentinos v Ampro SA* (1965)). Thus, Augustus is entitled to nominate a second ship.

The pinto beans deteriorate before loading and Augustus refuses to load the consignment on this basis. The implied terms as to satisfactory quality and as to fitness for a particular purpose under **ss14(2)** and **(3)** of the **Sale of Goods Act 1979** apply to an fob contract, and breach of either term may entitle the buyer to reject the goods and claim damages, provided the breach is not so slight that it would be unreasonable for him to reject the goods (**s15A** of the **Sale of Goods Act 1979**).[3] Since the seller is responsible for the goods prior to loading, it appears that Augustus is *prima facie* entitled to refuse to accept delivery of the defective pinto beans on 28 May.

If the pinto beans deteriorate due to unsuitable packaging, this would amount to a breach of **s14(3)**. Where the seller knows that goods are to be shipped, he is under an obligation to ensure that the goods are packaged in such a way that they can endure the sea transit (*Wills v Brown* (1922)). It seems, therefore, that Augustus may be able to reject the pinto beans and will be entitled to recover damages for non-delivery from Aurelia.[4]

KIDNEY BEANS

Aurelia is not able to send the consignment of kidney beans to the docks until three days after *The Gaul* is ready to load. In a 'classic' fob contract, it is the buyer who has the option of when to ship within the contract period (*Bowes v Shand* (1877)) and, once shipping instructions have been received, the seller must load within a reasonable time. It seems

---

2   The measure of damages will be that set out under **s50(3)** of the **Sale of Goods Act 1979** for non-acceptance.

3   Damages will be for non-delivery of goods under **s51(3)** of the **Sale of Goods Act 1979**.

4   If the question had not included a reason for the goods deteriorating, the issue would be whether a seller can recover damages for losses incurred because the buyer substitutes another ship (see *J&J Cunningham v Monroe* (1922), in particular Lord Heward's comments).

that 12 days' notice is reasonable in this question, since we are told that the delay in sending the kidney beans to the docks was due to a strike at the farm. A failure to load on 20 May is a breach of a condition of the contract and is a ground for rejection (*The Mihalis Angelos* (1971)), because time is of the essence in commercial contracts.

Marcus could have chosen to affirm the contract and claim damages for the loss occasioned by the delay but, due to the drop in the market price of kidney beans, it seems more likely that Marcus will wish to reject the goods.[5] He will also have a claim against Aurelia in damages for non-delivery.

MUNG BEANS

As for the consignment of mung beans, we are told that Aurelia is only aware of the recent prohibition on the export of such goods without a licence when she tries to load the goods on 30 May. It appears that the prohibition was imposed after the conclusion of the contract. Such a prohibition does not make the contract illegal *ab initio*, but may discharge it under the doctrine of frustration. Since the contract specifically provides that the mung beans are to be exported from Southampton (and within the country which is imposing the prohibition), the contract between Aurelia and Caesar may be frustrated (*Tsakiroglou v Noblee Thorl* (1962)). However, where the prohibition is qualified, as in this question (making a previously unrestricted export of goods subject to a licensing requirement), the contract is not automatically discharged. The court may decide to impose a duty on one of the parties to make reasonable efforts to obtain the licence. In the absence of an express provision as to licence, there is no general rule putting the burden of obtaining a licence on one party or another, and each case would depend on the facts.[6] *Pagnan SpA v Tradax Ocean Transportation* (1986) provided that in such cases, the court will ask itself whether the duty imposed on the seller to obtain a licence is absolute or is only to use due diligence. If the duty is to be imposed on Aurelia, then Aurelia will only be able to rely on the prohibition as a ground of discharge if she can show that reasonable efforts to procure the licence would have failed. Certainly, Aurelia only knew of the prohibition on 30 May, giving her only 24 hours to obtain the licence before the end of the shipment period.

The prohibition, however, is only partial, in that the regulations merely restrict the amount of mung beans a seller is allowed to export without a licence to 1,000 tons. In the circumstances, although in the normal course of events a buyer is not obliged to accept a smaller quantity of goods than that contracted for, the contract is not discharged but the prohibition may excuse partial performance. Aurelia must supply 1,000 tons of mung

....

5 Explaining why a course of action might be preferable will attract additional marks.

6 See *Brandt & Co v Morris & Co* (1917) (where the court held that the buyers were obliged to obtain the export licence on the basis that a ship which could not legally carry goods was not an effective ship) and *Pound & Co Ltd v Hardy & Co Inc* (1956) (where the court found that the sellers were obliged to obtain the export licence since the licence could only be obtained by persons registered in the exporting country and, as between the parties, it was the sellers who were registered).

beans but is excused from supplying the remaining 500 tons.[7] If Caesar refuses to accept delivery of 1,000 tons of mung beans, Aurelia will be entitled to recover damages under **s 50(3)** of the **Sale of Goods Act 1979**.

Common Pitfalls

Where a question involves various issues, do not waste time by writing out the facts of the question.

QUESTION 33

Bridget agrees to sell to Gwen in Bristol 1,000 kilograms of anchovies packed in boxes, 25 kilograms in each box, fob Hamburg, payment by letter of credit on tender of documents to Birken Bank. The contract called for October shipment. On 3 October, Gwen nominates *The Enterprise* to take the goods and Bridget arranges for the consignment to arrive at the docks shortly afterwards. Gwen had not booked shipping space on *The Enterprise* but Bridget finally manages to persuade the master to take the goods on 31 October. The following day, a fire breaks out on *The Enterprise* and the boxes containing the anchovies are wetted while the fire is being extinguished. The boxes are unloaded and repacked in boxes of 50 kilograms. They are reloaded on 2 November. The master of the ship issues a bill of lading for '20 x 50 kilograms anchovies shipped on 31 October'.

When Bridget presents the documents to Birken Bank, she is refused payment on the ground that the bill of lading shows incorrect packaging. Bridget takes the bill of lading back to the master of *The Enterprise*, who agrees to have the anchovies repacked on the voyage and issues a fresh bill of 40 boxes of 25 kilograms of anchovies.

When the boxes arrive in Bristol, Gwen discovers that the anchovies had been infected with fungus, causing the anchovies to deteriorate.

▶ Advise the parties.

How to Answer this Question

Although Gwen nominates a ship, she has not booked shipping space. This is not a fundamental breach of the contract, since Bridget does manage to load the goods on the ship nominated by Gwen. The problem is that the goods are damaged and then unloaded and the question of risk will need to be addressed.

Shipping documents have always played a key role in international sale contracts and the second part of this question requires you to discuss whether the bank may refuse to pay against documents which indicate incorrect packaging. The issue of packaging falls squarely within the implied term as to description under **s 13** of the **Sale of Goods Act 1979**. Because the anchovies deteriorate, **s 14** of that Act will also need to be discussed.

---

7 The effect of the partial prohibition is the same as that of physical impossibility caused by the failure of a specified crop.

Applying the Law

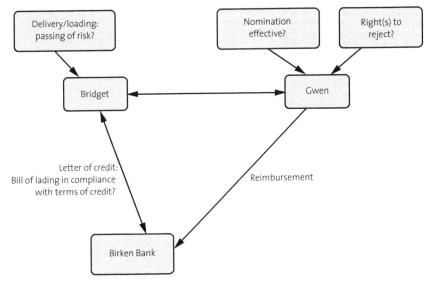

This diagram focuses on the parties involved in this scenario and the relationship between them. As well as issues of compliant and non-compliant documents the rights of rejection in relation to documents and goods must be dealt with separately.

ANSWER

In the absence of further information about the express terms, the contract between Bridget and Gwen is a 'classic' fob contract. The primary duties of the buyer are to nominate an effective ship to carry the goods, to notify the seller of such nomination in time for the seller to load goods and to pay the agreed price (*Pyrene & Co v Scindia Navigation Co Ltd* (1954)). The seller's primary duty is to deliver goods which comply with the terms of the contract once the seller has given his shipping instructions.

Where documentary credit is involved, the rule is that the letter of credit must be opened at the very latest before the first day of the shipment period. This is clear from *Pavia & Co SpA v Thurmann-Nielsen* (1952). In this question, we are not told when Birken Bank advised Bridget of the opening of the credit and, if this was on or after 1 October, Bridget is entitled to refuse to ship the goods and may treat the contract as discharged and claim damages against Gwen. We are told that Bridget does in fact ship the goods, thus choosing not to treat the late opening of credit (if indeed it was opened on or after 1 October) as discharging the contract.

Although Gwen nominates *The Enterprise*, she has not in fact booked shipping space for the goods. It is the prime duty of an fob buyer to give 'effective' shipping instructions, that is, it must be possible and lawful for the seller to comply with them (*Agricultores Federados Argentinos v Ampro SA* (1965)). The essential point is that the seller must be instructed as to the way in which he can perform his duty to put the goods on board. Bridget, nevertheless, manages to persuade the master of *The Enterprise* to take the goods. Gwen's nomination of *The Enterprise* is therefore adequate since the named ship can in fact take the goods, irrespective of her failure to make advance arrangements with the master. Nothing turns on this point, since if Gwen had not reserved shipping space in advance, she runs the risk that her shipping instructions may be ineffective, but she does not commit any breach of contract as long as Bridget is in fact able to ship the goods in accordance with the shipping instructions. Despite the fact that Bridget only managed to persuade the master of *The Enterprise* to take the goods on the last day stipulated within the contract shipment period, all the boxes were in fact loaded by the end of that day.

A fire breaks out on *The Enterprise* the next day, 1 November, and the boxes are unloaded. Once goods have been loaded, risk normally passes to the buyer because the seller has fulfilled his obligation to deliver the goods and nothing remains to be done by him under the contract except to tender the shipping documents for payment. Thus, Bridget need not have involved herself with the events that occurred after 31 October, and it would have been Gwen's decision whether or not to claim for any damage against the underwriters if she had taken out an insurance policy.[8] Because the goods are unloaded, a problem has arisen. For whatever reason, the anchovies have now been packed in boxes of 50 kilograms per box whereas the contract had stipulated for 25 kilograms per box. The bill of lading issued by the master states '20 x 50 kilograms anchovies shipped on 31 October'.

The requirement that goods must correspond to their description used to be a strict one, entitling the buyer to reject for quite trivial discrepancies, and to do so even though the failure of the seller to deliver goods of the contract description does not in the least prejudice the buyer (*Arcos Ltd v Ronaasen & Son* (1933)).[9] This is no longer the case due to **s 15A** of the **Sale of Goods Act 1979**. The buyer can no longer reject where the breach is so slight that it would be unreasonable for him to do so.

Birken Bank was entitled to refuse to pay against the documents which Bridget presented, since the bill of lading does not comply with the terms of the credit because it indicates incorrect packaging. This stems from the principle of strict compliance in documentary financing. As Lord Sumner said in *Equitable Trust Co of New York v Dawson Partners Ltd* (1927): 'There is no room for documents which are almost the same, or which will

---

8   An fob seller is not obliged to take out insurance cover for the goods, but **s 32(3)** of the **Sale of Goods Act 1979** imposes on him an obligation to 'give such notice to the buyer as may enable him to insure [the goods] during their sea transit'. If the seller does not do so, the goods are deemed to be at the seller's risk. However, *Wimble Sons & Co v Rosenberg* (1913) established that in a classic fob contract, that is, where the buyer nominates the vessel and gives the shipping instructions, the buyer will normally have sufficient information to enable him to insure so that the seller need not give further notice under **s 32(3)**.

9   In *Re Moore & Co and Landauer & Co* (1921), it was held that goods did not comply with their description when the contract called for 3,000 tins of fruit to be packed 30 tins to a case and the seller delivered the correct number of tins, but some were packed 24 tins to a case.

do just as well.'[10] Birken Bank has no discretion, in that it must comply strictly with the buyer's instructions as to payment.[11] Birken Bank's duty is to examine all the documents with reasonable care to ascertain whether they appear on their face to be in accordance with the terms of credit. It is not responsible for the genuineness or accuracy of the documents, merely whether they comply, and Birken Bank has rightly refused to pay Bridget.

The bank's right to reimbursement from Gwen depends on it taking up a faultless set of documents and, since the bill of lading indicates incorrect packaging, Birken Bank was entitled to refuse to pay Bridget, no matter how minor the discrepancy may appear.

It appears that Birken Bank has notified Bridget of the reason for rejection and Bridget does have an opportunity to put right any defect and present the documents again, provided that there is time to do so in accordance with the contract of sale and the credit. Bridget therefore takes the bill of lading back to the master of *The Enterprise*, who issues a fresh bill now stipulating that the cargo is of 40 boxes each containing 25 kilograms of anchovies as was required under the contract.

We are not then told what the parties' actions were, but it is reasonable to assume that Bridget then retenders the documents to Birken Bank which then pays against them, since the bill of lading now indicates the correct packaging. As far as the date of shipment is concerned, the bill of lading shows 31 October and thus the documents appear on their face in apparent good order and comply with the terms of the credit. In order for Gwen to have taken possession of the goods on arrival, Gwen must have reimbursed Birken Bank because a bank will not release the documents until payment is made by its principal. Once Birken Bank has taken reasonable care in scrutinising the documents, it will not be liable to Gwen if the documents later turn out to be defective.

Gwen discovers that the anchovies have deteriorated due to fungus infection. Although she has previously accepted documents, Gwen may be entitled to reject the goods. An fob buyer has two distinct rights of rejection. As Devlin, J made clear in *Kwei Tek Chao v British Traders and Shippers* (1954), the right to reject documents arises when the documents are tendered, and the right to reject goods arises when they are landed and when, after examination, they are not found to be in conformity with the contract.

This would be the case if the goods suffered from some qualitative defect not apparent on the face of the documents. In *Mash & Murrell v Joseph Emanuel* (1961), Cyprus horsebeans were sold cif Southampton. The horsebeans were sound when shipped but were found to be rotten on arrival. On the facts of the case, it was found that the deterioration was a result of fungus infection before or at the time of shipment. The court held that the

---

10 The inclusion of a direct quote by a judge or by a noted expert in the field is not only a good starting point for a wider discussion of the relevant issues but also serves as evidence both of your wider research efforts and of your knowledge of the area in question.

11 Lord Wilberforce in *Reardon Smith Line Ltd v Hansen Tangen* (1976) described some of the older cases as 'excessively technical', but that the need for certainty, particularly in international sales, outweighs the need for flexibility.

seller was liable for the deterioration. As Diplock, J said in that case: 'when goods are sold under a contract such as a cif contract or fob contract which involves transit before use, there is an implied warranty not merely that they shall be [satisfactory] at the time they are put on the vessel, but that they shall be in such a state that they can endure the normal journey and be in a [satisfactory] condition on arrival.'

It therefore seems that because anchovies are normally capable of enduring a sea transit, Bridget will be liable for any deterioration apparent on arrival.[12] This implied warranty is distinct from the implied term under **s 14** of the **Sale of Goods Act 1979**, the former relating to an undertaking that the goods can endure sea transit as opposed to **s 14(2)** and **(3)**, which are implied terms relating to satisfactory quality and fitness for purpose.

Gwen may thus be entitled to reject the goods for breach of the implied terms as to satisfactory quality and fitness for purpose under **s 14** of the **Sale of Goods Act 1979**, provided that the breach is not so slight so as to treat it as a breach of warranty (**s 15A** of the **Sale of Goods Act 1979**). If the anchovies no longer have commercial value, as it appears in this case, Gwen is likely to be entitled to reject the goods despite the fact that Bridget has already been paid against documents.

Furthermore, according to the House of Lords in *Bowes v Shand* (1877), stipulations as to the time of shipment form part of the description of the goods and breach of such stipulations entitles the buyer to reject. Although *Bowes v Shand* was decided before the **Sale of Goods Act 1893**, subsequent cases have acknowledged that the time of shipment is part of the description of the goods and is within **s 13** of the **Sale of Goods Act** (*Avon & Co v Comptoir Wegimont* (1921)). Since the goods were not in fact shipped within the contract period, Gwen may be able to reject the goods on the ground that they did not constitute an October shipment. However, it is arguable whether Gwen can reject the goods, since **s 15A** of the **Sale of Goods Act 1979** provides that where the breach is so slight that it would be unreasonable for the buyer to reject the goods, the breach is to be treated as a breach of warranty and not as a breach of condition. Since time is of the essence in commercial contracts (*The Mihalis Angelos* (1971)), it is submitted that the breach will not be perceived as so slight for it to be treated as a breach of warranty.

QUESTION 34

Cednex plc, wholesalers based in London, enters into two separate contracts for the purchase of 5,000 (3,000 superior models and 2,000 standard models) Blu-ray players cif London from Kanazawa (Japan) Ltd, and the purchase of 10,000 Selfie Jewellery kits fob Amsterdam from Glamclub. Both contracts called for September/October shipment and payment by irrevocable letter of credit at Saga Bank on presentation of the shipping documents. The contract with Glamclub contained a clause requiring the Selfie Jewellery kits to be delivered in time to catch the Christmas trade.

---

12 Remember to draw conclusions from your analysis; this evidences your understanding of how to apply the law.

An irrevocable letter of credit in favour of Kanazawa (Japan) Ltd was opened on 5 September and the bank paid on presentation of a received for shipment bill of lading, an insurance policy and an invoice. When the Blu-ray players arrived in London, the 2,000 standard models were immediately delivered to Precision Ltd, which had agreed to buy them from Cednex plc, and the superior models were transferred to Cednex's warehouse. Three weeks later, Precision returned all 2,000 Blu-ray players on discovering that the electrical wiring was faulty.

A revocable letter of credit in favour of Glamclub was opened on 27 August and the bank paid on presentation of the shipping documents, which included a bill of lading dated 31 October and a certificate of quality dated 1 November. The Selfie Jewellery kits arrived in London on 28 November but, due to a shortage of staff at the docks, Cednex plc was not notified of this until 26 December.

Both contracts are governed by English law.
❱ **Advise Cednex plc as to its remedies.**

How to Answer this Question
Both parts of the question require you to discuss the opening of the documentary credit. Although the cases do not lay down a conclusive rule in the cases of either fob or of cif contracts, you will need to discuss the time at which documentary credit must be available to the seller.

The bank's position needs to be dealt with. Both Kanazawa and Glamclub have presented the shipping documents to Saga Bank, but neither set of shipping documents is in accordance with Cednex's instructions to the bank. The contractual nature of the bank's undertaking to Cednex and the bank's entitlement to reimbursement will need to be discussed.

It is not uncommon to find international sale questions involving certain provisions of the **Sale of Goods Act 1979**. In this question, you will need to discuss the buyer's remedy where there has been a breach of **s 14(2)** and **(3)** but where he may have accepted the goods under **s 35**.

The final part of the question involves stipulations as to time of delivery in fob contracts.

Applying the Law

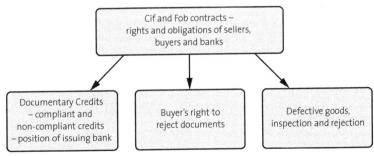

ANSWER --

The general rule is that the documentary credit must be opened in accordance with the contract of sale. The contracts with Kanazawa and Glamclub do not provide a date for the opening of the credit. They do, however, stipulate a period for the shipment of the goods. It is clear from *Pavia & Co SpA v Thurmann-Nielsen* (1952) that in these circumstances, the documentary credit must be opened at the very latest on the first day on which shipment may take place. The reason for this is that the seller is not bound to tell the buyer the precise date when he is going to ship, but whenever he does ship the goods, the seller must be able to draw on the credit.[13]

As far as Kanazawa is concerned, the documentary credit was not opened until 5 September. Following the *Pavia* case, Kanazawa is not obliged to ship the goods and may terminate the contract and claim damages.[14] However, we are told that Kanazawa presents the shipping documents to the bank for payment. Thus, Kanazawa must have shipped the goods, although the credit was not opened until 5 September, and may be taken to have waived the breach or at least agreed to a variation of the contract.[15]

The credit in favour of Glamclub was opened on 27 August, and this appears to have allowed a reasonable time before the shipment date (*Sinason-Teicher Inter-American Grain Corp v Oilcakes and Oilseeds Trading Co Ltd* (1954)).

However, the contract stipulated that the credit to be opened is to be an irrevocable credit, whereas the credit that was actually made available is a revocable one, that is, one where the bank is free to revoke its undertaking to pay the beneficiary at any time before payment is due. In these circumstances, Glamclub is entitled to claim damages for a breach of the terms of the contract, such a breach qualifying as a condition. As with Kanazawa, Glamclub appears to have either waived the breach or agreed to a variation to the contract, because Glamclub does ship the goods and presents the documents to the bank for payment.

We are told that the contracts are governed by English law. It is also assumed that, as is usual, the documentary credits expressly incorporated the **Uniform Customs and Practice for Documentary Credits** (UCP) published by the International Chamber of Commerce. It

---

13 This principle applies to both cif and fob contracts. It has been argued that, since an fob buyer had the option as to the time of shipment, the documentary credit needs to be opened at a reasonable time before the date nominated by the buyer in the shipping instructions. Lord Diplock in *Ian Stach Ltd v Baker Bosley Ltd* (1958) thought that such a rule would lead to uncertainties and concluded that the *prima facie* rule is that the credit must be opened, at the latest, on the first day of the shipping period.

14 The measure of damages, it seems, is not limited by the market price rule in **s 50(3)** of the **Sale of Goods Act 1979**, but may extend to the seller's lost profits, provided that they are not too remote under the rule in *Hadley v Baxendale* (1854); *Trans Trust SPRL v Danubian Trading Co Ltd* (1952).

15 The difference between a waiver and an agreement to a variation is that the former entitles the seller to reinstate the requirement on giving the buyer reasonable notice, and the latter will prevent the seller unilaterally to reverting to the original position. The significance of the distinction does not arise in this question.

appears from the question that Kanazawa has already been paid on presentation of the shipping documents and nothing turns on the fact that some of the goods are faulty.[16] However, it seems that the bank has paid against a received for shipment bill of lading. Such a bill of lading is not good tender under a cif contract because the buyer cannot confirm that the goods have been loaded within the shipment period. The bank's duty is to examine all documents with reasonable care to ascertain that they appear on their face to be in accordance with the terms of the credit.[17] Saga Bank does not seem to have scrutinised the documents carefully. Therefore, Cednex is not bound to take the shipping documents from the bank.[18] However, we are told that Cednex has taken physical delivery of the goods. This in turn means that Cednex must have ratified the bank's actions (otherwise the bank would not release the shipping documents to Cednex), and such ratification prevents Cednex from treating the shipping documents as anything but regular as against the bank.

Precision returns the 2,000 standard model Blu-ray players. Faulty electrical wiring renders the goods unsatisfactory and will give Cednex a remedy for breach of **s 14(2)** of the **Sale of Goods Act 1979** against Kanazawa. Furthermore, the use of Blu-ray players is well known, so that faulty electrical wiring would render Kanazawa in breach of the implied term under **s 14(3)** whereby goods should be reasonably fit for that use. The often sought remedy for breach of **s 14(2)** and **(3)** is rejection of the goods and damages. However, this is subject to **s 15A**, which provides that where the breach is so slight that it would be unreasonable for a buyer to reject the goods, the breach may be treated as a breach of warranty.

Faulty electrical wiring, even if easily put right, would hardly appear to be a slight breach. However, rejection will not be available for those goods which have been accepted. **Section 35** of the **Sale of Goods Act 1979** provides that the buyer may be deemed to have accepted the goods, thus losing the right to reject, where *inter alia* he does some act 'inconsistent with the seller's ownership' or where after a reasonable period he retains the goods without indicating that he rejects them. It is unclear whether before the delivery to Precision, Cednex had an opportunity to examine the standard model Blu-ray players for the purpose of seeing whether they conformed to the contract.[19] If Cednex resells the goods, having inspected them, and Precision then rejects them, it might be argued that Cednex has lost the right to reject the goods, it being argued that it had retained them for more than a reasonable length of time before rejecting them. On the other hand, it has been held (*Truk (UK) Ltd v Tokmakidis* (2000)) that where goods are bought for resale, the reasonable period of time before the right to reject the goods is lost will normally last for the time it takes to resell the goods, plus a further period of time for the ultimate purchaser to test the goods.

....

16 Even if the bank knew that the goods were faulty at the time Kanazawa presented the shipping documents, it is well established that the courts will not allow revocation at all where the credit is irrevocable.

17 **Article 14** of **UCP 600**.

18 The bank is also prevented from returning the documents to the seller.

19 Considering ambiguities in the question demonstrates understanding and will attract a higher mark.

Thus, in determining whether Cednex has accepted the goods, the important factor becomes one of whether Precision has accepted the goods vis-à-vis Cednex. This in turn depends upon whether the three weeks which it took Precision to reject the goods amounts to more than a reasonable period of time and, since **s 35** was amended by the **Sale and Supply of Goods Act 1994**, one of the relevant factors is whether that period allowed Precision a reasonable opportunity to examine the goods for the purpose of ascertaining whether they complied with the contract. Whereas, prior to the 1994 amendment, a three-week period was held to amount to more than a reasonable period of time (*Bernstein v Pamson Motors*), it seems likely that the court would now find that it does not.[20] Thus, Precision, it is submitted, is not restricted to a claim for damages but was entitled to reject the goods, and Cednex was similarly entitled. If, as soon as Precision intimated to Cednex its rejection of the goods, Cednex immediately informed Kanazawa that it was rejecting the goods, then Cednex will not have lost its right to reject the goods. If, on the other hand, Cednex failed for some time to inform Kanazawa that it was rejecting the goods, that delay will have increased the chances of Cednex being held to have accepted the goods.

Assuming that Precision validly rejected the goods, Precision will also have a claim for damages against Cednex. The *prima facie* measure of those damages will be the difference between the contract price of the goods and (if it is higher) the market price (of goods that comply with the contract) on the day of delivery. If Cednex has also validly rejected the goods, that will also be the *prima facie* measure of damages that Cednex can claim against Kanazawa. If Cednex has not validly rejected the goods, then it is entitled only to damages. Those damages will, however, include any consequent losses which Cednex has incurred in relation to the sub-sale to Precision. In the case of a breach of term as to quality in a contract where goods are bought for resale, the courts are prepared to take into account the effect of a sub-sale upon the losses incurred by the buyer (*Bence Graphics v Fasson UK* (1997)).

As discussed above, the opening of the credit on 27 August was not too late.[21] However, Cednex is in breach of the contract in that the credit was not an irrevocable one, but Glamclub ships the goods and is paid by the bank on presentation of the shipping documents.

Saga Bank is only entitled to be reimbursed sums it pays out if it pays on receipt of documents which strictly comply with Cednex's instructions. Saga Bank has paid against the bill of lading which is dated 31 October (and thus appears to fall within the shipment period) but also a certificate of quality dated 1 November. On the face of the documents, read together, the goods could not have been shipped on 31 October. The bank is thus liable to Cednex, since the documents do not comply with the terms of the credit which stipulate for a September/October shipment (*Soproma v Marine and Animal By-Products*

---

20 Showing an awareness of the development of the area of law in question demonstrates both knowledge and understanding.

21 Build upon points you have raised previously; this gives your answer structure.

(1966)). Because Cednex appears to have ratified the bank's wrongful act, does Cednex have a second right to reject, that is, to reject the goods themselves on the ground that they are not of contract description? The general rule is that where a buyer who accepts documents in ignorance of a defect in them and later discovers the defect and takes delivery of the goods, he will be taken to have waived his right to reject not only the documents, but also the goods on account of that defect (see *Panchaud Fréres v Establissements General Grain* (1970)). However, since Saga Bank acts as principal when accepting the shipping documents, and not as Cednex's agents, Cednex can reject the goods on arrival on the ground that they are not of contract description (even if Saga Bank accepted the documents which showed they were defective on the face of them).

May Cednex reject the goods since they did not arrive in time to catch the Christmas trade? In *Frebold and Sturznickel (Trading as Panda OGH) v Circle Products Ltd* (1970), German sellers sold toys to English buyers under an fob contract on terms that the goods were to be delivered in time for the Christmas trade. The goods arrived at the destination on 13 November. Due to an oversight (for which the sellers were not responsible), the buyers were not notified of the arrival of the goods until 17 January. The court held that the sellers were not in breach, since they had delivered the goods in such a way that would normally have resulted in the goods arriving in time for the Christmas trade. Applying this case to the question,[22] the Selfie Jewellery kits did in fact arrive in London on 28 November and therefore in time for the Christmas trade but, because of a shortage of staff at the docks, which could not have been the fault of Glamclub, Cednex did not know of the arrival until some time after. It seems, therefore, that Cednex will have no remedy against Glamclub, since Glamclub had delivered the goods in accordance with the requirements of the contract. Cednex's remedies may be in suing the port authorities, the carriers or their agents or other parties responsible.

---

22 In order to attract a good mark you need to ensure that you don't merely describe the law; you need to explain and apply it to the requirements of the question.

12

Cif Contracts

INTRODUCTION

Under a cif (cost, insurance and freight) contract, the seller is required to arrange the carriage of the goods and their insurance in transit, and all costs of such arrangements are included in the contract price. The essential duties of a cif seller are to obtain a bill of lading, a policy of insurance and any other document required by the contract, and to forward them to the buyer who pays on the invoice when he receives the shipping documents.

Shipping documents play a central role in cif contracts, particularly where documentary financing is concerned. Because the buyer in international sale contracts has two rights of rejection, he retains his right to reject the goods on arrival if they do not conform with the terms of the contract, even if he has paid against shipping documents.

Cif contracts are often concerned with the sale of unascertained goods, and issues concerning the passing of risk and property are often involved. A particular problem arises where unascertained goods are lost before the cif seller has appropriated the goods to the contract.

This chapter deals mainly with cif contracts, although questions often have parts involving other types of international sale contracts (**Questions 34, 37** and **38**, for instance, deal with both a cif contract as well as an fob contract).

QUESTION 35

Discuss the rights of the parties in all of the following situations:

(a) Zeus bought a quantity of silk from Hades, a Belgian silk manufacturer, 'cif Southampton'. The contract did not stipulate the type of vessel to be used. Hades was unable to find a cargo ship, but knew that Zeus needed the silk urgently, and so sent it on a canal barge, which was not designed for sea journeys. As a result, the silk was damaged by sea water.

(b) Zeus bought a quantity of wool from Poseidon 'cif Bristol'. Poseidon bought the wool from Rhea, who claimed to have shipped it. Poseidon tendered to Zeus a bill of lading which recorded that the wool was on a ship called *The Titans*. When this ship arrived there was no wool on board, and it was discovered that no wool had ever been carried on the ship.

(c) Zeus bought a quantity of cotton from Cronus, 'cif London'. Shortly afterwards, Zeus found a cheaper supplier and so rejected the documents tendered by Cronus. When Cronus threatened to bring a claim, Zeus responded by correctly stating that when the cotton arrived it was not of satisfactory quality.

How to Answer this Question

Part (a) requires a clear grasp of the fundamental principles of cif contracts and that contracts are subject to the express terms agreed between the parties.

Part (b) raises the time-honoured argument that a cif contract is more akin to a sale of documents than a sale of goods. The consensus, however, is that a cif contract is a genuine sale of goods contract which the seller performs using documents.

Part (c) raises the issue of whether a buyer who wrongfully rejects the documents may rely on a subsequent right to repudiate on the grounds that the goods are defective to justify his initial wrongful repudiation. The general rule set out in *Gill and Duffus v Berger* (1984) needs to be discussed.

Applying the Law

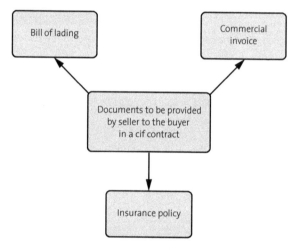

This mind map shows the main documents required. You will also have to consider the nature of the vessel on which goods were shipped and rejection issues in relation to first documents and then the goods.

ANSWER

(A) HADES

According to the House of Lords in *Johnson v Taylor Bros* (1920), the duties of the cif seller are to ship the goods, to procure proper shipping documents and to tender the documents to the buyer. Thus, Hades fulfils its part of the bargain by tendering to Zeus proper shipping documents. Although the goods have been damaged by sea water, in cif contracts this is irrelevant. A buyer must still pay against the proper documents. Unless the contract stipulates otherwise, Hades must tender three documents: the bill of lading, the insurance policy and the commercial invoice. We are not told whether or not Hades has tendered these documents to Zeus.

We know that Hades was unable to find a suitable cargo ship, hence a barge was used instead. Unless the contract between Zeus and Hades specified what type of vessel was to be used, as long as Hades makes a reasonable contract of carriage, Hades is not in breach of its cif duties and Zeus must pay against the documents (**s 28** of the **Sale of Goods Act 1979**). However, Hades is the seller of silk, and ought to have been aware of the nature of the goods being shipped. It is therefore questionable whether shipping silk using a barge is a reasonable method of carriage. Certainly, Hades needs to tender a bill of lading. If the terms of the contract of carriage for barges are approximate to those for cargo ships, it may be that Hades has fulfilled its duties.

Zeus needs to be assured of its rights against the carrier (under the contract of carriage) and the insurer (under the insurance policy). Therefore, if Hades makes a reasonable contract of carriage with the barge owners and the endorsement to Zeus of the bill of lading provides Zeus with rights under **s 2(1)** of the **Carriage of Goods by Sea Act 1992** (that is, a lawful holder of the bill of lading can sue the carrier as if he were a party to the original contract of carriage) and satisfies all other requirements of the bill of lading (such as providing continuous documentary cover (*Hansson v Hamel and Horley* (1922)), and the insurance policy satisfies the terms of the cif contract, then Zeus needs to pay Hades against the documents. Zeus' claim will be against the carrier and/ or the insurer.

On the other hand, if the contract of carriage is not a reasonable one, Zeus can reject the documents at the time they are tendered to him for payment. The goods in that situation remain at Hades' risk and Hades bears the loss of the silk being damaged by sea water.

(B) POSEIDON

The cif seller has a choice. He either ships goods in accordance with the contract, or he buys goods afloat. We are told that, as between Zeus and Poseidon, Poseidon has bought goods afloat, that is, the original shipper was Rhea. If the cloth was lost in transit, Poseidon is entitled to tender the proper shipping documents to Zeus, and Zeus must pay even though both parties know that the goods have been lost (*Manbre Saccharine v Corn Products* (1919)). If this was the case, Zeus' remedy is against the carrier under contract of carriage or against the insurer under the insurance policy.

However, it seems that no cloth had ever been shipped. Because a cif seller can demand payment against shipping documents, some argue that the cif contract is more akin to a sale of documents than a sale of goods. The consensus, however, is that a cif contract is a genuine sale of goods contract which the seller performs using documents. A seller who tenders a bill of lading showing goods have been shipped when this is not true has not performed his contractual duties. It makes no difference that Poseidon is not the shipper but an intermediate seller in a chain of contracts. Professor Goode argues that a buyer can reject tender of documents in these circumstances.[1] This is because even a cif buyer is contracting primarily to buy goods, not claims. So, if goods are lost or damaged before the contract of sale is made, a cif buyer cannot be made to accept the tender of documents, because there were no goods conforming to contract at the time the contract was made. Thus, Zeus can reject the documents against Poseidon.

However, it sounds as though Zeus has already paid against the documents. Although Zeus cannot now reject the documents, he does have a second right of rejection. According to Lord Devlin in *Kwei Tek Chao v British Traders* (1954), the buyer's right to reject goods arises when they are landed and when after examination are found to be not in conformity with the contract. Assuming the fact that no cloth was ever shipped was not apparent on the face of the shipping documents, Zeus may rely on his second right to reject. There has been a total failure of consideration, and Zeus will be entitled to the return of the purchase price he has paid and damages for non-delivery, which is assessed by reference to the difference between the market price and contract price at the due date for delivery (**s 51**). Alternatively, since, as against the indorsee, the bill of lading is conclusive evidence of the facts contained, Zeus may wish to claim against the shipowner of *The Titans*, who is estopped from denying that the cloth was shipped. Similarly, Poseidon can make his claim against Rhea.

(C) CRONUS

As discussed above, the cif buyer has two distinct rights of rejection (*Kwei Tek Chao v British Traders*).[2] We are told that Zeus has rejected the shipping documents because it found a cheaper supplier. The courts do not question a party's motive for rejection. If Zeus had the right to reject, then Zeus had that right irrespective of market price movements. However, nothing in the question suggests that the documents were defective, so Zeus should have accepted the documents and paid against them. Zeus' wrongful rejection of conforming documents amounts to a repudiatory breach, entitling Cronus to **s 50** of the **Sale of Goods Act 1979** damages for non-acceptance (since the bill of lading represents goods).

Zeus, however, claims that the goods were defective. The question is whether Zeus' wrongful rejection of the documents is justified on the ground that the goods are subsequently found to be defective. The general rule is set out in *Gill and Duffus v Berger* (1984). The House of Lords in that case made it clear that a buyer's rejection of conforming documents is a wrongful repudiation. This is true even if the buyer subsequently discovers that the goods themselves are not in accordance with the contract.

---

1   The inclusion of academic references rather than the 'mere' consideration of case law shows not only that you have researched and read more widely but also adds to the criticality of your analysis.

2   By referring to a previously drawn conclusion or explanation you link different stages of your analysis and thus present a more complete answer.

As Lord Diplock said, the duties to ship goods and to present documents are separate and independent duties. Thus, Zeus' wrongful rejection amounts to a repudiatory breach.[3]

Aim Higher

It should be noted, however, that Professor Goode submits that this principle ('pay now, argue later') is open to serious objection. He argues that the idea that the buyer's remedy to pay against documents and then later reject goods on arrival and sue for the recovery of the purchase price lacks commercial realism. He questions the rationale of insisting that the buyer go through the exercise.

QUESTION 36

Callaghan buys 3,000 tons of wheat germ from Heath, October shipment, cif Irani. Irani is a port in the Middle West where war has been raging continuously for many years.

The wheat germ is put on board *The Askari*. On 27 October, the master, believing the loading will have been completed by the end of October, issues a bill of lading to Heath dated 31 October. In fact, loading was not completed until 1 November.

The wheat germ is in good condition on shipment but deteriorates on the voyage and by the time the consignment arrives, the wheat germ is unsuitable for use in the manufacture of bread. The wheat germ would not have deteriorated on the voyage but for the fact that *The Askari* was forced to make a substantial detour in order to avoid hostile submarines which were known to be patrolling the area. Such detours are normal in the Middle West. The bill of lading contained a deviation clause.

Heath tenders the bill of lading and a certificate of insurance (which is customary in the wheat germ trade). Callaghan discovers that the wheat germ is insured against ordinary marine risks, but not against war risks.

The general market price of wheat germ has unexpectedly dropped.

▶ **Advise Callaghan as to whether he must accept the shipping documents.**

How to Answer this Question

This question involves the importance of shipping documents, in particular, the bill of lading and the insurance policy. The key issues in relation to the bill of lading are whether the false date of shipment and the deviation clause entitle Callaghan to reject the

---

3   There is a controversial decision of the High Court of Australia (*Henry Dean & Sons (Sydney) Ltd v O'Day Pty Ltd* (1927)) which suggests that a buyer may be entitled to reject documents where the documents are, but the goods themselves are not, in accordance with the contract. The sellers, when refusing to pay against documents, are taking a risk but one that was 'justified by the result'. This problem is yet unresolved in the English courts.

document. A buyer of goods under a cif contract is not entitled, as against the seller, to reject shipping documents merely because the ship has deviated. The buyer's remedy is usually against the carrier. However, the problem in this question is that the bill of lading contains a deviation clause entitling the carrier to deviate. What is the effect of such a clause as between Heath and Callaghan?

The part of the question involving the insurance policy requires discussion of what type of policy the cif seller is entitled to expect, taking into account what is usual in the trade in question.

Applying the Law

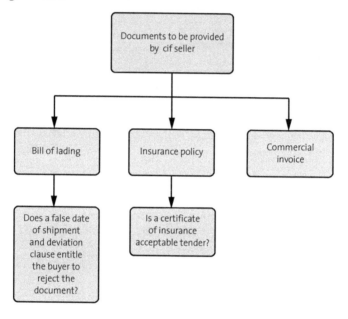

ANSWER

If the documents tendered by Heath accord with the contract, Callaghan must accept them and pay the agreed price (*Biddell Bros v Clemens Horst Co* (1912)). A wrongful rejection amounts to a repudiation of the contract (*Gill & Duffus SA v Berger & Co Inc* (1984)).

As far as the bill of lading is concerned, it is clear that it must show that the goods were loaded at the time required by the contract of sale. We are told that the bill of lading is erroneously dated 31 October whereas, in fact, loading was not completed until after the contract shipment period. The general rule is that the bill of lading must be 'genuine' (*James Finlay & Co Ltd v Kwik Hoo Tong* (1929)), and a bill of lading which contains a false date of shipment is a bad tender entitling the buyer to reject the shipping documents. If Callaghan is certain that he can prove the goods were not shipped until 1 November, then he has the right to reject the bill of lading.

Callaghan may have the right to reject the goods themselves on the ground that the wheat germ was not of contract description. According to the House of Lords in *Bowes v Shand* (1877), stipulations as to the time of shipment form part of the description of the goods and that breach of such stipulations entitles the buyer to reject. Although *Bowes v Shand* was decided before the **Sale of Goods Act 1893**, subsequent cases have acknowledged that the time of shipment is part of the description of the goods and is within **s 13** of the **Sale of Goods Act 1979** (*Avon & Co v Comptoir Weigmont* (1920)). However, **s 13** is affected by **s 15A**, introduced by the **Sale and Supply of Goods Act 1994**. According to **s 15A**, where the breach is so slight that it would be unreasonable for the buyer to reject the goods, a breach is not to be treated as a breach of condition but as a breach of warranty. The issue here is whether time of shipment is to be treated as a slight breach and hence as a breach of warranty. Since time is of the essence in commercial contracts, it is unlikely that the time of shipment will be treated as a breach of warranty.[4] It seems that Callaghan would be entitled to reject the goods even though he previously accepts documents which were, on the face of them, in accordance with the contract. In *Suzuki & Co v Burgett & Newsam* (1922),[5] peas were sold under a cif contract which called for shipment by January. The seller tendered a 'received for shipment' bill of lading, which was usual in the trade, dated 31 January. Although the goods had been received for shipment on 31 January, actual shipment took place in February. The court held that the buyer, who had accepted the bill of lading (which was in accordance with the contract), was entitled to reject the goods as they did not constitute a January shipment (*Kwei Tek Chao v British Traders and Shippers* (1954)). Applying this to the question, Callaghan is thus advised not to reject the bill of lading unless he is sure that he can prove that the goods were in fact shipped on 1 November. He may be entitled to reject the goods themselves.

We are told that the wheat germ deteriorates during the voyage due to the need to make a substantial detour. Since risk in the goods passes to the cif buyer on shipment (irrespective of the time at which property passes) (*Law and Bonar Ltd v British American Tobacco Ltd* (1916)), Callaghan cannot reject the goods on the basis that they have deteriorated during carriage. Objection may nevertheless be taken to the bill of lading on the ground that it contains a deviation clause permitting the carrier to depart from the route of shipment. This rule is subject to contrary custom or usage (*Burstall v Grimsdale* (1906)). It seems likely that a bill of lading relating to a shipment to the Middle West, where hostilities have been apparent for years, will contain a deviation clause permitting the carrier to make such detours as are necessary to avoid danger. If the clause is not drafted in unusually wide terms, Callaghan is advised that the bill of lading is a good shipping document as the bill is 'usual and customary'. This bill of lading may be governed by the **Hague-Visby Rules**, which allow for express deviation clauses (*Stag Line Ltd v Foscolo, Mango &*

4　Time of shipment is generally regarded as part of the description of the goods, due to the crucial role that time plays in commercial contracts. Time for both the seller and buyer is important for sorting out payment arrangements. The buyer may also wish to fulfil his contractual obligations with other parties (see Lord Cairns' judgment in *Bowes v Shand* (1877), at p 463).

5　Outlining the facts of a particular case is a good way to illustrate the relevant legal rules and thus strengthens your argument.

Co (1932)). Under the **Rules**, deviation is also permitted to save life, to save property and where it is reasonable.

Callaghan is therefore required to accept the bill of lading.

It appears that there are two problems with regard to the policy of insurance: first, Heath tenders a certificate of insurance (and not a policy); second, war risk cover has not been obtained.

In respect of the first problem, it is established that a cif seller does not perform his obligations by procuring and tendering a certificate of insurance (*Maine Spinning Co v Sutcliffe & Co* (1917)).[6] Of course, a document may be a policy even though it does not contain all the terms of the insurance, but incorporates a reference to an identified or identifiable policy or perhaps makes reference to terms known in the trade.[7] It is unlikely that these requirements are satisfied in this question. The fact that it is customary in the wheat germ trade to tender certificates of insurance rather than policies is unlikely to be sufficient to require Callaghan to accept the certificate of insurance tendered by Heath, unless there was an express provision in the contract to the contrary.

As for the second problem, if Heath tenders a policy which is usual or in accordance with the express requirements of the contract, it is immaterial that the policy does not cover the loss which has actually occurred. We are not told of any express terms in the contract requiring Heath to obtain war risk cover. In the absence of any contractual term, the general rule is that the seller must tender such policy as is usual in the trade to cover the goods and voyage in question (*Burstall v Grimsdale* (1906)).[8] It is not clear if the risks covered must be those usual at the time of the contract of sale or at the time the policy is issued. In *Groom Ltd v Barber* (1915), a policy not covering war risks was held to be a good tender on the basis that at the time of the contract of sale, it was not usual to cover war risks.[9] The decision in this case makes it clear that the time of tender of the documents is not decisive, but the court did not indicate whether the relevant time is that of the sale or the time at which the policy of insurance was taken out. There was no interval between

....

6 One of the reasons behind this rule is that the certificate usually makes reference to the policy, and the person to whom tender is made will be unable to determine from the certificate what the terms of the insurance are (*Donald H Scott Ltd v Barclays Bank Ltd* (1923)). A certificate of insurance is not transferable like a policy to the buyer by endorsement, which means that the buyer will not have a right of action against the insurers (*Diamond Alkali Export Corp v Fl Bourgeois* (1921)).

7 There is, however, authority to support the proposition that an insurance certificate or other document entitling the insured to demand the formal delivery of an insurance policy will suffice.

8 Incoterms 2010 (in force since 1 January 2011) require a seller to arrange minimum cover, that is, Institute Cargo Clause (C). But this is a very low standard, essentially only covering huge disasters, such as total loss of cargo. A buyer needs to expressly agree that the seller provides additional 'bolt-on' cover, for example, cover by Clause (A) or (B). If the buyer wants 'bolt-on' insurance, the buyer must expressly provide for this in sale contract, otherwise the seller is only obliged to arrange for the lowest level of cover under Clause (C)

9 Unless otherwise provided, cif policies are only for commercial rather than war risks.

these two points in *Groom v Barber*. The better view might be that the relevant time should be the time at which the insurance policy is effected. Either way, we are told in this question that war had been raging continuously for many years in the Middle West. It would appear, therefore, that it was usual to insure against war risks. Heath's tender of the certificate of insurance is probably defective, entitling Callaghan to refuse to accept the documents on the basis that a certificate (rather than a policy) is not sufficient and that Heath failed to insure against war risks. However, this will only be so on the basis that there was no express provision to the contrary in the contract.

QUESTION 37

Pugwash agrees to buy 10,000 tons of garbanzo beans from Jake out of the 15,000 tons of garbanzo beans currently in Jake's warehouse in Portsmouth, cif Hong Kong. Shortly afterwards, Jake sells to Barnabas the remaining 5,000 tons of garbanzo beans, fob Bristol, Jake to make the shipping arrangements to Hong Kong. Payment is to be in cash against shipping documents on both contracts.

Jake ships all 15,000 tons on board *The Flying Dustman* and the cargo of garbanzo beans is put into two separate holds – 10,000 tons in hold No 1 and 5,000 tons in hold No 2. The master of *The Flying Dustman* is hesitant in signing clean bills of lading because he knows of the rumour that the garbanzo beans were suspect, having been lying in Jake's warehouse for some time. The gossip is that the garbanzo beans are unlikely to be usable by the time the cargo arrives in Hong Kong. Nevertheless, he is persuaded by Jake and signs two clean bills of lading, one relating to hold No 1 and the other to hold No 2.

Before the ship sails, the garbanzo beans are severely wetted due to an exceptionally heavy storm. Water penetrates into both holds due to inadequate sealing of the hatch covers. The master notes on both bills of lading as follows: 'Cargo wetted by rain after shipment.'

After the ship sails, Jake tenders the bill of lading relating to hold No 1, with the insurance policy and the invoice, to Pugwash who, having now heard about the rumours regarding the garbanzo beans, refuses to pay on the ground that the bill of lading is not 'clean'. Jake tenders the bill of lading relating to hold No 2 to Barnabas, who also refuses to pay on the ground that because he had not been given any information about the shipping arrangements, he had not taken out an insurance policy covering the sea transit.

▶ Advise Pugwash and Barnabas as to their legal position.

How to Answer this Question

Shipping documents have always played a key role in international sale contracts, and the first part of this question requires you to discuss the time when the bill of lading must be 'clean'. The fact that Pugwash has heard of rumours concerning the cargo does not entitle him to reject the documents, but he does have the right to reject the goods on arrival. The cif buyer's two rights of rejection are separate and distinct.

As far as Barnabas is concerned, this is a straightforward question about the fob seller's statutory duty under **s 32(3)** of the **Sale of Goods Act 1979**.

Applying the Law

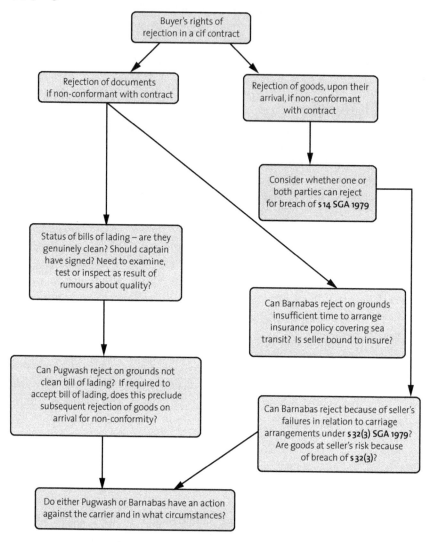

This diagram shows how the right of rejection can be understood in this scenario.

ANSWER

Both Pugwash and Barnabas are refusing to pay against shipping documents. If these documents conform to the contract, then Pugwash and Barnabas must accept them, otherwise they will be in breach of contract even if the goods themselves do not comply with the contract when they arrive (*Gill and Duffus SA v Berger & Co Inc* (1984)).

PUGWASH

Pugwash is refusing to pay on the ground that the bill of lading is not 'clean'. A clean bill of lading is one that does not contain any reservation as to the apparent good order or condition of the goods or the packing (*British Imex Industries Ltd v Midland Bank Ltd* (1958)). The time to which such a reservation must relate to prevent the bill of lading from being clean is that of shipment. In *The Galatia* (1980), a bill of lading was issued stating that the goods had been shipped in apparent good order and condition, but bore a notation that they had been subsequently damaged. The court held that the notation did not prevent the bill from being clean.

Applying *The Galatia* to this question, Pugwash cannot reject the bill of lading on the ground that the bill is not clean. The master of *The Flying Dustman* is neither bound to take samples of the garbanzo beans nor to have them analysed, nor otherwise investigate the cargo even if he is aware of rumours concerning the quality of the cargo. The master is justified in issuing a clean bill of lading. The note that was added referred to damage that occurred after loading. Thus, the bill of lading is still clean.

If Jake has tendered the shipping documents (which, in a cif contract, will include an insurance policy and an invoice in addition to a bill of lading (*The Julia* (1949)) in accordance with the contract, Pugwash must pay against them. It seems that Pugwash has wrongfully refused to do so. It should be said, however, that a buyer in international sales contracts has two rights of rejection. For non-compliance with the contractual terms, he may have a right to reject documents, and a right to reject the goods on delivery where the breach is not slight (**ss 13, 14** and **15A** of the **Sale of Goods Act 1979**). These two rights of rejection are quite distinct (*Kwei Tek Chao v British Traders and Shippers* (1954)). A cif buyer to whom documents have been tendered is not entitled to refuse to pay until he has examined the goods for the purpose of determining whether the goods are of the contract quality. Even if Pugwash hears of the rumours and suspects that the garbanzo beans are not in accordance with the contract, he is nevertheless bound to pay on tender of documents which are in accordance with the contract.[10]

Pugwash is thus advised to pay against the shipping documents because by doing so, he retains his possible right to reject the goods on arrival provided that the breach is not so slight as to be treated as a breach of warranty (**s 15A** of the **Sale of Goods Act 1979**). Certainly, even if the garbanzo beans are of satisfactory quality on shipment but are in such a state that they cannot endure a normal sea transit, Jake will be in breach of an implied warranty entitling the buyer to claim damages (*Mash and Murrell Ltd v Joseph Emanuel* (1961)). This implied warranty is distinct from the implied term under **s 14** of the **Sale of Goods Act 1979**, the former relating to an undertaking that the goods can endure sea

---

10 There is a controversial decision of the High Court of Australia (*Henry Dean & Sons (Sydney) Ltd v O'Day Pty Ltd* (1927)) which suggests that a buyer may be entitled to reject documents where the documents are, but the goods themselves are not, in accordance with the contract. The sellers, when refusing to pay against documents, are taking a risk but one that was 'justified by the result'. This problem is yet unresolved in the English courts.

transit, as opposed to **s 14(2)** and **(3)** which are implied terms relating to satisfactory quality and fitness for purpose. If the garbanzo beans at the outset were of satisfactory quality and usable, then no action arises under **s 14**. But, because garbanzo beans are normally capable of enduring a sea transit, Jake will be liable for any deterioration apparent on arrival.

Even if the garbanzo beans were of satisfactory quality at the time of shipment and were in such a state that they could have endured the sea transit, the cargo was damaged due to rain penetrating through improperly sealed hatches. It may be that Pugwash will have an action against the carrier (but if, as we are informed, this is due to exceptionally heavy weather, the carrier might be covered by the excepted perils under the **Hague-Visby Rules**). It must be said, however, that in order to take the benefit of the contract of carriage, Pugwash must be the holder of the relevant documents and the only way Pugwash will be the holder of the documents is to have paid Jake for them. If Pugwash does pay Jake, Pugwash will have the right to sue the carrier for breach of his duty to take proper care of the goods, as is required under the contract of carriage.[11] Since Jake is under a duty to make a reasonable contract of carriage (**s 32(2)** of the **Sale of Goods Act**), Pugwash will have a good action against the carriers.

Furthermore, once Pugwash has paid against the shipping documents, he will have the insurance policy assigned to him and he will be able to claim against the underwriter if he can show that the damage to the garbanzo beans by heavy storm conditions is a peril insured against.[12]

BARNABAS

As for Barnabas, he is refusing to pay against the shipping documents because he did not receive information from Jake as to the shipping arrangements and so he has not insured the cargo. In an fob contract, a seller is not obliged to obtain insurance cover for goods, but **s 32(3)** of the **Sale of Goods Act 1979** provides that the seller must give such notice to the buyer as may enable the buyer to insure the goods during the sea transit. If the seller fails to do so, the goods are at the seller's risk during sea transit. In a 'classic' fob contract, it is the buyer who makes the shipping arrangements and thus a seller need not give notice under **s 32(3)** where the buyer already has enough information to be able to insure (*Wimble Sons & Co v Rosenberg & Sons* (1913)).[13] The contract between Barnabas and Jake appears to be an fob contract with additional services, obliging Jake to make the necessary shipping arrangements. If Jake has not given Barnabas notice to enable him to

---

11 Under **s 2(1)** of the **Carriage of Goods by Sea Act 1992**, the lawful holder of a bill of lading has the right to sue the carrier under the contract of carriage 'as if he had been a party to that contract'.

12 Marine insurance is not usually found in undergraduate commercial law syllabuses and students will not be expected to discuss the implications of whether or not Jake, who arranges the policy, has disclosed the rumours that surround the quality of the garbanzo beans. Remember that contracts of insurance are contracts *uberrimae fidei*, that is, of utmost good faith, so that even if a non-disclosure does not relate to the loss, an insurer may decline to pay against a claim.

13 Explaining a legal rule before applying it to the requirements of the question gives structure to your answer.

insure, then although the cargo will be at Jake's risk during the sea transit, Barnabas is not entitled to refuse to pay against the shipping documents. **Section 32(3)** imposes a statutory duty and not a contractual duty. Thus, if the goods arrive safely, Barnabas has no cause of action because of the lack of insurance cover. As was discussed in relation to Pugwash, however, if the goods are not of satisfactory quality or unfit for their purpose, Barnabas may have a second right of rejection, that is, against the goods on arrival, provided the breach is not so slight that it would be unreasonable to treat it as a breach of condition (**s 15A** of the **Sale of Goods Act 1979**).

In order to have an action against the carrier for breach of the contract of carriage, Barnabas must, like Pugwash, have paid against the shipping documents. If Barnabas does not accept the documents but wishes to claim damages against the carrier in tort, the position following *Leigh and Sillivan v Aliakmon Shipping, The Aliakmon* (1986) is that he must show that at the time of the damage, he had legal ownership of the goods. Because he will not be able to do so (having refused to pay against the documents), Barnabas does not have a claim in tort and must pursue his claim in contract against Jake. Barnabas is thus advised to pay against the documents and reserve the possibility of rejecting the goods on arrival. If the cargo is damaged during the sea transit, Barnabas will then have a claim against either the carrier for breach of the contract of carriage or Jake for breach of **s 32(3)**.

QUESTION 38

Brixton agreed to buy the following goods under separate contracts:

(a)   1,000 tons of oats cif Antwerp from Angel;
(b)   2,000 potatoes fob Yarmouth from Vauxhall;
(c)   3,000 staves of Latvian timber cif Mumbai from Chelsea.

Each contract stipulated for payment by irrevocable letter of credit at Southern Bank on presentation of the shipping documents, and called for shipment in August/September.

The following events have occurred and you are asked to advise Brixton:

(i) Angel has the oats ready to load by 10 September, but discovers that no credit has been opened and hence refuses to load. The credit was in fact opened on 28 September, and although Angel begins to load the oats, loading was not completed until 1 October. The bank refused to pay against the shipping documents, which included the bill of lading showing a shipment of 1 October.

(ii) Southern Bank informed Vauxhall that the credit was opened on 30 July. Brixton contacted Vauxhall to say that he wanted his local representative to inspect the potatoes before shipment, but Vauxhall refused to allow the representative to do so. The bank paid on presentation of the shipping documents. On arrival of the vessel, the potatoes were found to have been damaged due to severe storms during the voyage. The shipment date was 10 August, but Brixton knew nothing of this.

(iii) On 7 August, the Latvian authorities announced that the exportation of timber was prohibited as from 1 September. Since the market price for timber was rising, Chelsea used the prohibition announcement as an excuse for not being able to ship the contract goods.

How to Answer this Question

Part (a) concerns the opening of credit, which comes too late to enable Angel to load the goods within the contract shipment period.

Part (b) involves a discussion as to an fob buyer's right to examine the goods. In relation to this, a comparison to domestic sale contracts must be made since in that situation, the point of delivery is the normal place of inspection, whereas in international sale contracts, there is no such rule. Was Brixton entitled to insist on an inspection at the point of shipment (which in international sale contracts is the point of delivery)? What are the effects of Vauxhall's refusal to allow Brixton's representative to inspect?

The answer should also deal with the fob seller's statutory duty under **s 32(3)** of the **Sale of Goods Act 1979**.

Part (c) asks you to discuss whether Chelsea is entitled to rely on the prohibition of timber as justifying her refusal to deliver (for instance because the contract has been frustrated).

Applying the Law

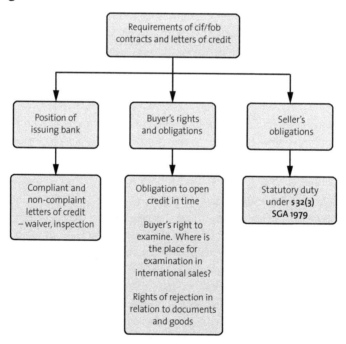

As well as position of the buyer and seller you will have to consider the legal position of the bank issuing the letter of credit.

ANSWER

(A) ANGEL

The general rule is that documentary credit must be opened in accordance with the terms of the contract of sale. The contract between Brixton and Angel does not provide a date for the opening credit but it does, however, stipulate a period for the shipment of goods. It is clear from *Pavia & Co SpA v Thurmann-Nielsen* (1952) that in these circumstances, the documentary credit must be opened at the very latest on the first day on which shipment may take place. In a cif contract, the seller is not bound to tell the buyer the precise date on which he is going to ship, because it is the seller who has the option as to the time of shipment. Whenever the seller does ship, he must nevertheless be able to draw on the credit. Thus, Angel is entitled to refuse to load the goods if the credit has not been opened, and may treat the contract as discharged because of Brixton's breach and claim damages for loss suffered.[14]

The credit is opened on 28 September and Angel begins to load. However, there is insufficient time before the end of the shipment period to complete the loading. *Bunge & Co Ltd v Tradax England Ltd* (1975) involved an fob contract where the buyer nominated a ship which was not ready to load until two hours before the end of the last working day of the shipment period. It was held that the seller could have rejected the nomination. Although Angel is a cif seller, and thus has the option of when to load, her option was restricted to that part of the shipment period when the letter of credit was open. By loading part of the goods within the available period, she has not waived her right to treat the contract as repudiated because of Brixton's failure to comply with the contractual stipulations as to payment.

When Angel tenders the shipping documents to Southern Bank, the documents are rejected. Since the bill of lading gives the shipment as 1 October, as far as the bank is concerned, it is not obliged to pay the seller because the documents do not comply with the terms of credit (*Equitable Trust Company of New York v Dawson Partners Ltd* (1927)). Southern Bank's right of reimbursement depends on it taking up a faultless set of documents and since the bill of lading indicates a shipment date outside that permitted under the terms of credit, Southern Bank is entitled to refuse to pay Angel. Angel's remedy is against Brixton for failure to have the documentary credit opened in her favour in time for her to load the goods before the end of the shipment period.

(B) VAUXHALL

Vauxhall refuses Brixton's request for an inspection of the potatoes to be carried out before shipment. There is no 'right' to inspect the goods before shipment but, under **s 35(2)** of the **Sale of Goods Act 1979**, if the buyer had not done so, there is no legal acceptance when the goods are shipped until the buyer has had a reasonable opportunity to inspect them upon delivery.

---

14 The measure of damages in these circumstances is not limited by the market price rule in **s 50(3)** of the **Sale of Goods Act 1979**, but may extend to the seller's loss of profits, provided that they are not too remote under the rule in *Hadley v Baxendale* (1854); *Trans Trust SPRL v Danubian Trading Co Ltd* (1952).

The fact that the buyer here was not afforded an opportunity to inspect the goods before shipment does not deprive him of his right to inspect at the contractual place of examination. This means that although Brixton was not given an opportunity to look at the goods when he asks to do so, he is nevertheless entitled to ask to inspect (and be allowed to do so) at the contractual place of examination.

Where is this contractual place of examination in Brixton's case? **Section 35(2)** refers to the place of delivery and this reflects the rule at common law, where it was held in *Perkins v Bell* (1893) that there is a presumption that the place of examination is the contractual delivery point.

'Delivery' in this instance is to be construed according to the terms of the fob contract. Where it is a classic or a strict fob case, namely, where the buyer acts as shipper of the goods, then the buyer is entitled to inspect the goods or have the local representative look at the goods before the ship sails. Where it is an fob contract with extended services, then the seller acts as the buyer's agent in shipping and hence the contractual (note: not necessarily coinciding with the statutory!) point of delivery for the purposes of **s 35(2)** would be at the point of arrival. So, unless the contract provides otherwise, the assumption is that inspection and examination of the potatoes is postponed until the consignment arrives at the destination, and that is the place for examination. Even then, if Vauxhall knows that the potatoes are being resold to Brixton's sub-buyer, then the opportunity to examine goods is postponed until his sub-buyer has had an opportunity to examine.

We will need to inquire as to whether the buyer had waived the right to inspect. If Brixton was requesting inspection at a non-contractual time, Vauxhall was acting within his rights not to let Brixton inspect the goods. If, however, Brixton did not purport to exercise his right to inspect at the contractual time, it is possible that such an omission might be construed as a waiver. In *B&P Wholesale Distributors v Marko* (1953), when the goods arrived, the buyer was given an opportunity to inspect the goods at the docks, but the buyer did not avail himself of the opportunity. Instead, the buyer transported the goods to his depot and there examined the goods. The court held that the buyer had not lost his right to reject. He would only be deemed to have waived his right to examine the goods if he had been given a genuine and practical opportunity to make a proper examination of the goods at the docks.

If Brixton had been offered a real and practical opportunity to inspect the goods, then he may not be able to quibble with any defects or deficiencies which that inspection could have revealed. However, where the goods deteriorated as in the present case and it is possible that an inspection could not have revealed the inherent vice in the goods, then the buyer retains his statutory and contractual right to damages for unfit goods as long as the deterioration was caused by the state of the goods as they were at shipment: *Mash & Murrell Ltd v Joseph Emanuel* (1961).[15] Deterioration caused by the sea passage shall naturally be borne by

---

15 It is not always necessary to provide details of the cases you cite as you are merely using them as authorities for the legal principles you have explained/referred to.

the buyer (as he is the shipper) and any claim (if any) would have to be brought against the carrier under the contract of carriage.

It is also possible that Brixton wished to inspect the potatoes in order to discover matters necessary for him to take out effective insurance. There is no information in the question leading to the suggestion that Vauxhall must have made the shipping arrangements. Unless the fob contract stipulated otherwise, Vauxhall is not obliged to obtain insurance cover for the goods. It is Brixton's responsibility to ensure that insurance cover was in place if he required it. We are told that the goods are damaged during the voyage, but we are not told whether or not Brixton had insured the potatoes.[16] Since Brixton only knew of the date of shipment after the damage occurred, it may be that under the contract, Vauxhall had the responsibility to make the shipping arrangements. Thus, if Brixton had not taken out effective insurance cover because he did not have sufficient information to insure, then **s32(3)** of the **Sale of Goods Act 1979** places the risk of damage after shipment on the seller, Vauxhall. Although in a 'classic' fob contract, it is the buyer who makes all shipping arrangements (*Pyrene Co Ltd v Scindia Navigation Co Ltd* (1954)), it seems in this question that Vauxhall might have made them, otherwise Brixton would have had sufficient information on which to insure the goods.

Thus, if Vauxhall is in breach of **s32(3)** by failing to give notice to Brixton and Brixton has not insured the goods, although the risk in goods normally passes on shipment, Vauxhall bears the damage to the potatoes during the voyage.

(C) CHELSEA

Once the contract has been concluded, a contract may be frustrated because of supervening governmental prohibition rendering the contract illegal. However, the prohibition operates as a frustrating event only if it is final and extends to the whole time still available for the performance of the contract. Chelsea will not be able to rely on the prohibition of export to excuse performance, since the Latvian authorities had indicated in advance that the export of timber would only be prohibited from a future date within the shipment period.

In *Ross T Smyth & Co Ltd (Liverpool) v WN Lindsay Ltd* (1953), the contract provided for the shipment of horsebeans from a Sicilian port, cif Glasgow during October/November. On 20 October, the Italian authorities announced that the exportation of horsebeans was prohibited as from 1 November except under special licence. The sellers failed to ship. The court held that the buyers were entitled to claim damages, since the prohibition did not operate as a frustrating event.[17] Applying this case to the question, although Chelsea has

---

16 Pointing out omissions in the information provided by the question and considering the impact these omissions might have on the outcome of your analysis will attract a higher mark as it demonstrates your understanding.

17 If the prohibition of export had been instantaneous, it would have operated as a frustrating event. If, on the other hand, the Latvian authorities indicated that an export embargo might be imposed, then Chelsea would probably not be in breach if she did not ship between the time of that announcement and the subsequent date of the embargo: *Tradax Export v André & Cie* (1976).

the option of when to ship, she is not entitled to refuse to ship the goods before 1 September. The prohibition merely limited her option of when to ship from two months to one month and, when the announcement was made, Chelsea should have shipped the goods between the date of the announcement and 31 August. Brixton is thus entitled to claim damages from Chelsea.

QUESTION 39

Watson ships 10,000 tons of rapeseed oil from Southampton to Hamburg via Antwerp on board *The Bluenose*. While the goods are afloat, Watson enters into the following three separate contracts:

(a) to sell 5,000 tons of rapeseed oil to Charlotte cif Antwerp, payment to be made by letter of credit to be issued by Charlotte's bank;

(b) to sell 3,000 tons of rapeseed oil to George cif Hamburg, payment by cash against documents;

(c) to sell 2,000 tons of rapeseed oil to Alice *ex The Bluenose*, payment in full in advance.

The voyage between Antwerp and Hamburg is beset with difficulties and the master of *The Bluenose* informs Watson that 1,000 tons of rapeseed oil have been lost. Charlotte's bank accepts a bill of exchange on tender of documents which include a delivery order for 5,000 tons of rapeseed oil, but Charlotte refuses to take delivery of the goods, claiming that the rapeseed oil is of inferior quality. Watson couriers the shipping documents to George, who rejects them because they included a delivery order indicating that 500 tons of rapeseed oil have been lost. Alice refuses to pay Watson because only 1,500 tons of rapeseed oil had been discharged at Hamburg.

▶ **Advise Watson.**

How to Answer this Question

Shipping documents have always played a key role in international sale contracts and normally shipping documents include the bill of lading. In all three parts to this question, however, a delivery order is tendered. In the absence of an express term in the contract, is the seller entitled to tender such a document where the sale involves a part of a bulk quantity?

Part (a) also involves **s14** of the **Sale of Goods Act 1979**. Part (b) requires you to discuss whether goods must be appropriated to the contract before loss. Part (c) involves a straightforward discussion of **s30** of the **Sale of Goods Act 1979**. Note, however, that the contract with Alice is *ex* ship.

Applying the Law

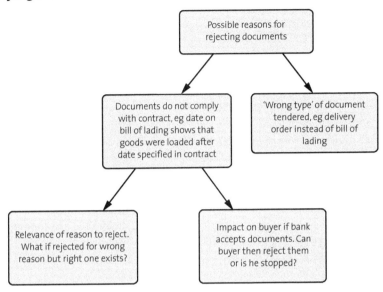

This diagram focuses on the two possible reasons for rejecting documents to be discussed in this answer. Important consideration in addition to this is which party bears the risk of any accidental loss or damage to the goods.

ANSWER

Neither the contract with Charlotte nor the contract with George requires Watson to supply goods from those on board *The Bluenose*. The contract with Alice, however, does so require. When did the loss of the 500 tons occur? Was it before risk passed to the buyer? Risk will, however, have passed under the first two contracts (with Charlotte and George) when the goods are loaded on the ship. Thus, assuming (as seems to be implied by the question) that the loss occurred during the voyage, the risk falls upon the buyer under a cif contract. Of course, that is so provided that the buyer has taken up, or has no legitimate reason for not taking up, the documents.

(A) CHARLOTTE

As far as Charlotte is concerned, her bank has taken up the documents and, it being her bank, Charlotte is presumably bound by what her bank has done. Thus, Charlotte – although she may have been entitled to reject the documents – cannot now resile from the acceptance of the documents by her bank. To put it another way, she is estopped from rejecting the goods on any ground which would have entitled her to reject the documents (*Panchaud Frères v Etablissements General Grain* (1970)). Thus, she is not entitled to reject the documents or the goods on the ground that she should not have been tendered a delivery order, but a bill of lading. In any case, it may be that the cif contract in this case expressly or impliedly provided for the tendering of a delivery order instead of the more normal bill of lading. This may be so especially if both buyer and seller (Charlotte and Watson) contemplated that the contract would be performed by delivery of documents relating to goods consisting of an undivided part of a cargo.[18]

As already indicated, however, even if Watson was not entitled to tender a delivery order, the documents tendered were accepted and Charlotte is estopped from relying on that non-compliance. On the other hand, a buyer under a cif contract has two rights of rejection: (i) to reject non-complying documents; and (ii) to reject goods which on arrival prove to be in breach of condition (except on any ground which would have entitled him to reject the documents) (*Kwei Tek Chao v British Traders and Shippers* (1954)). Thus, if the goods when tendered are in breach of condition, Charlotte is entitled to reject them. It is possible that the rapeseed oil being 'of inferior quality' means that: (i) there is a breach of an express term of the contract; and/or (ii) there is a breach of one of the conditions implied by **s14** of the **Sale of Goods Act 1979** (as to satisfactory quality or fitness for purpose).[19] In the case of (i), it is only if either: (a) the express term amounts to a condition; or (b) the breach is such as to deprive Charlotte of substantially the whole of the benefit of the contract, that the buyer will have a right of rejection. From the facts given, it is impossible to determine whether the goods being of inferior quality amounts to a breach of condition, express or implied.

If, in fact, Charlotte's bank has accepted documents which it was entitled to reject and which it ought to have rejected, then although Charlotte is estopped as indicated above, she will have a remedy against her bank if the bank has acted contrary to her instructions in accepting the documents.

(B) GEORGE

Unlike Charlotte, George has rejected the documents. The reason that motivated him to reject the documents is irrelevant. What is relevant is whether he had a valid reason to reject the documents. He can rely on a valid reason, even if at the time of his rejection he relied upon an invalid reason, and he was unaware of the existence of the valid reason (*Glencore Grain Rotterdam BV v Lebanese Organisation for International Commerce* (1997)). There are two possibly valid reasons: first, that he was tendered a delivery order rather than a bill of lading – though, as discussed in relation to Charlotte, it may be that the contract expressly or impliedly allowed tender of a delivery order; second, that the delivery order showed less than the contract quantity. It is unclear whether Watson had appropriated[20] the lost 500 tons of rapeseed oil to George's contract before the goods were in fact

---

18 Even if this were the case, the delivery order must be one issued by the ship so that the document should give the buyer some contractual rights against the ship. Under the **Carriage of Goods by Sea Act 1992**, this has the same effect as a bill of lading in transferring property.

19 It is unlikely to amount to breach of the condition implied by **s13**, since the matter of quality is not normally regarded as part of the contract description (*Ashington Piggeries v Christopher Hill* (1972)).

20 'Appropriation' here is used in the sense that the seller has contractually bound himself to deliver certain goods. There can be appropriation in this sense even though the goods remain 'unascertained' because they form part of a larger bulk.

lost. Cases such as *Re Olympia Oil and Cake Co and Produce Brokers Ltd* (1915) indicate that a seller can appropriate lost cargo since, in a cif contract, the buyer has the benefit of a contract of carriage and a policy of insurance so that, in the event of loss, the buyer has a claim against either the carrier or the insurer, even though the loss or damage to the goods occurred before those documents were tendered (*Manbre Saccharine Co Ltd v Sugar Beet Products Co Ltd* (1919)). There is academic opinion, however, that the seller *cannot* make a valid tender of documents after the loss of the goods unless, before the loss occurred, they had become fully identified as the contract goods. In this case, they appear not to have been fully identified. Indeed, the problem does not even state that the goods supplied to George must come from the cargo on *The Bluenose*. It would appear that Watson could have complied with the terms of his contract with George by buying a cargo of rapeseed oil afloat (cif Hamburg) and using that cargo to fulfil his contract with George. Thus, although the matter is not free from doubt, Watson is advised that his tender of documents to George was not valid and that accordingly George was entitled to reject them.

(C) ALICE

The difference between *ex* ship and cif contracts is that in the former, documents do not stand in the place of goods so that actual delivery of the goods must be made (*The Julia* (1949)). So far as Alice is concerned, the risk in an *ex* ship contract, unless the contract specifically provides otherwise, passes upon delivery from the ship against payment. According to **s 30(1)** of the **Sale of Goods Act 1979**, where the seller delivers a quantity less than he has contracted to sell, the buyer has the option of either rejecting them or to accept the part-delivery and pay for them at the contract rate. However, according to **s 30(2A)**, the buyer will not be able to reject the goods under **s 30(1)** if the shortfall is so slight that it would be unreasonable for him to do so. A shortfall of 500 tons, in the present instance, is not slight. There is no question of Alice getting her money back, since she has not yet paid the price. She has refused to pay. It seems, therefore, that Alice is entitled to reject the goods and to refuse to pay (**s 30(1)** of the **Sale of Goods Act**).

Common Pitfalls

Be careful not to spend too long on the first or the first two answers and run out of time for the last answer.

Index